The Implications of Brexit for East Asia

David W. F. Huang • Michael Reilly
Editors

The Implications of Brexit for East Asia

palgrave
macmillan

Editors
David W. F. Huang
Institute of European and American Studies, Academia Sinica
Nankang, Taipei, Taiwan

Michael Reilly
Taiwan Studies Program
University of Nottingham
Nottingham, UK

ISBN 978-981-13-0184-1 ISBN 978-981-13-0185-8 (eBook)
https://doi.org/10.1007/978-981-13-0185-8

Library of Congress Control Number: 2018942878

Cover illustration: © titoOnz / Alamy Stock Photo
Cover Design by Tjaša Krivec

Printed on acid-free paper

This Palgrave Macmillan imprint is published by the registered company Springer Nature Singapore Pte Ltd.
The registered company address is: 152 Beach Road, #21-01/04 Gateway East, Singapore 189721, Singapore

Contents

List of Figures

List of Tables

CHAPTER 1

Introduction

Michael Reilly and David W. F. Huang

On 23 June 2016, the UK electorate voted by a narrow majority in favour of the country withdrawing from the European Union (EU). The debate was often bitter and acrimonious; shortly before the vote one MP who campaigned for the country to remain in the EU was murdered by a right-wing extremist, an almost unprecedented event in British politics. The narrowness of the outcome—51.9% voted for leaving the EU, 48.1% for remaining—divided the country as perhaps never before. Scotland, Northern Ireland and most metropolitan centres voted to remain in the EU, as did the great majority of younger people. English rural areas, the old, the less well-educated and the poor voted to leave. British politicians who interpreted the outcome as a clear mandate to pursue a clean break from the EU as quickly as possible soon received a reality check. Just under one year later the new Prime Minister, Theresa May, called a snap general election confident she would receive a large majority in support of her clean break or 'hard Brexit' approach, only to suffer a damaging blow. Far from increasing her parliamentary majority she lost it, winning fewer

M. Reilly (✉)
Taiwan Studies Program, University of Nottingham, Nottingham, UK

D. W. F. Huang
Institute of European and American Studies, Academia Sinica, Nankang, Taipei, Taiwan
e-mail: wfhuang@gate.sinica.edu.tw

D. W. F. Huang, M. Reilly (eds.), *The Implications of Brexit for East Asia*, https://doi.org/10.1007/978-981-13-0185-8_1

seats than previously held and now governing only with the support of Northern Ireland's Democratic Unionists (DUP).

It was not meant to be like this. Referendums in the UK are rare: this was only the third such nationwide referendum ever and there was no constitutional or other compelling reason to hold it. David Cameron, the then British Prime Minister, had announced his intention of holding a referendum on the country's membership of the EU in January 2013 if his Conservative Party, then governing in coalition with the pro-European Liberal Democrats, won an overall majority in the next general election. At the time, opinion polls suggested this was unlikely—indeed the opinion polls continued to suggest it was unlikely right up to election day itself in 2015, when the Conservatives actually won a small overall majority, the first time they had done so in a general election since 1992.

The issue of EU membership had divided the Conservative Party throughout that period. It was a major contributory factor in the party's comprehensive defeat by Tony Blair's re-energised and re-vamped Labour Party in 1997. Some members of then Prime Minister John Major's Cabinet had both openly and privately worked to undermine his European policies, either oblivious to or contemptuous of the damage it was doing to the party domestically. Still officially known as the Conservative *and Unionist* Party, by the early years of this century it had become largely a party of English nationalism, having first distanced itself from the Unionists in Ulster as they fragmented and became more extreme in the 1970s and 1980s, then being all but wiped out electorally in Scotland, where for 20 years from 1997 to 2017 they held only one seat in the Westminster parliament.

By 2013, after three years back in office, albeit in coalition, the anti-EU faction within the Conservative Party was once again becoming vocal. And after three years of austerity measures brought in by Cameron's Chancellor (Finance Minister), George Osborne, which had a disproportionate impact on the poorest in society, the far right -wing UK Independence Party (UKIP) was gaining in the opinion polls. Cameron's announcement of the referendum was a tactical decision, aimed at cementing the support of his own right wing and undermining public support for UKIP. As such it was a major blunder, serving only to galvanise the anti-EU groups into mobilising support, a blunder further compounded by his insistence on going ahead with the referendum when he did. His fundamental errors of judgement have proved to be almost certainly the biggest political mistakes in recent British history.

The nature of the referendum debate was often surreal. Possibly anxious to avoid being labelled *Little Englanders*, some of the most passionate advocates within the Conservative Party for leaving the EU sought to portray it as an opportunity for the UK to adopt a more 'global' posture, as if EU membership was somehow constraining this. Indeed, this became the stated position of the British government, Prime Minister Theresa May declaring at the meeting of the World Economic Forum in Davos in January 2017 that henceforward the UK would be the strongest and most forceful advocate for business, free markets and free trade. In a perceptive analysis, Professor Linda Colley of Princeton has described this view as a *persistent chimera haunting post-war British foreign policy*: the inability of many in the UK's governing classes, the Conservative Party in particular, to make the adjustment from world power to regional power status.[1]

There was little serious analysis of such visions and attempts by outsiders to warn of possible consequences or to urge continued membership of the EU were either ignored or dismissed as interference in domestic matters. An example of the former was Chinese Premier Li Keqiang's statement in a joint press conference with David Cameron in London in June 2014, that *China all along supports the EU integration process*, that it welcomed a strong and prosperous EU and that China hoped that its bilateral relationship with the UK would stay at the forefront of its relations with European countries.[2] The clearest example of the latter was then US President Barack Obama's warning that in the event of a vote for 'Brexit' the UK would be at the back of the queue in negotiating any replacement trade agreement with the USA, a position rejected by a 'Brexit' campaigner as *a lame-duck American President doing an old British friend a political favour*.[3]

But the consequences of the outcome of the referendum reverberate far beyond the UK itself. Immediate concerns focused on the likely reaction in the rest of Europe, where it inevitably emboldened other right-wing nationalist, populist and anti-EU parties, most immediately and obviously Marine le Pen's *Front National* in France and Geert Wilders' *Partij voor de Vrijheid*—PVV or Freedom Party—in the Netherlands. But both did less well in subsequent national elections than they had hoped, or their opponents feared, and with centrist Emmanuel Macron's victory in the 2017 French presidential election and the strong position of Angela Merkel in Germany, most of the rest of the EU breathed a sigh of relief.

Within the UK itself, there appears to have been something of an anti-populist swing in the aftermath of the referendum. UKIP, the loudest and most persistent advocate of leaving the EU, saw its share of the vote collapse in the 2017 election, while ironically Theresa May owes her continued position as Prime Minister to a surge of support for her party in Scotland, due largely to a reaction there against the continuing campaign for independence by the Scottish National Party. But for this, the outcome of the 2017 election would have been even worse for the Conservatives. In a further irony, the Conservatives were traditionally allied in Northern Ireland with the Ulster Unionists but now depend on support from the DUP, the more extreme and hard- line of the two Unionist parties. While the DUP campaigned to leave the EU, a position rejected by the majority of Northern Irish voters, it also recognises the importance of an open border with the Republic of Ireland. All this has only added to the challenges faced by the May government in agreeing a clear position for its future relations with the rest of the EU, which can only view the UK's continued discombobulations with growing bemusement but also frustration.

But the impact of the referendum result was felt further afield too, including in East Asia. This should not have been a surprise, after all the UK is one of the five permanent members of the UN Security Council, with a history of engagement in the region (some might see it as meddling) since at least the Opium Wars of the nineteenth century until the handover of Hong Kong to China in 1997.

The security aspects of the relationship may now be consigned to history but East Asia remains of major—even critical—importance to the UK's prosperity, arguably even more so in the 'post-Brexit' future. It contains the world's second and third largest economies, some of the UK's biggest bilateral trading partners and in Japan, South Korea and China, significant sources of foreign investment into the UK's infrastructure, manufacturing and financial services. A neutral observer might therefore have reasonably expected the implications of the referendum outcome on the UK's future relations with the region to feature prominently in the debate. In practice, they were barely mentioned. The limited attempts to warn of the potential consequences on foreign investment from the region were usually dismissed as 'scaremongering' for example.

But there will inevitably be an impact. How deep or how wide it is too early to tell, not least because at the time of writing the British government's position on its future relationship with the EU remains unclear. Mrs. May's original stated aim in January 2017 was to pursue a 'hard Brexit,' withdrawing the country not just from the Single Market but also from the Customs Union and even the jurisdiction of the European Court of Justice, which extends beyond specifically EU matters. Without a parliamentary majority, it is far from clear that she can get enough domestic support for this stance, let alone conclude an acceptable agreement with the EU. By August 2017 some recognition of the enormity of the challenges ahead was becoming apparent, the UK's official position paper on the future relationship proposing a transition period '*which would mean close association with the EU Customs Union for a time-limited period,*' of up to three years after the formal break expected in March 2019 (the two-year timeframe set out for doing so under Article 50, which Mrs. May invoked in March 2017). The government also set out three key objectives for negotiations over future trading arrangements: to ensure trade with the EU is as frictionless as possible, to avoid any form of hard border between Ireland and Northern Ireland and to *establish an independent international trade policy* (emphasis added).[4]

The third of these is key to the UK's future relations with countries outside the EU, including those in East Asia. The paper explains that:

> *The UK would intend to pursue new trade negotiations with others once we leave the EU, though it would not bring into effect any new arrangements with third countries which were not consistent with the terms of the interim agreement.*[5]

It remains to be seen whether the UK can achieve this and if so on what terms: it seems to assume that the EU will agree to the UK pursuing bilateral trade deals with third countries even before a final settlement has been agreed. This is far from certain. The paper also seems unclear as to the basis on which such deals would be pursued: on the one hand, it talks of *ambitious new trade arrangements and comprehensive trade deals that play to the strengths of the UK economy of today and the future,* on the other it states that: *we will seek continuity in our existing trade and investment relationships.*[6]

The upbeat official language carefully skirts the complexities of modern trade deals. The reality of these is that there is far from being a single model and the government makes no mention of its preferred approach, beyond continuity of current relationships. The paper does recognise the importance of services to the UK economy but makes no mention of the Trade in Services Agreement (TiSA) negotiations ongoing within the World Trade Organisation (WTO). The EU, Japan, Korea and Taiwan are all members of

TiSA but not China (although it has applied to join) or Singapore. Would the UK seek to join in its own right after leaving the EU? As another example, the government's paper highlights the importance of China in international trade, with a strong inference that negotiation of a free trade agreement (FTA) with China would be a priority. But what would be the agreed objectives of such an agreement? Would it seek to replicate the EU's comprehensive agreement with Canada, the Comprehensive Economic and Trade Agreement (CETA) which encompasses mutual recognition of standards and regulations, or be closer to a traditional FTA focusing almost exclusively on tariffs, like Switzerland's agreement with China? Or something in between these, perhaps like the EU's agreement with Korea?

While the UK government's preferences remain unclear, analysis of a country's pre-referendum relations with the UK and the initial reactions of its government and businesses to the outcome can surely offer a guide to the future. The chapters in this book seek to do just this by considering some pointers as to the likely medium- and long-term impact of the referendum outcome on the UK's relations with countries in East Asia. They do so not through the at times Panglossian views of pro-'Brexit' campaigners or the sometimes equally Martinian pessimism of the 'Remainers' but predominantly through analysis from within the countries concerned. From this perspective, the preferences of the UK government are secondary: the primary issue for consideration is how the countries of the region see their future relations with the EU and UK and following from this, what sort of future trading agreements with the UK they are willing to envisage. The UK may see an FTA with China as a priority, for example, but is that how China sees the relationship? The East Asian countries or economies covered are China, Japan, Korea, Taiwan, Hong Kong and Singapore. Some discussion of responses of member states of the Association of Southeast Asian Nations (ASEAN) is also included.

Given the still highly uncertain nature of the final outcome, inevitably some assumptions have had to be made. Rather than simply present two scenarios, a 'hard Brexit' and a 'soft' one, the authors of the respective chapters were asked to consider and evaluate each of these. How would one or the other affect a country's relations with the UK and EU in the future? Each author examines the initial responses of government and business in his or her own country from this perspective. How far will their business sectors continue to engage with the UK and EU markets after Britain actually leaves the EU? What might the new political relationship between the UK and the EU on the one hand and East Asian countries on the other hand look like? In East Asia, are there any differences in government and business sectors' preferences with respect to 'hard Brexit' and 'soft Brexit'? Another chapter discusses the region-wide implications of 'Brexit' for East Asia. Finally, countries in East Asia are anxious to know what will happen to the EU and European integration after 'Brexit.' One chapter is therefore devoted to some theoretical speculation from an Asian scholar's perspective about future EU governance. While not all chapters adhere narrowly to this common framework, they do cover the above topics and follow a common broad approach. A summary of each chapter follows.

Much has already been written about the referendum, mainly from an openly partisan viewpoint with little if any attempt at objectivity. Books by Arron Banks, the main backer of the right-wing 'pro-Leave' UKIP, and Daniel Hannan, another ardent 'Leave' campaigner, fall firmly into this category and the 'Leave' campaign would doubtless say the same of Denis MacShane's book, given that he is a firm Europhile.[7] The first of these is primarily about the campaign itself, while Hannan unabashedly paints a picture of a bright future for the UK at the centre of a new world of bilateral FTAs, a future that most of the authors in this book show has little basis in fact. MacShane looks more at why the UK electorate voted the way it did but concentrating mainly on political aspects and the UK's long-ambivalent relationship with its partners in the EU. The contributory reasons, the geographical divisions, the disillusion with the political classes and more have been covered extensively in the news media and periodicals. Among academic studies, Andrew Glencross' is prominent in considering the basic strategic mistakes, blunders even, committed by David Cameron that led to the referendum outcome.[8]

It is not necessary, nor indeed relevant, to repeat this coverage which has already been examined in detail. But a reminder and explanation of the context are still appropriate. In Chap. 2, Chien-yi Lu places the reasons for the vote firmly in the context of wider reaction to the impact of globalisation, or more particularly the consequences of the 2008 financial crisis and its aftermath, arguing that the outcome reflected anger, fear, disillusion and frustration with the political and business establishment. Much of this was driven by concerns about immigration but based, she argues, on a high degree of misunderstanding about its real level and impact. This should not be surprising as public opposition to immigration in the UK is almost as well-established as immigration itself, as reflected in anti-Irish protests and riots in the mid-nineteenth century, anti-Chinese riots immediately after the First World War, the Notting Hill riots of 1958 and efforts by successive British governments since the 1980s to limit immigration. Arguably what was surprising given this history was the apparent failure of the Cameron government to realise the effect fear of immigration would have on the referendum campaign, especially as he had first won office on a pledge to reduce annual net immigration to the 'tens of thousands,' a pledge that the statistics showed his government was failing to achieve.

The 'Leave' campaigners argued that only by withdrawing from the EU could the UK control immigration as growing numbers of immigrants were from within the EU and therefore free to come to the UK. This resonated with the linked claim that withdrawal would allow the country to 'take back control' of its own affairs and regain sovereignty allegedly handed over to the European Commission and European Court of Justice. 'Leave' campaigners within the Conservative Party frequently linked this claim with Margaret Thatcher's often public and vocal opposition to aspects of EU membership, arguing that pulling out of the EU was consistent with her vision and would finally achieve her goal.

But this was—perhaps intentionally—a highly selective interpretation of her views, for Thatcher was a firm advocate for the Single Market and in Chap. 3 Michael Reilly argues that the combination of Thatcher's wider views and the advent of the Single Market were the foundation stones of the UK's current relations with East Asia. Historically these had been based on trade but the combination of the Single Market with the UK's language, legal framework and, by European standards, low-cost and flexible labour markets made it an attractive base to invest in for Asian companies seeking ready access to the huge new European market. By the time of the referendum, Japanese companies alone employed more than 5% of the entire UK manufacturing industry labour force. The impact of this was highly concentrated, notably in Sunderland where the Nissan car factory was the town's largest employer, the UK's biggest such factory and Europe's most productive. Some 80% of the entire output of the UK car industry, rejuvenated through investment by Nissan and other Japanese manufacturers, was exported, mostly to the rest of the EU. Yet Sunderland voted in favour of leaving the EU, apparently discounting or dismissing fears that by doing so the long- term future of the Nissan plant may have been jeopardised.

Given the efforts Thatcher had made to encourage such investment and its contribution to the UK economy over the last three decades, far from being the culmination of Thatcher's vision, the vote to leave the EU was therefore a rejection of that vision. Faced with this, the strategy of the May government appears to be to replace the comfort and benefits of the Single

Market by an ambitious series of bilateral FTAs. Given the relative importance of their bilateral trade for the UK, most North East Asian countries could be expected to be high on the list for opening such negotiations. But Reilly argues that this emphasis on trade by the UK government is misplaced and that East Asian countries, with the notable exception of Taiwan, are unlikely to accord it the same level of priority. Shorn of the attraction of the Single Market, and no longer able to offer the sorts of defence guarantees provided by the USA, he argues that the UK may therefore struggle to maintain its influence and standing in the region.

If the importance of foreign investment to the UK economy was given only passing consideration in the referendum debate, the same could hardly be said for the possible consequences for the UK's financial services industry. Although employing fewer people than manufacturing, the sector contributed an estimated £66.5 billion to the UK government through taxes in 2014/15, or roughly 11% of the government's total tax revenue.[9] Pivotal to much of this has been the City of London's pre-eminent role within the EU, including in handling Euro-denominated trades. Government determination to preserve the City's pre-eminent global status was a major factor in its relationship with China, a relationship characterised by Sam Beatson in Chap. 4 as 'zealously transactional.' He argues that this policy was predicated on a desire to increase Chinese investment into the UK and to leverage the UK's position as a leading world financial centre by ensuring that London was at the forefront of Chinese plans for making the renminbi (RMB) a truly international currency. This would give the City a further advantage in the competition to help China develop its own financial sector.

Following the referendum outcome, Beatson further argues that the UK government seems to have taken the view that the country will remain as open as ever to international trade and that forging ties with trade partners further afield would be a natural progression upon leaving the EU. But in the case of China he suggests that this is far from obvious. While the levels of RMB trade through London and the numbers of Chinese banks opening there in the last few years have been impressive, as a proportion of overall currency settlement and trading they remain very small. Their real significance lies in their potential but this in turn, he argues, is dependent on London being a European centre, not just a British one. Without the freedom to undertake business throughout the rest of the EU, the attractions of London to the Chinese as a financial centre are likely to be considerably less.

'Leavers' might argue that some of this would be offset by the signing of a bilateral FTA with China. But Beatson demonstrates that China has shown in recent years that it is adept at reaching deals which are in its own interests, and that the UK would engage with China in any negotiations on an FTA on a highly asymmetrical basis. Within the EU, at least it has a level of protection and is part of a massive bloc which matters to the Chinese. Alone, it becomes a second rank player, and one which is in a relatively weak position. He concludes that the UK will therefore have to make great efforts to nurture its relationship with China during its negotiations with EU partners over 'Brexit' if it is not to become less relevant to China.

If this seems a rather gloomy prognosis, 'Leavers' may draw some comfort from Wai Ting's analysis. In Chap. 5, he characterises the vote as a 'lose-lose' outcome for the UK and the EU and shares similar conclusions to Beatson over the consequences for the City of London, suggesting that there will be negative consequences for China's external economic actions and financial arrangements in view of London's importance as an RMB clearing centre. But more optimistically, he argues that outside the EU, Chinese companies will treat the UK as a close partner in its own right and that the Chinese government will continue to treat the UK as a great power politically.

By contrast, he cites Chinese scholars as believing that 'Brexit' will encourage the rise of populism and Euro-scepticism within the EU, which will become more conservative, more protectionist and less stable. China will therefore work to strengthen further its relations with the Central and Eastern European (CEE) members of the EU under the '16+1' arrangements, rather than with the EU as a whole. A weakened EU will strengthen the global influence of the USA by default, encouraging China to work more bilaterally with the USA. At the time of writing it is too early to judge this with any confidence: it could turn out to be highly prescient or simply wishful thinking. The first months of Donald Trump's presidency saw the USA-China relationship beset by uncertainty, while the 'Brexit' referendum may have turned out to be the high- water mark for right-wing populism in Europe. Not only did centrists regain the ascendancy in France and the Netherlands but in the UK itself, UKIP, arguably the driving force behind the vote to 'Leave' saw its share of the popular vote collapse in the 2017 election.

While both Beatson and Ting highlight the importance of the financial sector and RMB trading in London as a recent driving force behind the bilateral relationship, as Beatson and to a lesser extent Ting point out, direct investment from China has also been an important factor. In this respect, the UK has been little different from its EU partners, most of whom have been keen to attract some of China's surplus capital since the financial crisis of 2008 wrought havoc with their national budgets. The policy has been far from uncontroversial within the UK, mainly because of two high-profile investments: the first was by Chinese IT company Huawei, barred from both Australia and the USA, two of the UK's closest allies, on national security grounds; the second was the involvement by the China General Nuclear Power Corporation (CGN) together with EDF of France in the financing and construction of a new nuclear power station at Hinkley Point in Somerset.

Amidst all the publicity not only about Huawei and Hinkley Point but also about the UK's bilateral relationship with China more generally, especially following Xi Jinping's state visit to the UK in Autumn 2015, it is easy to forget that cumulative foreign direct investment (FDI) by Japan in the UK far exceeds that by China and that this has been continuing. The most notable recent example was the opening by Hitachi in 2015 of a new railway rolling stock manufacturing facility, while both Hitachi and—before its financial difficulties—Toshiba have also been assessing investing in the UK's nuclear power sector. Although Hitachi built its factory initially to construct trains for the UK market, it did not hide its European ambitions and its chairman, Hiroaki Nakanishi, was unequivocal that a vote to leave the EU would likely mean a scaling back of its investment plans in the UK.

In this respect, Hitachi was no different from the majority of other Japanese companies which had made significant investments in the UK over the previous 30 or so years, all of whom had based their decisions on the assumption of continued access to the Single Market, a point made by Japanese Prime Minister Shinzo Abe in the unprecedented memo he gave to Theresa May at the G20 meeting in Hangzhou in September 2016, as Michael Reilly and Daisuke Ikemoto both point out in their chapters. For Ikemoto however, the Japanese reaction is about more than commercial interests, important though these are. In Chap. 6, he argues that Japan is growing increasingly worried about the real commitment of the USA to its security while at the same time facing an increasingly assertive and expansionist China. Japan's response to 'Brexit' is therefore likely to be twofold.

The nature of the business response will depend on the details of the eventual 'divorce' agreement reached between the UK and the rest of the

EU and the ability of companies such as Nissan, Toyota, Honda and Hitachi to continue to supply the European market from their British factories. The closer these terms are to current practice, the more likely they are to remain in the UK and invest further. Meanwhile, until the referendum the EU and Japan had been discussing a bilateral FTA but in a somewhat desultory fashion, with neither side appearing to consider it the highest priority. But with Japan's hopes of a major regional agreement embracing the USA in the Trans-Pacific Partnership (TPP) dashed by President Trump's withdrawal of the USA from it, together with the 'Brexit' vote in the UK, both sides appear to have seen the benefits of reaching an early agreement and duly announced that they had done so in principle in spring 2017.[10]

But in Ikemoto's eyes this is unlikely to do much to strengthen the EU-Japan relationship on its own. Rather, he sees 'Brexit' as putting an end to any Japanese expectations of being able to build a stronger political relationship with the EU. Nor does he expect there to be strong interest in Japan in a new bilateral relationship with the UK. He concedes that it could remain attractive for Japanese companies if it becomes more business-friendly after 'Brexit' but British hopes or expectations of being able to negotiate an early bilateral FTA with Japan are unlikely to be reciprocated; on its own the UK is simply not sufficiently important in Japanese eyes. Intriguingly, however, nor does Ikemoto expect any new diplomatic initiatives from Japan, for example, seeking to build its own regional partnership or counter Chinese ambitions although Abe's apparent determination to press ahead with the TPP even without US membership appears to run counter to this. Instead, he expects Japan to cling even more closely to the security relationship with the USA. What effect the Trump Presidency will have on this remains to be seen.

Like Japan, the Republic of Korea has steadily developed its relationship with the EU while remaining dependent on the USA for security guarantees. And like both China and Japan, it is one of the EU's strategic partners but unlike these two, it already has an FTA with the EU, concluded in 2011. Contrary to widespread expectations at the time it was agreed, in headline terms EU countries appear to have benefited from it much more than has Korea, the overall balance of trade shifting in the EU's favour for the first time. In Chap. 7, Sunghoon Park and Michael Reilly argue that the real picture is rather different once account is taken of exchange rate variations, commodity and energy price fluctuations and other factors. But not surprisingly, the apparent outcome remains politically sensitive in Korea and this will inevitably have a bearing on any future negotiations.

On the one hand, there is likely to be pressure within Korea, especially from the automotive and petrochemical sectors, to negotiate a new bilateral FTA with the UK. It would also be in the UK's interests given the current volume of its bilateral trade with Korea. But this would in all likelihood lead to demands to renegotiate the existing agreement with the EU to try to secure more favourable terms for Korea than are thought to pertain at present. Whether the EU would be willing to do this is another matter. So, for Korea probably more than other countries in East Asia, the details of the UK's final agreement with its EU partners will be of the utmost importance in determining the nature of the future bilateral relationship. The less change there is to current trading arrangements within the EU, the easier it will be to agree new bilateral arrangements outside it. With this also comes recognition that none of this will happen quickly and that the original declared timetable of the UK government in 2017 is simply unachievable. Interim arrangements will be essential not just between the UK and its erstwhile EU partners but also between the UK and its other trading partners, including Korea, to minimise disruption to established trade and investment patterns until new long-term agreements can be concluded.

Singapore is even more dependent on trade than Korea, so it is striking that Lay Hwee Yeo in Chap. 8 suggests that the political repercussions and implications are likely to weigh more heavily on both Singapore and ASEAN than the economic ones. Part of this is because the same factors of immigration, stagnant wages and rising inequality that were perceived to be so important in the 'Brexit' referendum are also prevalent in Singapore, indeed were reflected in voting patterns in the 2011 general election there, together with a feeling that the elite and policy makers are increasingly out of touch with ordinary people. For Singapore's leaders, the outcome of the referendum was further demonstration that 'economics is global but politics is local.' Unlike their counterparts in Westminster, however, they cannot pass the blame on to technocrats elsewhere. The worrying implications for Singapore's rulers go further: for a country that has long prided itself on technocratic administration, cries of 'take back control' and the rejection of expert advice and views when casting votes are disturbing.

While the underlying philosophies of the EU and ASEAN as regional associations have been very different, Yeo also sees lessons for ASEAN from the outcome, arguing that the EU had too often overlooked or ignored its key principles of subsidiarity and proportionality. ASEAN must heed this she feels, keep its intergovernmental character and consensual decision-making and not be too ambitious as it considers moves to deeper regional integration. As with Korea, the future of Singapore-EU, Singapore-UK and ASEAN-EU relations will be influenced heavily by the final settlement between the UK and the EU.

In Chap. 9, Michael Reilly, Jyun-yi Lee and Chih-Mei Luo examine the likelihood of negotiating both a bilateral investment agreement (BIA) between the EU and Taiwan and a bilateral FTA between the UK and Taiwan after 'Brexit.' Although 'Brexit' creates a new strategic environment for Taiwan to pursue FTA negotiations with the UK, the authors argue that the UK government is unlikely to embark on FTA negotiations with Taiwan in the near future. Not only does the UK need to complete unfinished business with the EU regarding its 'divorce' but it also has to fine-tune or re-negotiate existing trade arrangements with third countries (around 44 in total) once a 'Brexit' deal is secured. After 'Brexit,' the UK is likely to give priority to agreements with the USA, China, Japan and other big trade partners before agreeing to FTA negotiations with Taiwan. The authors further argue that Taiwan has no incentive to put forward serious domestic reforms or improved market access purely for a bilateral deal but without these such an FTA would be of little benefit to the UK. A further obstacle, they argue, comes from China, which will try to insist that the UK first concludes an FTA with it before agreeing one with Taiwan. Taiwan's agreements with Singapore and New Zealand are both precedents, as indeed is China's accession to the WTO ahead of Taiwan. It is questionable whether the UK would ignore these precedents and Taiwan would do better to concentrate on negotiating a BIA with the EU as its top priority.

This, however, is subject to progress between the EU and China in negotiating their own BIA as well as to the EU's wider trade negotiation priorities. With the USA seeming to turn towards protectionism, or least bilateralism, however, the EU could become the global champion for free trade. The Taiwanese government hopes that such a change of stance by the EU would encourage it to launch BIA negotiations with Taiwan earlier than previously intended. However, concern about possible Chinese opposition and legal aspects of a BIA may slow down the progress of otherwise 'low-profile' consultations between the EU and

Taiwan. Furthermore, the EU may itself be distracted by internal problems, such as debt issues or refugee and migrant flows, and hence delay negotiation of a BIA with Taiwan.

A turn inwards by the EU would be understandable at one level. In addition to the need to resolve its own problems, the rise of anti-EU populism is a real concern. Despite the defeat of populist parties in subsequent European elections, people in East Asia are wondering whether 'Brexit' will be the start of a domino effect, leading to a total collapse of the EU, as it will become dysfunctional if key member states leave or block its common policies in response to their own populist demands. David Huang in Chap. 10 argues that the future of EU governance will depend on the balance of two forces, namely, identity mobilisation and the path-dependent nature of EU institutions. As an Asian scholar observing from afar, he anticipates an increasing use of referendums by European politicians to resolve their own inter- or intra-party disputes. He also observes a growing trend of anti-EU, anti-globalisation and anti-establishment parties gaining seats in local and national elections. Both the growing use of referendums and the rise of anti-establishment parties contribute to the politicisation of EU affairs. The EU is no longer governed by 'permissive consensus,' allowing cosy elites to set common policies. Instead, European elites must take into account popular demands through a more transparent decision-making process.

As a result, the community method, the most effective driving force of European integration, will be less applicable to new policy fields. In its place, there will be different modes of governance depending on the nature of the policy in question. In the aftermath of 'Brexit,' member states are likely to highlight diversity within the EU, leading to an entrenchment of existing forms of governance. Moreover, because of this kind of 'flexible integration' and the path-dependent nature of EU institutions, 'Brexit' is not likely to unleash a domino effect, leading to the total collapse of the EU. Nevertheless, the EU's negotiation mandate for 'Brexit' and remarks by its chief negotiator Michel Barnier in the early rounds of talks seem to suggest a tough and unified stance by the EU in dealing with the UK's demands. Huang argues that the EU's seemingly tough position towards 'Brexit' may go beyond a simple rationale of making 'divorce' work as soon as possible. Rather, the EU and its member states have incentives to consolidate internal coherence.

That the British electorate should not have considered foreign relations when casting its votes in the referendum is only to be expected. But the international impact of their momentous decision was brought home to them in no uncertain terms with the collapse of the pound on foreign exchange markets in the aftermath of the result. Their politicians had no excuses, however, and should have known better, especially those who promised the arrival of sunlit uplands if the country would vote to leave the EU.

The British government's mantra appears to be 'Reject Europe, embrace the world.' But in an increasingly interdependent world the countries of East Asia seem in agreement that their interests are better served by the UK remaining in the EU, not leaving it. For them, the EU has been a driving force of globalisation and they are likely to take much convincing that the UK alone can replace it in this respect. They may differ considerably in size, culture, development and political model. But they have all been major beneficiaries of globalisation and a common thread in all the chapters is the fears East Asian governments now hold for the future of globalisation. This does not just affect economic development. For while all countries in the region have prospered from the global economy, so old and sometimes bitter national rivalries and arguments have been held in check. Will they therefore seek to sustain globalisation, as Chinese President Xi Jinping called for at Davos in January 2017? Will they withdraw into themselves, as Ikemoto suggests Japan may do? Or will they find a third way? The UK may find the sunlit uplands turn out to be a dream. But its voters may also have opened a Pandora's Box in terms of the future of globalisation and what it might mean for East Asia.

Notes

1. Linda Colley: *May's global ambitions for Britain disguise a diminished status,* Financial Times, 21 January 2017.
2. David Cameron and Li Keqiang press conference: 17 June 2014, https://www.gov.uk/government/speeches/david-cameron-and-li-keqiang-press-conference-june-2014, retrieved 10 February 2017.
3. *Barack Obama says Brexit would leave UK at the 'back of the queue' on trade,* BBC News 22 April 2016, http://www.bbc.co.uk/news/uk-36115138, retrieved 10 February 2017. The 'Brexit' campaigner in question was Dominic Raab, a Conservative MP (now Minister) and former junior official in the Foreign Office.
4. *Future customs arrangements—a future partnership paper,* https://www.gov.uk/government/publications/future-customs-arrangements-a-future-partnership-paper, retrieved 21 August 2017.

5. Ibid.
6. Ibid.
7. Arron Banks: *The Bad Boys of Brexit,* London 2016; Daniel Hannan: *What Next: How to Get the Best from Brexit,* London 2016; Denis MacShane: *Brexit: How Britain Left Europe;* London 2016.
8. Andrew Glencross: *Why the UK Voted for Brexit? David Cameron's Great Miscalculation,* Basingstoke 2016.
9. Total tax contribution of UK financial services, eighth edition, https://www.cityoflondon.gov.uk/business/economic-research.../Total-Tax-2015.aspx, retrieved 13 February 2017.
10. *EU Japan Economic Partnership Agreement,* http://ec.europa.eu/trade/policy/in-focus/eu-japan-economic-partnership-agreement/, retrieved 31 July 2017.

CHAPTER 2

Brexit and the Anti-establishment Mood

Chien-Yi Lu

Preface

Attesting to Peter Gourvitch's insights of "second image reversed," "Brexit" is at the same time a product of domestic politics affecting regional politics and regional politics affecting domestic politics. The anger and frustration of British voters that propelled them to deliver the exit verdict had many sources, among which were a worsening of wealth distribution and diminishing possibilities of social mobility. This chapter examines the role of the anti-establishment mood in the Brexit referendum. It begins by identifying who voted how, and surveys the reasoning provided by major campaigns in both the Remain and the Leave camps. To determine which cues were more appealing to voters, I examine the context in which cue-taking took place. One of the main features of the context was an austerity-inflicted socio-economic condition characterized by a relatively high level of poverty and marked inequality. Such a condition has brewed an anti-establishment mood as well as fed xenophobic sentiments. It was within such a context that arguments put forth by the Leave camp, which had strong anti-establishment undertones, resonated with voters.

C.-Y. Lu (✉)
Institute of European and American Studies, Academia Sinica,
Taipei, Taiwan
e-mail: chienyilu@gate.sinica.edu.tw

D. W. F. Huang, M. Reilly (eds.), *The Implications of Brexit for East Asia*, https://doi.org/10.1007/978-981-13-0185-8_2

Identifying Leavers and Remainers: Who Voted How

Building on the literature on Euroscepticism, Sara Hobolt tests the approaches—*utilitarian, identity, cue-taking and issue-voting*—used for explaining variations in attitudes towards European integration for their influence on the Brexit vote. The *utilitarian approach* examines support for European integration based on an individual cost-benefit analysis. If the removal of barriers to trade through the Single Market is seen or perceived as beneficial to an individual, she is expected to be supportive of an "ever closer union." The *identity approach* seeks to explore the linkage between individuals' attachment to their nation and the erosion of boundary and self-determination through European integration. Individuals with a strong national identity and pride, who conceive of their national identity as exclusive of other territorial identities, are less supportive of European integration. The *cue-taking approach* takes the complexity and remoteness of the EU as its main features, resulting in a lack of interest, awareness or emotional attachment on the part of individuals towards the EU, and focuses on the role of political parties and other intermediaries, such as the media, in shaping support for the EU.[1] The *issue-voting approach* takes into account the fact that an individual's attitude towards the EU is not monolithic but varies according to the salience of an issue to the individual and her policy preference with reference to. It is possible, in other words, for an individual to be supportive of the EU on one issue but not on another.[2]

Using the rich data contained in the 7th Wave of the British Election Study, Hobolt built regression models with a Leave vote as a dependent variable and found that the utilitarian hypothesis has strong explanatory power, European identity is a powerful predictor of the Remain vote, party cue-taking does matter, albeit not necessarily as expected, and issue-voting had a strong presence in the Brexit referendum.

In order to investigate the importance of socio-demographic position in vote choice, Hobolt examined the impact of level of education, household income and age and found that those who are most likely to have benefitted from European integration—the better educated, the young and the well-off—were less likely to vote Leave compared to the low-skilled, the old and the poor. Deep-seated identities, too, are unsurprisingly a reliable predictor of vote choice: the more strongly "European" an individual sees herself the less likely she is to have voted to leave. In contrast, the more strongly one identifies with "being English" the more likely she is to have voted to leave. The relevance of party cues is clearly present in the

Brexit referendum, particularly when key figures within a party are united in their positions: UKIP (UK Independence Party) supporters are 88% more likely to have voted Leave compared to voters with no preferred parties. Labour supporters, in contrast, are 25% more likely to have voted in favour of Remain. In the Conservative camp, whose elites had different views, supporters were 12% more likely to have voted for Brexit compared to people with no party preferences. Hobolt highlights that while party cues do matter, many voters also use referendums as an opportunity to punish the political class in its entirety and vote against the *status quo*. Hence the impact of lack of trust in politicians is clearly discernible in the "Leave" vote. The more distrustful of politicians an individual is in general the more likely she is to have voted "Leave." Finally, individuals' policy preferences and attitudes towards salient issues are found to have had a strong correlation with their Brexit voting choice. On the issue of immigration, for instance, individuals who thought Britain should have fewer EU migrants were more likely to vote to leave. On the economic impact, individuals who believed that Brexit would reduce trade and employment were more likely to vote to remain.

Identifying Voices in Brexit Campaigns

Hobolt's analysis is useful for *identifying* who the Leavers and Remainers were but falls short of providing an in-depth and comprehensive explanation for *why* a majority of individuals' utilitarian analysis, identities, cues received and issue attitudes were the way they were, resulting in their preferring exiting over staying. In other words, why did so many people think they had lost out by being part of the EU? Why did some of those who used to identify with Europe cease to? Why did so many cues that the voters received send the signal that leaving was better? Why were the policy choices of the EU at odds with the issue attitudes of so many voters? Before answering these questions, I first lay out the supply of reasoning behind both the Remain and Leave camps (Fig. 2.1).

The Remain Camp

Centre Remain: "Britain Stronger in Europe"

Consisting of Conservative, Liberal Democrat and Labour "Remainers," the "Stronger In" campaign had as its central selling point the unbearable

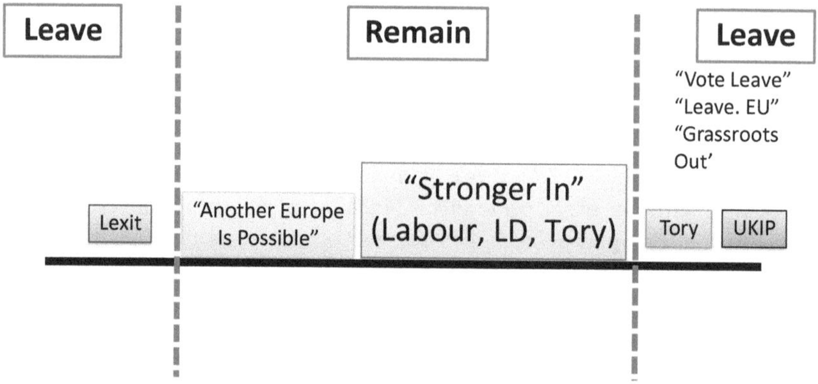

Fig. 2.1 Campaign groups in Brexit referendum. (Drawn by author)

economic costs of leaving the EU. This was deliberate and based on the previous referendum on Scottish independence, in which analysis showed that it was economic arguments that persuaded Scots to remain in the UK. The campaign was so non-partisan that even with Tory heavyweights on the team its script included statements like "Brexit would finish the job that Thatcher started." Convinced that as long as Brexit was narrowly framed as all about economic security the Leave camp would not even have a chance, the "Stronger In" campaign relied on the following core messages to persuade swing voters: "The choice in this referendum is economic security and global influence as part of the EU, or a leap in the dark. A vote to stay is a vote for certainty." Brexit meant: "Jobs aren't safe, prices will rise, mortgages will be at risk, and funding for your local school or hospital will fall. It is a risk not worth taking."[3] Hence, the "Stronger In" campaign stressed that:

- Nine out of ten economic experts predicted economic damage for the UK if it left the EU.
- One in ten jobs in the UK, that is, over 3 million, were linked to trade with the EU, and staying in the EU would create an extra 790,000 jobs by 2030.
- Every day, the British economy benefited from investment worth £66 million from EU countries.
- Staying in the EU allowed one to study abroad on the Erasmus programme, find work, take holidays and retire abroad all without a visa.

- Leaving the EU could translate into the evaporation of up to 950,000 jobs, and the average wage would fall by £38 a week.
- Staying in the EU would save an average family £350 a year due to lower prices for food, petrol, energy bills, flights and mobile roaming charges.
- Brexit would lead to a recession, meaning dramatic public spending cuts, job losses and years of financial insecurity for ordinary families.
- Brexit would result in the value of the pound to fall, causing the cost of merchandise and mortgage rates to rise, and the value of homes and pensions to fall.
- Leaving the EU would mean that the UK would lose vital EU funding for the farming, scientific and medical research programmes.[4]

Left Remain: "Another Europe Is Possible"

Much like progressive Clinton bashers might in the end have voted for Hillary Clinton only out of fear that Donald Trump would become the President, the left-wing campaign for Britain to remain in the EU—"*Another Europe is Possible*"—made its case largely by highlighting the appalling consequences of the rise of the far right. Supporting Brexit was portrayed as indistinguishable from legitimizing xenophobia and racism. For the Left "Remainers," the EU was a force against the xenophobic and nationalist UKIP and the "Brexit" Tories who used nationalism to cover up for their Thatcherite economic views and support for permanent austerity programmes. Britain should therefore stay in Europe to fight the far right.[5] In contrast with Lexit's view (see below) that it was a myth that the EU defended workers, the Left "Remainers" considered the EU the guardian of UK workers' rights, including limits on working hours, breaks during working hours, paid parental leave, equal pay for women, paid holidays and fairness for all. While it was true that some of these rights predated the EU, the EU did enhance them. Once Britain leaves the EU, so the argument went, in the absence of EU's control the Tories would be freed to move further right and would take away these basic workers' rights.[6]

Mirroring Lexit's emphasis that their goal was different from the xenophobic, racist, UKIP- and Tory-type Brexit, "*Another Europe is Possible*" had to stress that the "Remain" they envisioned was different from the EU membership that big business elites had in mind, being based instead on progressive reasons. Instead of walking away from the EU because it served mainly the interests of big corporations, the British Left needed to work with progressive movements across the continent to build a better Europe. The Left "Remainers" contended that there was nothing inherent in the EU that compelled it to advocate austerity policies, and that through an anti-austerity movement across Europe, austerity programmes could be overturned. For the Left "Remainers," the democratization of the EU was achievable, mainly through movements such as The Democracy in Europe Movement (DiEM) 2025 that strove to push for full transparency in EU decision-making.[7]

The Leave Camp

Vote Leave

The cross-party "Vote Leave" campaign was dominated by Conservatives. In contrast with the "Leave.EU" that focused on immigration (see below), "Vote Leave" placed more emphasis on the economic aspects of the disadvantages of staying in the EU. Pointing out that the country had sent over half a trillion pounds to the EU since 1973, the campaign claimed that by leaving the EU, the UK would be able to save £350 million a week to spend on things like the National Health Service (NHS), schools and housing. A total of £350 million a week was almost £20 billion a year, which was equivalent to half the entire English schools budget, or four times the annual Scottish schools budget and four times the science budget. In addition to breaking free from the fiscal constraints, leaving the EU would also eliminate obstacles to signing trade deals with countries such as Australia, New Zealand and fast-growing economies like India, China and Brazil. By leaving the EU, the UK would be free to trade with the whole world and therefore create more jobs. By staying in, in contrast, not only would the UK lose these opportunities, but would also continue to be outvoted on economic policy by Euro members and be forced to pay the prices for their failure. The campaign claimed that EU regulations were highly damaging to the British economy, costing small businesses millions every week, and that only 5% of British businesses exported to the EU but 100% suffered the burden of EU red tape.[8]

"Leave.EU"

Closely associated with UKIP's Nigel Farage, "Leave.EU" argued that by leaving EU British citizens would be able to enjoy better care from the NHS not only because of the re-allocation of funds from the EU budget but also through reduced hospital waiting times as controls on immigration would reduce demand for treatment. Controls on immigration would also mean less competition for jobs, resulting in a wage rise in the UK. By taking back control, politicians would become more accountable and help strengthen communities most damaged by EU policies, not only on immigration but affecting farming, fishing and industries like steel. "Leave. EU" emphasized, however, that leaving the EU did not mean leaving Europe: "We love Europe, its people, and its culture. We love its diverse mix of countries and enjoy the access we have to them. We have voted to leave an undemocratic state of disunion which is called the European Union."[9]

Lexit: Left Leave Campaign

Lexit, the "Left Leave" Campaign, urged voters to vote Leave. Contrasting to the slogan of the left for "Remain" that "*Another Europe is Possible*," Lexit believed that the EU was "unreformable." Being dominated by unelected bodies such as the European Commission and the European Central Bank (ECB) and with corporate interests to protect, the EU was not only undemocratic but anti-democratic,[10] with those running the unelected bodies contemptuous of democracy. The Lexit campaign also stressed that, unlike the Leave.EU campaign, it was emphatically not motivated by racism or nationalism, but was committed to democracy, social justice and environmental sustainability and was outward-looking, international and anti-racist.[11]

The cue that the Lexit campaign wished to convey to voters was that the EU itself, as well as the trade deals it struck, was part of a big business agenda, responsible for many of the negative distributional consequences of the country. For instance, the Transatlantic Trade and Investment Partnership (TTIP), on which the EU was in negotiations with the USA, would result in further privatization, lowering of corporate standards on both sides of the Atlantic and job losses. By being a member of the EU, nation states have been deprived of the ability to fight this business agenda and to rescue industries, nationalize railways or reverse austerity programmes. The Lexit team argued that the fact that the rich and powerful overwhelmingly supported British membership was an indicator of whose interests continued British membership of the EU would serve. Not only did the City and the Confederation of British Industry support the *status quo*, at least two-thirds of large British firms surveyed by the *Financial Times* also supported the "Remain" ticket.

Which Cues Were Voters More Likely to Take?

Given the array of cues for the Brexit referendum, how could we determine which ones stood out as more appealing and played a critical role in tipping the results? I argue that this question cannot be answered properly without taking into consideration the context and the situation voters lived in. Pollster Andrew Cooper's foundational research showed that voters were more or less equally divided into three categories: about one-third of British people were internationalist in outlook, socially liberal and positive about globalization, immigration and multiculturalism. Another one-third were nationalist in outlook, socially conservative and opposed to globalization, immigration and multiculturalism. The last third were torn between the idea of freeing the UK from the pressures of an open world and fear of an isolated Britain: their hearts told them to leave but their heads told them leaving was risky. The first category largely voted to remain, the second overwhelmingly to leave and the third split their votes.[12] Given the worldviews of the three-way, equally divided voters, and given the cues provided by different campaigns outlined in the previous section, what cues would appear more appealing to voters considering the social situation in which they were living? I argue that anger, fear, disillusion and frustration led enough voters to find resonance with anti-establishment voices/cues—whether from left or right—to tip the referendum results. But what were the sources of such anger and disillusion?

The Economic Background

Poverty

To trace the fear, anger and frustration of ordinary citizens, I begin with the economy. In 2014, 122.3 million people living in the EU were at risk of poverty or social exclusion (AROPE).[13] To reach the goal of the EU's "Europe 2020 strategy" launched in 2010, the EU needs to lift at least 20 million people out of the risk of poverty or social exclusion by 2020. That approximately one in four people living in the EU—the establishment of which was emphatically to make lives better through an integrated single market—is AROPE is itself stunning and disturbing; a closer look at the data further shows that many of those AROPE are living in countries commonly seen, for some long while, as being advanced, wealthy and prosperous (Fig. 2.2).

In the UK, one in three people experienced poverty between 2011 and 2014.[14] A total of 3.9 million children were living in "relative poverty"[15]

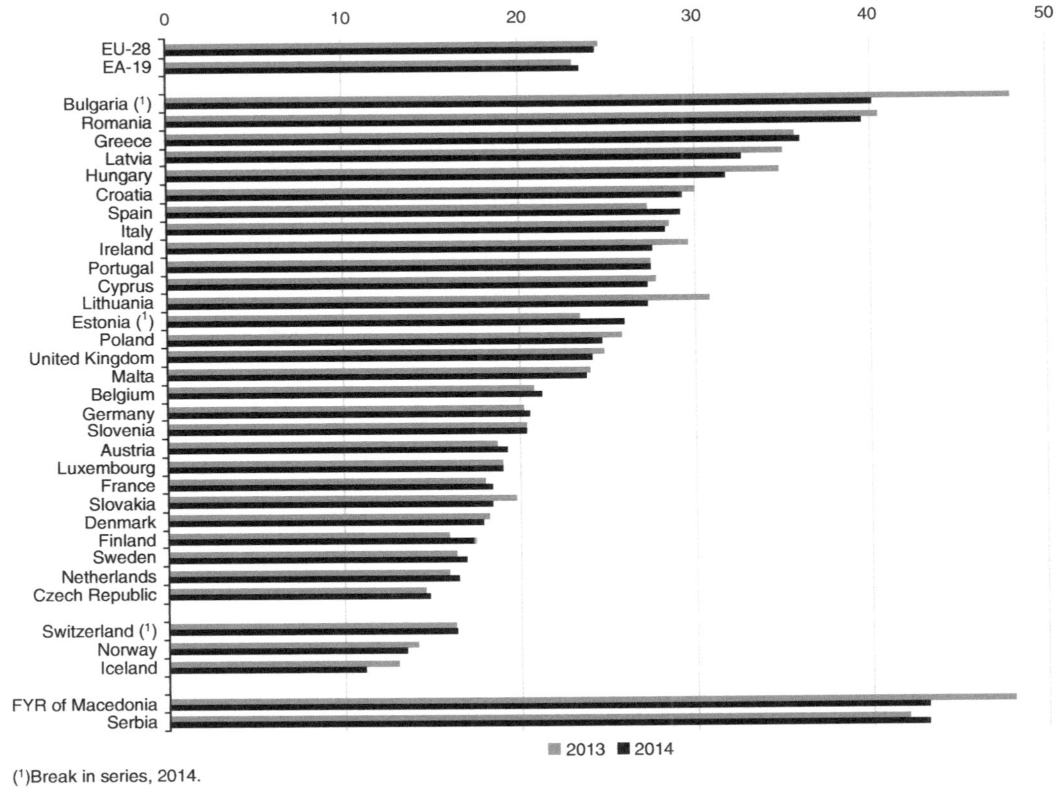

Fig. 2.2 At-risk-of poverty or social exclusion rate, 2013 and 2014. (Source: *Eurostat*: http://ec.europa.eu/eurostat/statistics-explained/index.php/People_at_risk_of_poverty_or_social_exclusion)

in the 2014–2015 period according to figures from the Department for Work and Pensions.[16] When the figure hit 3.5 million in 2012, the London-based charity "Save the Children" that raises funds mainly for helping children overseas published a report titled "Child Poverty in 2012: It Shouldn't Happen Here"[17] and launched—for the first time in its 93-year history—a fundraising campaign to help children in poverty in the UK.[18] Figures 2.3, 2.4, 2.5, 2.6, 2.7, 2.8, 2.9, 2.10, 2.11, 2.12, 2.13, and 2.14 demonstrate that, with the exception of London and Northern Ireland, the higher the rate of child poverty[19] the lower the voter turnout and the vote for Remain.

In some areas the inverse relationship between child poverty and the Remain vote is less evident than others. The reason might be the high degree of overlap between wealth and poverty concentration in metropolitan areas such as London. Mike Savage and Cunningham's study—based on the Great British Class Survey, for instance—shows that boroughs such as Enfield, Redbridge, Waltham Forest, Islington and Hackney have a high

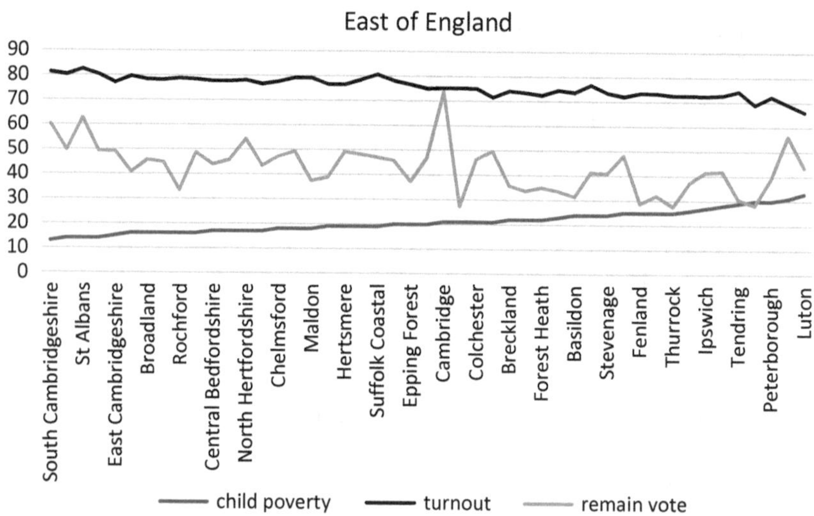

Fig. 2.3 Child poverty, voter turnout, and remain votes: East of England. (Source: End Child Poverty, 2014: http://www.endchildpoverty.org.uk/images/ecp/Report_on_child_poverty_map_2014.pdf; The Electoral Commission: https://www.electoralcommission.org.uk/find-information-by-subject/elections-and-referendums/past-elections-and-referendums/eu-referendum/electorate-and-count-information)

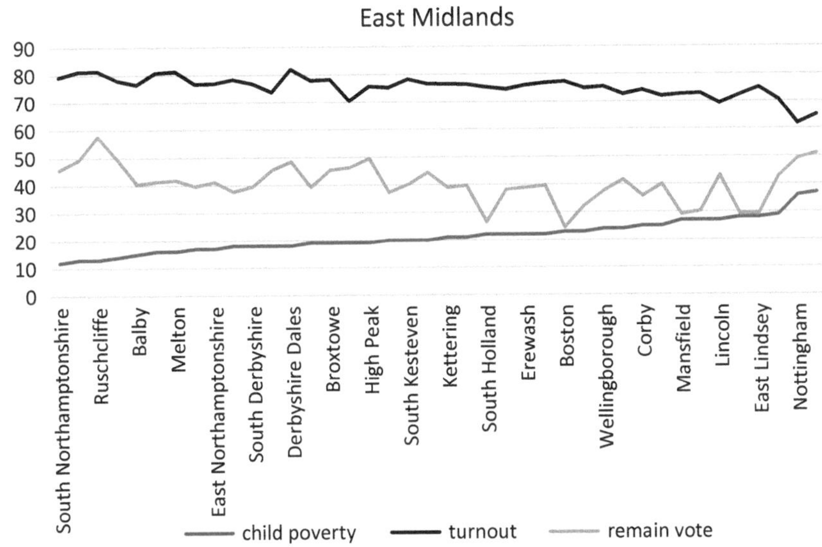

Fig. 2.4 Child poverty, voter turnout, and remain votes: East Midlands. (Source: End Child Poverty, 2014: http://www.endchildpoverty.org.uk/images/ecp/Report_on_child_poverty_map_2014.pdf; The Electoral Commission: https://www.electoralcommission.org.uk/find-information-by-subject/elections-and-referendums/past-elections-and-referendums/eu-referendum/electorate-and-count-information)

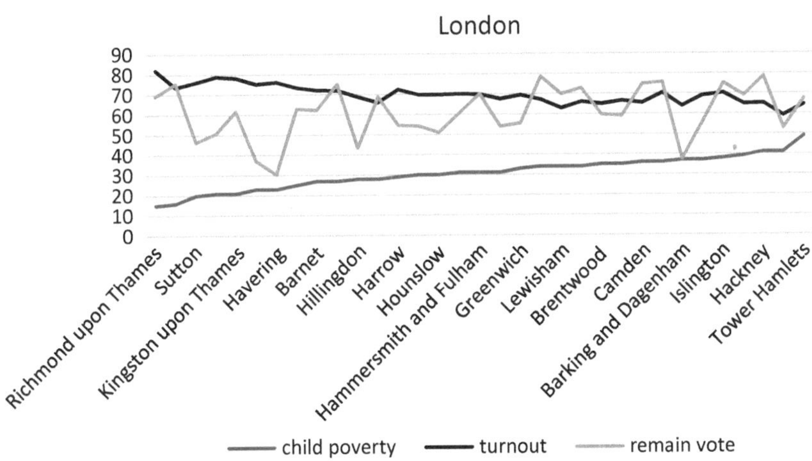

Fig. 2.5 Child poverty, voter turnout, and remain votes: London. (Source: End Child Poverty, 2014: http://www.endchildpoverty.org.uk/images/ecp/Report_on_child_poverty_map_2014.pdf; The Electoral Commission: https://www.electoralcommission.org.uk/find-information-by-subject/elections-and-referendums/past-elections-and-referendums/eu-referendum/electorate-and-count-information)

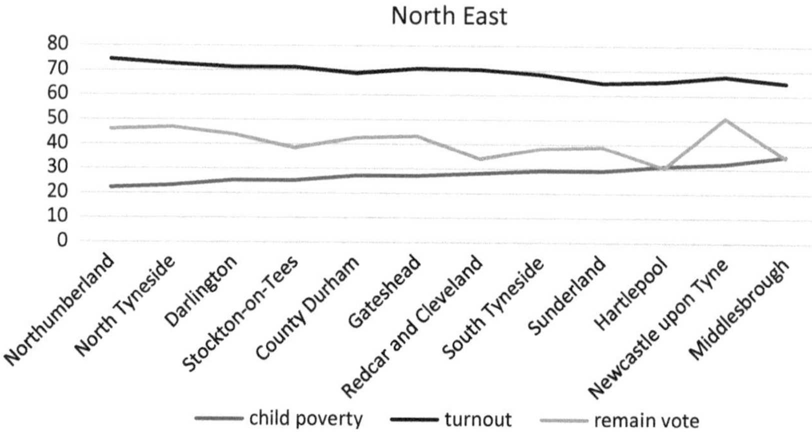

Fig. 2.6 Child poverty, voter turnout, and remain votes: North East. (Source: End Child Poverty, 2014: http://www.endchildpoverty.org.uk/images/ecp/Report_on_child_poverty_map_2014.pdf; The Electoral Commission: https://www.electoralcommission.org.uk/find-information-by-subject/elections-and-referendums/past-elections-and-referendums/eu-referendum/electorate-and-count-information)

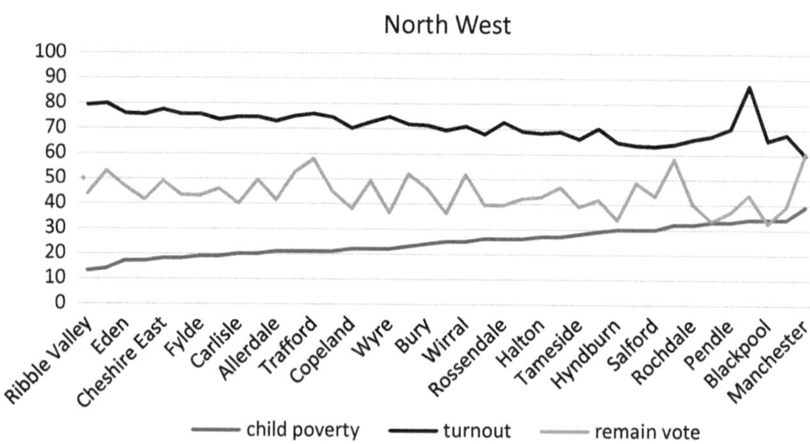

Fig. 2.7 Child poverty, voter turnout, and remain votes: North West. (Source: End Child Poverty, 2014: http://www.endchildpoverty.org.uk/images/ecp/Report_on_child_poverty_map_2014.pdf; The Electoral Commission: https://www.electoralcommission.org.uk/find-information-by-subject/elections-and-referendums/past-elections-and-referendums/eu-referendum/electorate-and-count-information)

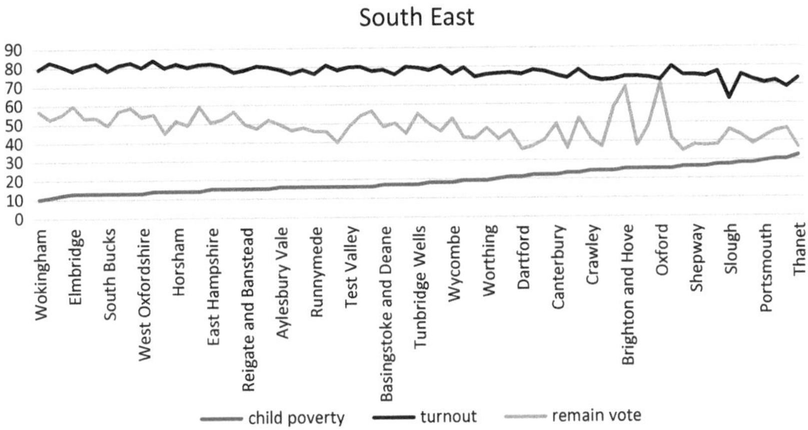

Fig. 2.8 Child poverty, voter turnout, and remain votes: South East. (Source: End Child Poverty, 2014: http://www.endchildpoverty.org.uk/images/ecp/Report_on_child_poverty_map_2014.pdf; The Electoral Commission: https://www.electoralcommission.org.uk/find-information-by-subject/elections-and-referendums/past-elections-and-referendums/eu-referendum/electorate-and-count-information)

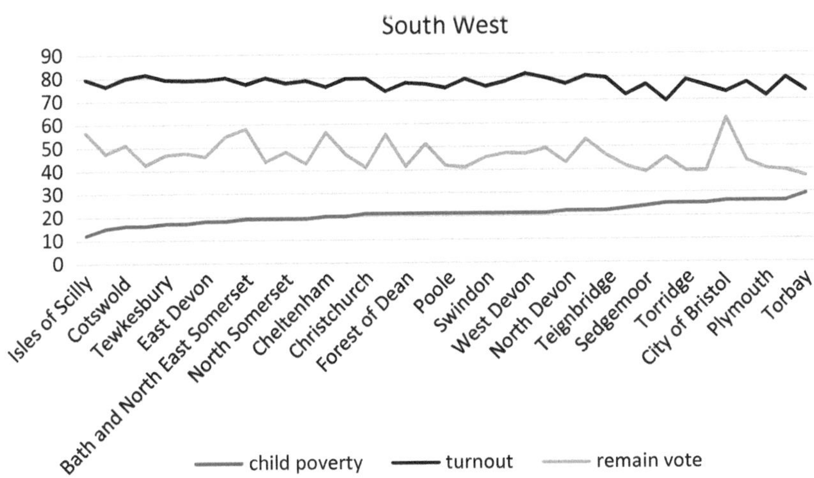

Fig. 2.9 Child poverty, voter turnout, and remain votes: South West. (Source: End Child Poverty, 2014: http://www.endchildpoverty.org.uk/images/ecp/Report_on_child_poverty_map_2014.pdf; The Electoral Commission: https://www.electoralcommission.org.uk/find-information-by-subject/elections-and-referendums/past-elections-and-referendums/eu-referendum/electorate-and-count-information)

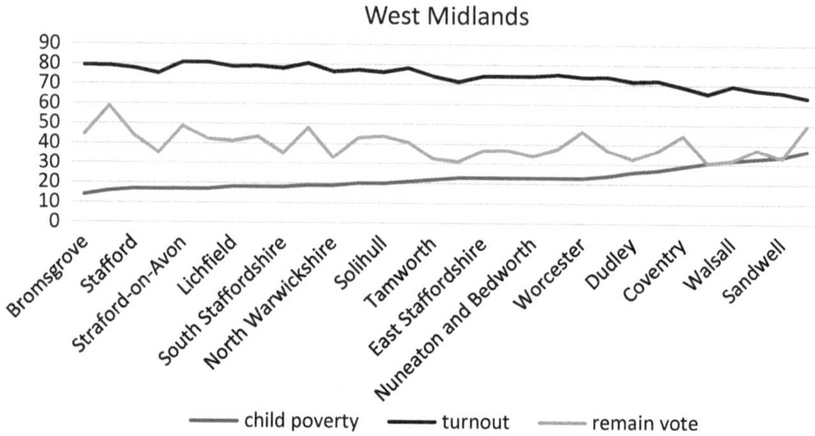

Fig. 2.10 Child poverty, voter turnout, and remain votes: West Midlands. (Source: End Child Poverty, 2014: http://www.endchildpoverty.org.uk/images/ecp/Report_on_child_poverty_map_2014.pdf; The Electoral Commission: https://www.electoralcommission.org.uk/find-information-by-subject/elections-and-referendums/past-elections-and-referendums/eu-referendum/electorate-and-count-information)

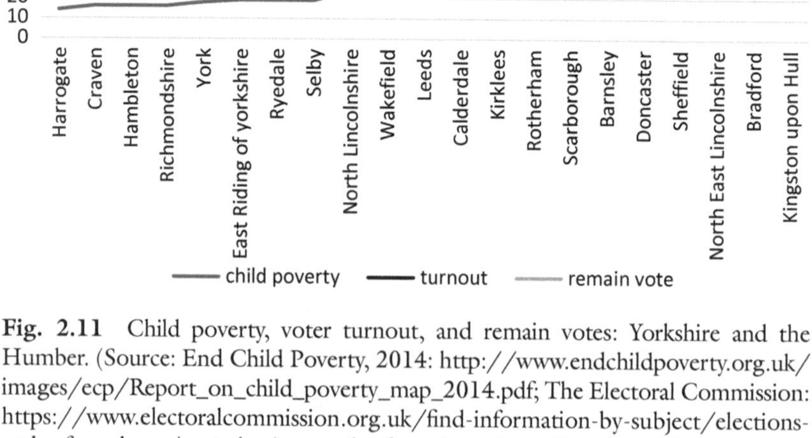

Fig. 2.11 Child poverty, voter turnout, and remain votes: Yorkshire and the Humber. (Source: End Child Poverty, 2014: http://www.endchildpoverty.org.uk/images/ecp/Report_on_child_poverty_map_2014.pdf; The Electoral Commission: https://www.electoralcommission.org.uk/find-information-by-subject/elections-and-referendums/past-elections-and-referendums/eu-referendum/electorate-and-count-information)

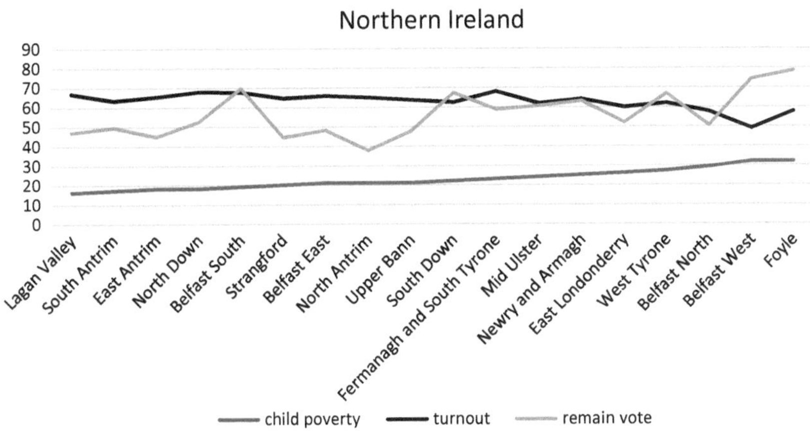

Fig. 2.12 Child poverty, voter turnout, and remain votes: Northern Ireland. (Source: End Child Poverty, 2014: http://www.endchildpoverty.org.uk/images/ecp/Report_on_child_poverty_map_2014.pdf; The Electoral Commission: https://www.electoralcommission.org.uk/find-information-by-subject/elections-and-referendums/past-elections-and-referendums/eu-referendum/electorate-and-count-information)

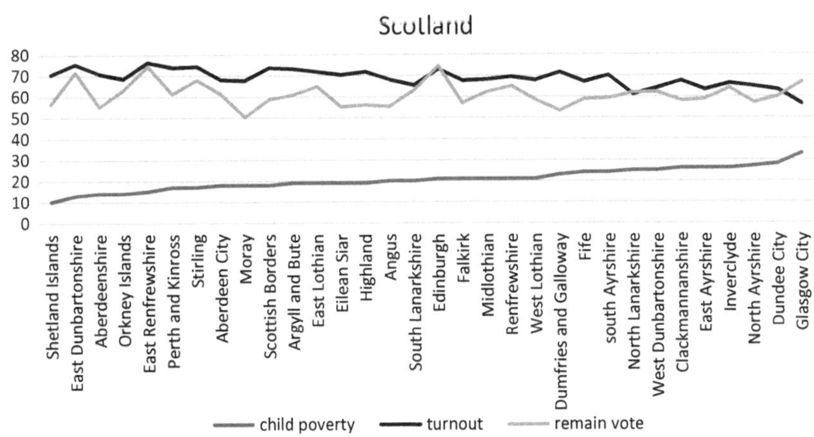

Fig. 2.13 Child poverty, voter turnout, and remain votes: Scotland. (Source: End Child Poverty, 2014: http://www.endchildpoverty.org.uk/images/ecp/Report_on_child_poverty_map_2014.pdf; The Electoral Commission: https://www.electoralcommission.org.uk/find-information-by-subject/elections-and-referendums/past-elections-and-referendums/eu-referendum/electorate-and-count-information)

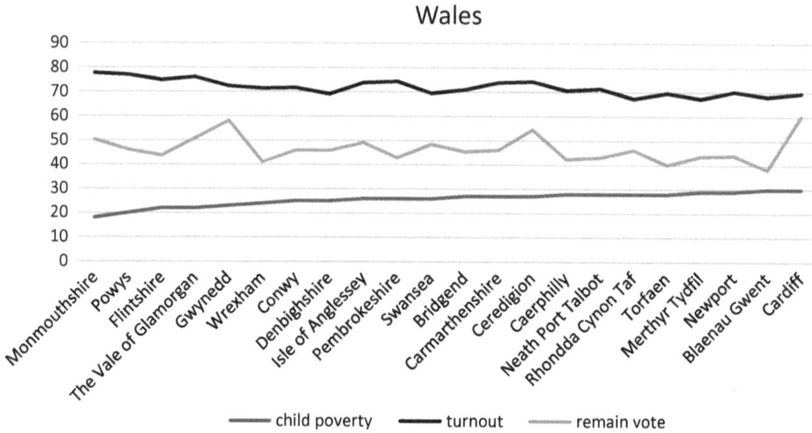

Fig. 2.14 Child poverty, voter turnout, and remain votes: Wales. (Source: End Child Poverty, 2014: http://www.endchildpoverty.org.uk/images/ecp/Report_on_child_poverty_map_2014.pdf; The Electoral Commission: https://www.electoralcommission.org.uk/find-information-by-subject/elections-and-referendums/past-elections-and-referendums/eu-referendum/electorate-and-count-information)

level of child poverty *as well as* a high level of economic capital (income, property and savings combined). In addition, Savage and Cunningham pointed out that some of the deviations of voting results from the pattern as predicted by economic status could be due to the presence of well-established universities in a city, as was the case in Manchester.

Complementary to economic status as an explanatory factor, Savage and Cunningham use cultural capital and social capital, factors closely linked to economic status, as additional factors helpful for predicting the voting results. By differentiating people more likely to attend classical music concerts, opera, to visit art galleries and museums from those who are less likely to do so, they found that the Remain vote was more associated with "highbrow" or "elite" culture.

Similarly, as was demonstrated in much of London, voters who have high social capital, for example, being in exclusive social networks of higher occupational status, were more likely to vote Remain. With the correlation coefficient being 0.790, exclusive social capital is the single best predictor of the Remain vote.

Using a more localized breakdown of votes from nearly half of the electoral wards in England, BBC News also found educational qualifications—

a factor inversely related to poverty—had a high correlation with the voting pattern, with wards where the population had lower levels of education more likely to have voted to Leave.[20]

Austerity

But why are the poor so poor? Why are there so many of them? Why are there an increasing number of them?

The financial crisis that began in 2008 and hit almost everyone in the financially integrated world had a huge impact on the UK as well. The government poured so much public money[21] into bailing out private banks, whose creative but toxic financial products caused the crisis to break out in the first place, that it deemed it justified to reach right into the shallow pockets of the very poor to fill the big hole in the public finance made by the banks.[22]

The BBC reported in October 2010 that, "[a]fter months of warnings, the UK's 'age of austerity' will begin in earnest on 20 October when the government announces the results of its spending review."[23] The biggest cuts in public spending since World War II introduced by the Conservative-Liberal Democrat coalition government were sugarcoated in language such as "rebalancing the economy," "we're all in it together," "balancing the budget" and "renewing prosperity through austerity."[24] At both central and local government levels, public services, investment in public infrastructures and expenditure on welfare were all targeted for deep cuts and retrenchment.[25]

Under his plans to reduce the budget deficit, George Osborne slashed welfare payments, cutting child benefit, for example, and raised VAT back to 20%, removing a reduction introduced by the previous government. But he also introduced a 5% cut to the top rate of tax and raised the threshold for personal income tax allowance.[26] This was in spite of the fact that cutting income tax and public spending combined with raising VAT had been proven to disproportionately harm the poor. A study by the Office for National Statistics (ONS) in 2010 had shown that, "for the richest fifth of the population, VAT added an extra 4 per cent to their tax bill. But the poorest fifth, often thought by the better off to pay no tax at all, actually pay 8.7 per cent of their income to the Treasury in VAT."[27] The Robin-Hood-in-reverse austerity measures ignited public anger. London saw the city's biggest protest since the 2003 Iraq War in March 2011 when more than 250,000 people took to the streets to protest against the measures. Protests lingered on and sprang up across the UK towards the end of 2011, echoing similar "Occupy" movements around the world.[28]

Five years into the austerity plan, instead of "savings estimated at about £83bn made over four years" as promised at the launch in 2010 of the austerity measures,[29] what the British government received was a letter signed by an army of economists, including Thomas Piketty, in June 2015 explaining why the plan could never have worked because it was not based on economics.[30] The British government received similar judgement on its austerity plan in the form of a "Leave" vote in the 2016 Brexit referendum.

Distribution

That the British economy is dependent on the EU is such an obvious fact that arguing or stressing it seemed redundant. Yet a *Financial Times* analysis[31] showed that regions most dependent on the EU economically had among the highest share of "Leave" votes in the Brexit referendum. Voters seemed to realize that the pie that they helped make bigger—the growth in GDP—was distributed in such a way that those at the top of the society receive almost the whole pie with only crumbs left for those at the bottom to share among themselves.

An Oxfam report published in March 2014, "A Tale of Two Britains" found that since the mid-1990s, the incomes of the top 0.1% had grown almost four times faster than the incomes of the bottom 90%. In money terms, this meant that while the richest 0.1% saw their income grow by around £24,000 a year, the incomes of the bottom 90% increased £147 a year.[32] The five richest British families listed in *Forbes* magazine—the Duke of Westminster, David and Simon Reuben, the Hinduja brothers, the Cadogan family and Sports Direct retail boss Mike Ashley—were wealthier than the bottom 20% of the entire British population.[33] Similarly, a survey by the Office for National Statistics (ONS) covering the 2012–2014 period showed that the top 0.1% of households saw a 21% increase in their wealth in comparison with the 2010–2012 period, while the poorest half of households saw their wealth rise by only 7%. The top 0.1% of households owned 45% of total wealth, while the bottom half owned 9% and the poorest 1% shared just 0.05% of wealth.[34] This extreme inequality is a cumulative effect of a long-term trend as Richard Wilkinson and Kate Pickett documented in their influential book, *The Spirit Level.* The book shows how badly the UK is doing in comparison with other developed countries in maintaining a fair system for distributing national wealth.[35] Figures 2.15, 2.16, 2.17, and 2.18 tell more of the same story, namely, how extremely and increasingly unequal the UK is.

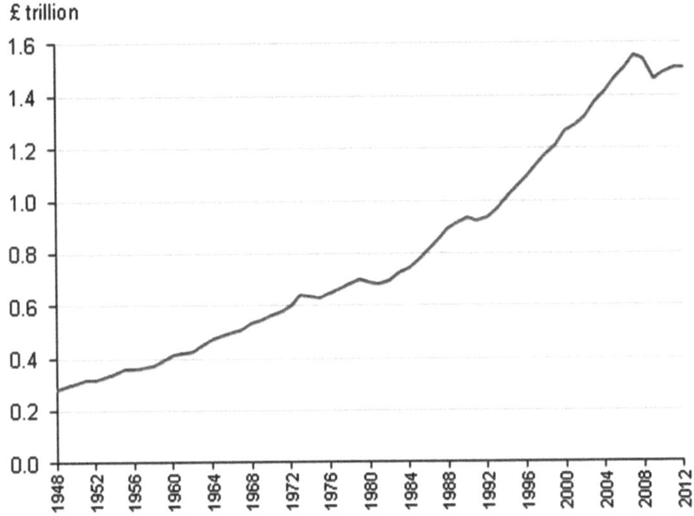

Fig. 2.15 Real GDP, UK. (Source: Office for National Statistics. http://webarchive.nationalarchives.gov.uk/20160105160709/http://www.ons.gov.uk/ons/rel/elmr/explaining-economic-statistics/long-term-profile-of-gdp-in-the-uk/sty-long-term-profile-of-gdp.html)

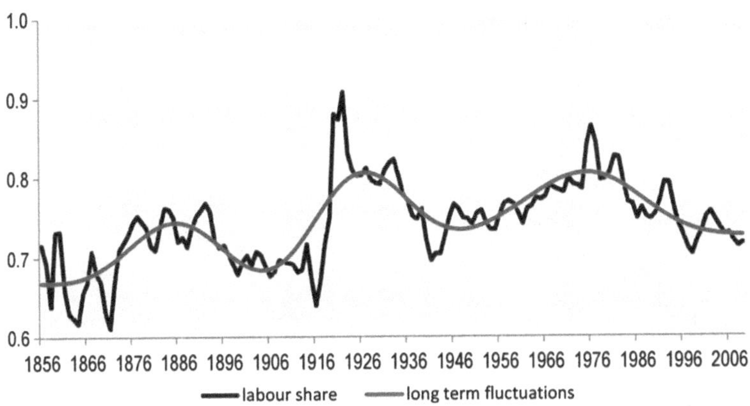

Fig. 2.16 The labour share in historical perspective: United Kingdom. (Source: OECD, https://www.oecd.org/g20/topics/employment-and-social-policy/The-Labour-Share-in-G20-Economies.pdf)

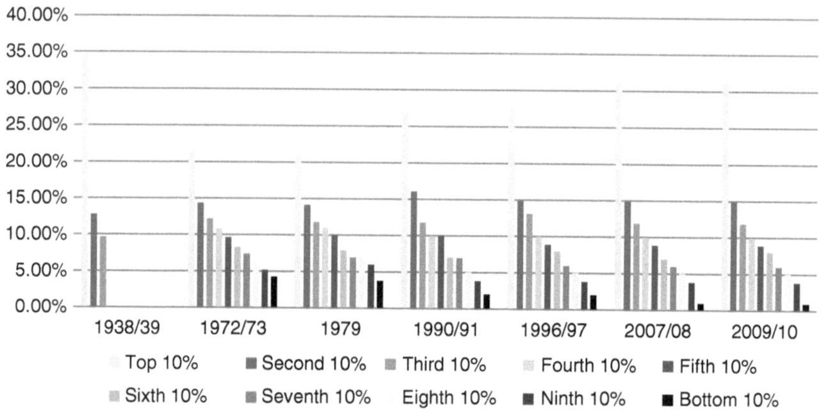

Fig. 2.17 Income share over time. (Source: The Equality Trust, https://www.equalitytrust.org.uk/how-has-inequality-changed)

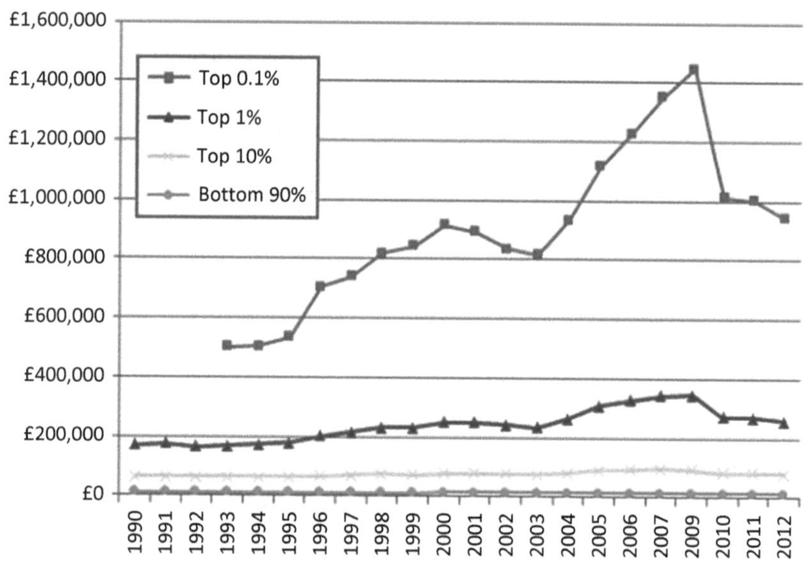

Fig. 2.18 Income growth at the top. (Source: The Equality Trust, https://www.equalitytrust.org.uk/how-has-inequality-changed)

As striking as the revelation of the widening distribution gap is, a common feature of statistics like these is the underestimation of the true wealth of the very richest due to their ability to hide wealth in offshore tax havens from Panama to Vanuatu, the establishment of which was often aided by the City of London.[36] In other words, on top of a worsening domestic labour/capital share ratio, wealth hiding practices, available only to the very top of the elite, further transfer wealth from ordinary taxpayers to offshore corporations and wealthy individuals, precipitating inequality in Britain. The revelation that David Cameron's family was listed in the scandalous Panama Papers likely heightened the public rage and contributed to the pervasive feeling that "the Brexit vote was a once-in-a-lifetime opportunity for exasperated people to kick Britain's rotten establishment in the teeth."[37] While Brexit may prompt the City of London to race even faster to the bottom to attract the world's hot money, such a plausible scenario[38] was neither common knowledge nor effective inhibitor for the negative emotions of leave voters, whose frustration was likely fuelled by how corrupt yet untouchable the British establishment had become.[39]

The Anti-establishment Mood

Given the social and economic reality that people were experiencing, it is not surprising that an anti-establishment mood had been easily and widely detected. This growing sentiment was reflected in the increasing support gained by the main anti-establishment party—UKIP—in local, European and general elections over the years. In the 2013 local elections, UKIP got its first significant breakthroughs when its equivalent national vote share reached 23% and its councillors increased from 8 to 147.[40] In the 2014 European elections, UKIP outperformed both the Conservative and Labour parties, receiving 26.77% of the votes, sending 24 MEPs to the European Parliament.[41] In the 2015 general elections, UKIP won 12.6% of the vote, making it the party with the third largest number of votes nationwide.[42]

UKIP, together with the right-wing Leave campaign, with their often false and at times xenophobic messages, was almost certainly the wrong solution for the social and economic predicament that its supporters were in. Nevertheless, UKIP, Brexit and Donald Trump in the USA present an attractive choice to some mainly because they appear to lie outside of an establishment perceived to be responsible for the hopeless situation their supporters find themselves in, and from which they struggle, but fail, to emerge. The very last thing these voters wanted was more of the same: the same group of elites—politicians from both the ruling and opposition parties, business leaders seeing nothing wrong with sharing among themselves just about the entire pie, policy analysts serving as the sounding board for those advocating the *status quo* to perpetuate the unequal distribution, media gurus behaving as though they were neutral but in fact caring more about their own share of the spoils and scholars either oblivious to or having something to gain from the existence of the establishment—telling them what to do and expecting them to obey as they had for four decades. More and more voters had fewer and fewer reasons left to trust the very people who had lured them by words through election rhetoric, only to harm them by deeds through policies decided on high up in the circle of the rich and the powerful day in day out.

For those who opposed to the establishment but nonetheless campaigned for "Remain," that is, the Corbyn faction of Labour and the "*Another Europe is Possible*" endorsed by the former Greek Finance Minister Yanis Varoufakis, Brexit was not just a choice between "business-as-usual/establishment-style prosperity and stability (Remain)" and "chaos and uncertainty (Leave)." For these progressive Remainers, business-as-usual/establishment-style prosperity and stability were not real prosperity and stability at all. While it was an imperative to expose the real agenda of the establishment, such an imperative should not by itself lend credibility to just anyone who claimed to be anti-establishment. From the perspective of the progressive Remainers, abandoning the establishment elites by embracing those on the far right was like refusing to be exploited by one group yet willingly offering oneself to be exploited by another. It was like saying "I refuse to be abused the old way, but please abuse me the UKIP way." The progressive Remainers therefore had the difficult task of highlighting that: "yes, prosperity and stability were important, but not the business-as-usual/establishment type; and no, voting Leave and inevitably boosting the bigoted UKIP will bring neither stability nor prosperity, and certainly not equality and social justice."

This was a very complicated message to convey. It was also an extremely demanding request for disillusioned voters to envision that another Europe was indeed possible. For people suffering non-stop pain, discontinuity and rupture were irresistible, while staying clear-headed in sorting out the cause of the pain was simply too difficult. The choices boiled down to continuity and discontinuity. Apart from this psychological aspect of the anti-establishment Leave vote, there was also a legitimate concern that another—a more progressive—Europe, involving the daunting task of forming a European-wide coalition of progressive movements, was just a pipe dream.

Alexander Betts addressed these deeper structural facts in his TED Talk and pointed out how the Brexit referendum exposed the deep divide as well as the shocking lack of awareness of this divide in British society. It was quite likely that many opinion leaders, even those who considered themselves to be inclusive, open, liberal and tolerant, had spent very little time in and knew very little about lives in the regions that had voted "Leave." Given the sharp differences in life experiences and life situations, it was hardly surprising that narratives about being open, tolerant, inclusive, European and global that made perfect sense for elites in their liberal bubbles sounded utterly unpersuasive or even irrelevant for those who struggled to survive.[43]

From this perspective, it is not surprising that Brexit was also a referendum on whether the British voters still trusted experts. The head of political and social research at YouGov, Joe Twyman, said "What we're seeing is a rise in the number of people who are dissatisfied, disapproving, distrusting of political institutions, political parties, the establishment, the media and, wrapped up with that, the experts." "A certain proportion of people don't believe a word of what they hear from those they consider part of the metropolitan elite."[44] As Figs. 2.19 and 2.20 show, Leave voters did not really trust anyone, while Remain voters believed that experts can sometimes get things right.

If past experiences played a role in voters' learning processes regarding their trust in experts, the Iraq War and the financial crisis served as good material that taught voters not to trust experts. The suspicion that experts may sometimes be captured by industries provided good reason for voters at least not to trust all the experts all the time. The high degree of distrust of newspaper journalists shown in Figs. 2.19 and 2.20 is a sign that voters did not consider the media as outside the establishment. NYU journalism professor Jay Rosen noted, "[j]ournalists today report on hostility to the political class, as if they had nothing to do with it... if the population—or part of it—is in revolt against the political class, this is a problem for journalism."[45]

Using the anti-establishment mood as a major explanatory factor for Brexit, however, seems to run counter to the widely shared impression that older voters voted to leave, while younger voters—the group stron-

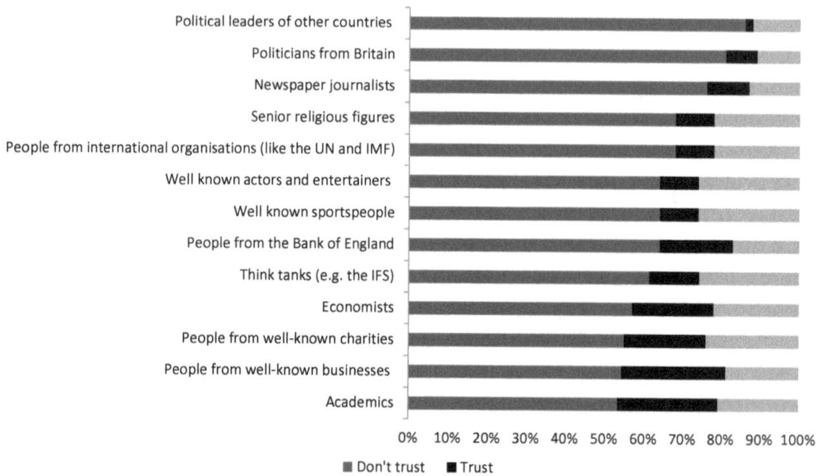

Fig. 2.19 How leave voters trust different groups. (Drawn by author. Source: YouGov https://d25d2506sfb94s.cloudfront.net/cumulus_uploads/document/x4iynd1mn7/TodayResults_160614_EUReferendum_W.pdf)

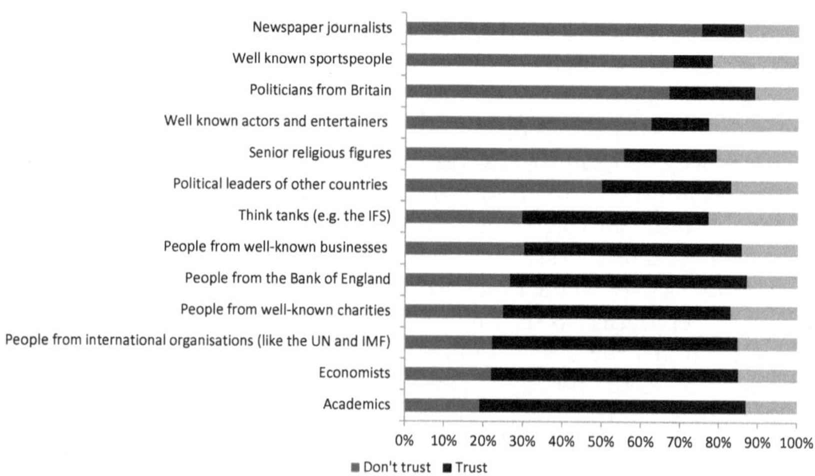

Fig. 2.20 How remain voters trust different groups. (Drawn by author. Source: YouGov https://d25d2506sfb94s.cloudfront.net/cumulus_uploads/document/x4iynd1mn7/TodayResults_160614_EUReferendum_W.pdf)

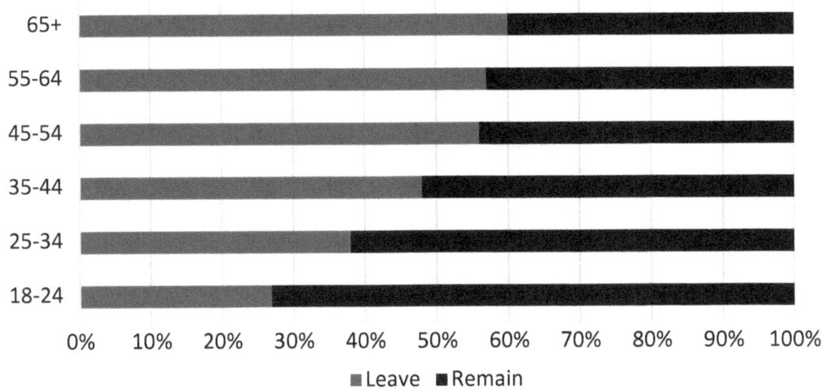

Fig. 2.21 How different age groups voted. (Drawn by author. Source: Lord Ashcroft Polls http://lordashcroftpolls.com/2016/06/how-the-united-kingdom-voted-and-why/)

gest hit by austerity and unequal distribution—voted to stay. It is true that "[t]he older voters were, the less faith they retained in the European Union. Nostalgia played a part in their decision, but so did lived experience. These are the same people, after all, who voted to join the Common Market in 1975."[46] Yet a closer look at the data reveals that the role of age in the Brexit referendum was presented, mainly by the media, in an overly simplified way. As is shown in Fig. 2.21, a clear majority of voters in the 45–54 group, a group not exactly "old," voted for Leave, while the 25–34 group was far from enthusiastic about remaining. If one takes into account the lower turnout rate in areas where a higher percentage of the population were young people,[47] it might be the case that the claim that young Britons wanted to stay, while old Britons had "screwed the younger generation" was neither accurate nor fair.[48] It is also worth noting that age ranked only fifth as an indicator of how people voted, trailing behind education, occupation (professional or not), possession of a passport and income.[49]

The Issue of Immigration

The economic situation and the resulting anti-establishment mood provided fertile ground for xenophobic ideology to spread. Two weeks into the Brexit campaign, immigration emerged as the top concern of voters, particularly among those who voted Leave. According to a Survation poll,

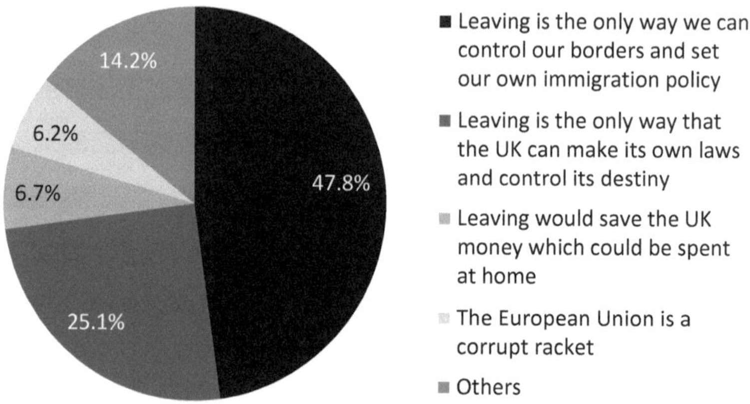

Fig. 2.22 Top reasons for voting leave. (Drawn by author. Source: Survation http://survation.com/wp-content/uploads/2016/10/Final-Brexit-Tables-101016JMDLL-1c0d0h2.pdf)

47.8% of Leave voters voted Leave because they believed it was "the only way we can control our borders and set our own immigration policy" (Fig. 2.22).[50]

There was evidence, however, that it was not "immigration" but "fear of immigration" that played a major role in the Brexit referendum. The highest levels of Remain votes were in areas with the highest levels of net immigration, while some of the areas with the strongest Leave votes have had the fewest new immigrants. In London, for example, the electorate voted resoundingly for Remain even though the city had absorbed 133,000 of the 330,000 net arrivals in 2015. A total of 78% in Lambeth in London voted to stay even though it had a net influx of 4598 immigrants. Castle Point in Essex had a net inflow of only 81 immigrants in 2015, but 72% voted to leave. Manchester, which had nearly double the level of net immigration (13,554) as Birmingham, voted to remain, while Birmingham voted to leave. According to Bobby Duffy of Ipsos Mori, "the actual direct impact on people's local areas and lives is much less widespread than the general concern…. It is… remarkable that the single most important factor driving the Leave vote actually only has a direct negative impact on one in five of the population."[51] In Alexander Betts' words, "the regions…that are the most tolerant of immigrants have the largest stock of immigrants."[52] Brexit, in other words, was to a significant degree determined by huge public misunderstandings about the levels of immigration. The socio-economic situation and the resulting anti-establishment mood served as the wind carrying misleading and confusing messages.

Notes

1. Sara B. Hobolt and Catherine E. de Vries. "Public Support for European Integration." *Annual Review of Political Science*, Vol. 19 (2016): 413–32.
2. Sara B. Hobolt. "The Brexit vote: a divided nation: a divided continent." *Journal of European Public Policy*, Vol. 23, No. 9 (2016):1259–1277.
3. Rafael Behr (2016), "How remain failed: the inside story of a doomed campaign," *The Guardian*, 5 July 2016.
4. "Stronger In" official website: http://www.strongerin.co.uk/get_the_facts#iSs3uhQwKhempQP8.97.
5. "Another Europe is Possible" official website: http://www.anothereurope.org/fight-the-hard-right/.
6. "Another Europe is Possible" official website: http://www.anothereurope.org/protect-our-rights/.
7. "Another Europe is Possible" official website: http://www.anothereurope.org/change-europe/.
8. "Vote Leave" official website: http://www.voteleavetakecontrol.org/why_vote_leave.html.
9. "Leave.EU" official website: http://leave.eu/en/our-campaign.
10. "Leftleave" website: http://www.leftleave.org/the-real-lexit-movie-part-1-feyzi-ismail-the-eu-is-not-just-undemocratic-its-antidemocratic/.
11. "Leftleave" website: http://www.leftleave.org/wp-content/uploads/2016/04/Lexit1_v1.2.pdf.
12. Andrew Cooper. (2016) "Thoughts on Brexit," *Populus*.
13. "At risk of poverty or social exclusion," abbreviated as AROPE, refers to the situation of people either "at risk of poverty" or "severely materially deprived" or "living in a household with a very low work intensity." The "at-risk-of-poverty" rate is the share of people with an equivalized disposable income (after social transfer) below the at-risk-of-poverty threshold, which is set at 60% of the national median equivalized disposable income after social transfers. "Material deprivation" refers to a state of economic strain and durables, defined as the enforced inability (rather than the *choice* not to do so) to pay unexpected expenses, afford a one-week annual holiday away from home, a meal involving meat, chicken or fish every second day, the adequate heating of a dwelling, durable goods like a washing

machine, colour television, telephone or car, being confronted with payment arrears (mortgage or rent, utility bills, hire purchase instalments or other loan payments). "Severe material deprivation rate" is defined as the enforced inability to pay for at least four of the above-mentioned items. The indicator "persons living in households with low work intensity" is defined as the number of persons living in a household having a work intensity below a threshold set at 0.20. Eurostat Statistics Explained. See: http://ec.europa.eu/eurostat/statistics-explained/index.php/Glossary:At_risk_of_poverty_or_social_exclusion_(AROPE).
14. Katie Allen. "A third of people in the UK have experienced poverty in recent years," *The Guardian*, May 16, 2016.
15. A household with income less than 60% of median income.
16. Angela Monaghan. "Number of UK children living in poverty jumps by 200,000 in a year." *The Guardian*, 28 June 2016.
17. Grahm Whitham. *Child Poverty In 2012: It shouldn't happen here*, London: Save the Children (2012).
18. Graeme Paton. "Save the Children launches first poverty campaign in Britain." *The Telegraph*, 05 September, 2012.
19. Child poverty data by Donald Hirsch and Laura Valadez, Centre for Research in Social Policy (CRSP) Loughborough University, compiled for End Child Poverty. Their estimates are based on official benefit and HMRC tax credit data adjusted to reflect unemployment rates and the differing risks of child poverty for in and out of work families.
20. Martin Rosenbaum (2017) "Local voting figures shed new light on EU referendum," *BBC News*.
21. According to The National Audit Office, support for the banks from public funds totalled more than £1 trillion at its peak. National Audit Office (2013). For more on this, see: http://www.nao.org.uk/wp-content/uploads/2013/07/HMT-Accounts-2012-13.pdf.
22. Michael Kitson, Ron Martin and Peter Tyler (2011) "The geographies of austerity," *Cambridge Journal of Regions, Economy and Society*, vol. 4: 293.
23. Edwin Lane (2010), "Q&A: Government Spending Review," *BBC News*, 18 October.
24. BBC (2012) "EU austerity drive country by country" 21 May 2012; Michael Kitson, Ron Martin and Peter Tyler (2011) "The geographies of austerity," *Cambridge Journal of Regions, Economy and Society*, vol. 4.
25. Michael Kitson, Ron Martin and Peter Tyler (2011) "The geographies of austerity," *Cambridge Journal of Regions, Economy and Society*, vol. 4: 293. For the magnitude and impact of the austerity programme, see Paul Johnson's opening remarks from an Institute of Fiscal Studies event on 27 June 2013 in London: http://www.ifs.org.uk/budgets/sr2013/paul_johnson.pdf.

26. *Ibid*; For more on this, see: James Meek (2014) *Private Island—Why Britain Now Belongs to Someone Else*, London: Verso, p. 22.
27. James Meek (2014) *Private Island—Why Britain Now Belongs to Someone Else*, London: Verso, p. 22.
28. BBC (2012) "EU austerity drive country by country" 21 May 2012.
29. Ibid.
30. Chang Ha-Joon, Thomas Piketty et al., Letter: "Osborne plan has no basis in economics," *The Guardian*, June 2015.
31. Financial Times: https://twitter.com/ft/status/746275255354818561.
32. Oxfam (2014) http://policy-practice.oxfam.org.uk/publications/a-tale-of-two-britains-inequality-in-the-uk-314152.
33. Larry Elliot (2014), "Britain's five richest families worth more than poorest 20%," *The Guardian*, 17 March 2014.
34. Heather Stewart (2015), "Almost half of Britain's private wealth owned by top 10% of households," *The Guardian*, 18 December 2015.
35. Richard Wilkinson and Kate Pickett. The Spirit Level—Why Greater Equality Makes Societies Stronger, New York: Bloomsbury Press, 2009.
36. Nicholas Shaxson (2016), *Treasure Islands—Tax Havens and the Men Who Stole the World*. London: Vintage, p. viii.
37. Ibid., p. x.
38. According to Shaxson, within hours of the Brexit vote, fantasists were already coming out of the woodwork to devise ways to form a united bloc to defend the interests of offshore finance. Ibid., pp. ix–x.
39. Shaxson quoted the response of a board member of a major high street bank to a former British Fraud detective's concern about the dangers of openly tolerating criminality in the financial system: "If you think Her Majesty's Government is ever going to prosecute people of my class, you are utterly mistaken. We are a protected species," Ibid., p. 309.
40. Karine Tournier-Sol (2015), "Reworking the Eurosceptic and Conservative Traditions into a Populist Narrative: UKIP's Winning Formula?" *Journal of Common Market Studies*, Vol. 53, no.1, pp. 140–156.
41. European Parliament results of the 2014 European elections website: http://www.europarl.europa.eu/elections2014-results/en/country-results-uk-2014.html.
42. BBC News results of 2015 election website: http://www.bbc.com/news/election/2015/results.
43. TED Talk: "Why Brexit Happened, and What to Do Next": https://www.ted.com/talks/alexander_betts_why_brexit_happened_and_what_to_do_next#t-608154.
44. Griff Witte (2016) "9 out of 10 experts agree: Britain doesn't trust the experts on Brexit," *The Washington Post*, June 21.

45. Glenn Greenwald (2016) "Brexit is only the latest proof of the insularity and failure of western establishment institutions," *Intercept*, June 25, 2016.
46. Ashton Applewhite. "Age Takes Center Stage Around The Brexit Vote--Not In A Good Way." *The Huffington Post*, 12 July 2016.
47. Financial Times http://blogs.ft.com/ftdata/2016/06/24/brexit-demographic-divide-eu-referendum-results/.
48. Ashton Applewhite. "Age Takes Center Stage Around The Brexit Vote--Not In A Good Way." *The Huffington Post*, 12 July 2016.
49. John Burn-Murdoch. "Brexit: voter turnout by age." *FT Data*, 24 June 2016: http://blogs.ft.com/ftdata/2016/06/24/brexit-demographic-divide-eu-referendum-results/
50. Jean-Christophe Catalon, "Immigration toped concerns for Brexit voters," *La Tribune*, 1 November, translated by Samuel White, *EurActiv*, November 1, 2016.
51. Alan Travis, "Fear of immigration drove the leave victory-not immigration itself." *The Guardian*, June 24, 2016.
52. Emily McManus, "I am British: Alexander Betts at TEDSummit," TEDBlog June 29, 2016: http://blog.ted.com/i-am-british-alexander-betts-at-tedsummit/.

CHAPTER 3

The Burial of Thatcherism? The Impact of Brexit on the UK's Relations with North East Asia

Michael Reilly

The UK and East Asia: A Relationship Shaped by Margaret Thatcher

The late Margaret Thatcher has a strong claim to having had a broader and deeper engagement with the countries of North East Asia than any other British Prime Minister before or since. For better or worse, she was the driving force behind the agreement with China on the handing over of Hong Kong in 1997 and made no secret of her admiration for Deng Xiaoping and the reforms he introduced in China. She was the first British Prime Minister to visit the Republic of Korea, in May 1986, and the only one to have visited Taiwan, albeit after leaving office, in September 1992.

Her relationship with her Japanese counterparts was more complex, reflecting trade frictions stemming from Japan's economic standing at the time. She reacted angrily when a Japanese-led consortium won the contract to build the Second Bosphorus Bridge in Istanbul in the mid-1980s, believing it to have received state-backed concessional finance in support of its bid. She reintroduced concessional financing arrangements into the

M. Reilly (✉)
Taiwan Studies Program, University of Nottingham, Nottingham, UK

D. W. F. Huang, M. Reilly (eds.), *The Implications of Brexit for East Asia*, https://doi.org/10.1007/978-981-13-0185-8_3

UK's bilateral overseas aid programme (the 'Aid for Trade Provision' or ATP) in response. But she was also thoroughly pragmatic and recognised the benefits that Japanese inward investment could bring to the British economy at a time when antipathy to foreign investment was widespread, not just in the UK but more generally.

Her relationship with the European Commission, especially under the leadership of Jacques Delors, was similarly complex. The UK tabloid press delighted in playing up their supposed differences, even heaping personal abuse on Delors. But Thatcher herself made clear that her opposition was not to the European Community as it then was, but to the notion of European federalism. She was happy to describe herself as a Gaullist and publicly supported the leading role of the Commission in setting European trade policy. Above all, she and Delors shared an objective in the creation of the European Single Market and she was quicker than other European leaders to realise the benefits this could bring to her own country.[1]

Her vision and engagement came together in grand form in the Nissan car factory in Sunderland in North East England. Opened in 1986 (the same year construction work started on the Second Bosphorus Bridge), at a time when the UK motor manufacturing industry was in seemingly terminal decline, its presence owes much to Thatcher, who helped persuade Nissan to commit to the investment. It fitted perfectly with her view of Europe and Britain's place in it: a community of nations with a genuinely single market allowing the free movement of capital and goods and in which the member countries would work more closely together, especially on trade policy and relations with the rest of the world. (The free movement of people within the EU, which was to prove such a contentious issue in the 'Brexit' debate, long predated the Single Market, being enshrined in the Treaty of Rome under which the EEC was created in 1957).[2]

Today Nissan's Sunderland plant claims to be Europe's most efficient car factory measured by output, making more than 500,000 cars annually or over 100 per employee—more than the annual output of the entire Taiwanese auto sector—and the majority for export to other EU countries. Nissan was the pathfinder in what turned out to be a remarkable two decades of foreign direct investment (FDI) in the British economy, much of it from North East Asia. It was followed by Toyota and Honda from Japan, Samsung and LG from Korea, Tatung and Taiwan Synthetic Rubber from Taiwan and over the years many, many more. For most if not all of them, the attractiveness of the UK lay in its membership of the huge new

European Single Market, combined with generally lower employment costs and more flexible labour regulations than in most other EU states at the time. It was an approach that has served the UK well. Almost 80% of the annual output of the UK car industry is exported, more than half going to other EU countries and Japanese companies alone now employ an estimated 140,000 workers in the UK.[3]

Today's EU is very much a reflection of Thatcher's vision and objectives. Not just in the creation of the Single Market but also in its enlargement to embrace former Soviet-bloc countries. Few European heads of government today see the future of the EU as other than *willing and active co-operation between independent sovereign states,* another of Thatcher's positions.[4] But in the bizarre and often unreal world of the 'Brexit' debate, it was those campaigning loudest to leave the EU that most frequently invoked the spirit of Thatcherism in arguing their cause. Another irony was that the city of Sunderland, so dependent on foreign investment and the Single Market for its own livelihood, was one of the majority of English areas that voted to leave the EU. Yet another, given the importance of foreign investment in creating domestic employment, was the near total lack of any consideration of the UK's relations with the wider world other than in the context of immigration. Insofar as foreign relations were raised at all, suggestions that inward investment might be affected were dismissed as scaremongering, too often along the lines of 'they need us more than we need them.'

If the Leave campaigners actually believed their own rhetoric, a reality check soon came in the aftermath of the vote to leave when in September 2016 Nissan's chief executive warned that further investment in the Sunderland plant was being placed on hold until the future of the UK's relationship with the EU was clarified. Prime Minister Shinzo Abe of Japan delivered an even clearer message to the new UK Prime Minister Theresa May at the G20 meeting in China earlier the same month, in the form of a 15-page memo setting out the concerns of Japanese companies about the outcome and the possible consequences.[5] So it was not surprising that Mrs May quickly sought to reassure Nissan that its trading relationship with the EU would not be changed by the UK's departure from the Union although whether she can actually deliver this in the negotiations now underway remains to be seen.[6]

This state of muddle and confusion reflected not only the essentially insular and inward-looking way in which the whole 'Brexit' campaign was conducted, with blithe and trite assumptions about reactions from elsewhere, but also the complete absence of any plan on the part of the Leave campaigners for what they would do if they won, leading to a new debate about the nature of the UK's divorce from the EU—whether it should be a 'soft Brexit,' seeking to retain as many links as possible with the EU, or a complete break and 'hard Brexit.' Mrs May eventually provided clarity about her planning in a speech on 17 January 2017 in which she stated that not only would the UK leave the Single Market but also the Customs Union, leaving it free to negotiate its own tariff arrangements with the rest of the EU. As she saw it, this could be through a completely new agreement, associate membership of the Customs Union, or as a signatory to some elements of it. The eventual outcome will not be known for another two years, possibly more, as she also recognised that a transitional phase to the new arrangements would be almost inevitable. But her statement points to it being a more complete break with the EU than was envisaged during the referendum debate by all but the most extreme 'Leave' campaigners.[7]

The Importance of Trade with North East Asia for the UK

The UK's relations with the countries of North East Asia are influenced primarily by three main strands: trade, investment, and what I call for want of a more precise term, influence. The last one is most diffuse and hardest to describe: the UK certainly is not able to offer the sorts of security guarantees hitherto provided by the USA but its permanent membership of the UN Security Council gives it influence and standing with other countries—but also brings certain expectations and even obligations. Insofar as this featured at all in the 'Brexit' debate, it was from an overwhelmingly isolationist perspective, reinforcing arguments that this status was another reason why EU membership was not relevant for the UK. Because membership of the EU was presented in such overwhelmingly negative terms, there was little, if any, consideration given to the fact that for many countries outside the EU, the UK's standing, particularly in bilateral terms, has often been judged by the way in which it has been able to use its status to influence broader EU policy. This is particularly true for countries in North East Asia. Outside the EU the UK will be far less likely to carry such influence.

I would also add a fourth, albeit lesser, strand: people-to-people links. These should not be underestimated: overseas students, especially from

Asia, make a vital contribution to the success of the UK's major universities while much of London's attraction, and increasingly that of cities such as Manchester and others, stems from their cosmopolitanism—arguably something that puts them at odds with other parts of the country in the Brexit debate. But I would argue that people-to-people links follow the other three—one only needs to look at the way bilateral trade with Korea or China or Taiwan preceded the surge in inward tourism, for example—so I have therefore concentrated on these three strands in trying to assess the future of the UK's relations with the region after Brexit.

Of the three, it was the future of the UK's trading relationships that received most of the attention in what passed for domestic debate in the referendum campaign. The advocates of a 'hard Brexit' appeared united in their conviction that membership of the EU constrains the UK's ability to trade freely with the rest of the world, not only in hampering British exports but also in raising the price of imports. It is a view advanced by Liam Fox, the current Secretary of State for International Trade among others.[8] Underlying this conviction seems to be a nostalgic view of the UK's history as a trading nation, of a global empire built on the back of trade. According to this, by leaving the EU the clock can simply be turned back and old trading patterns quickly and easily re-established. As one prominent 'Brexiteer' put it: *Why should we allow accident of geography to trump ties of language and law, habit and history, culture and kinship?*[9] Although not necessarily sharing the same nostalgic view, the future importance of trade for the UK was also emphasised by Theresa May in a speech on 14 November 2016 when she said that the UK would be the 'strongest global advocate for free markets,' although how she will reconcile this with her earlier commitment at her 2016 party conference to end the free movement of labour remains to be seen.[10]

North East Asia has featured more prominently in this context than most regions, not because of ties of language or law, much less culture and kinship but mainly because of the importance of China within the modern world economy, together with the history of the UK's trade links with the region in the nineteenth century, which fits well with the nostalgic vision of the UK as a great trading country.

It is a seductive picture. Hong Kong was a British colony until 1997 and Britain was at the forefront of opening up China to trade with the wider world in the nineteenth century. It was the first country to open a diplomatic mission in Taiwan and one of the first to do so in Korea, both in support of trade. But it is not a picture that bears scrutiny. The

'Brexiteers' argue that the lack of a free trade agreement (FTA) between the EU and China hampers UK businesses' ability to sell there. But it does not seem to constrain the UK's business rivals in other EU states. For most of this century, the UK's exports to China have been surpassed by those of Germany, France and Italy, the three other largest European economies. It is a pattern replicated in trade with other North East Asian economies. As Dr. Fox has admitted, for all the rhetoric about the UK's history as a trading nation, its export to GDP ratio is only 27.3%, compared to an average for the rest of the EU of 47.3%. The one real national success story in North East Asia for UK exporters in recent years has been in trade with the Republic of Korea (RoK, or Korea), exports to which jumped 131% between 2009 and 2015. But awkwardly for the 'Brexiteers,' this success came after the signing and entry into force of the EU-RoK FTA in 2011 (much of it too was due to increased oil imports from the UK, arising from wider changes in the oil market and strategic sourcing considerations, rather than from any broader change in trading patterns).[11]

Nor does wider evidence support the idea that the UK is any more outward looking today than its European counterparts. With English the lingua franca of international commerce it might be natural to assume that Britons must be well represented in commercial centres around the world. They certainly visit in large numbers. But to give two random but very different examples, in 2015 there were more than twice as many students from both France and Germany studying in Taiwan as there were from the UK, while in 2013 there were 50% more French nationals and 36% more German nationals resident in Shanghai than Britons. The Britons were even outnumbered by Shanghai residents from Australia, Canada and Singapore, all countries with smaller populations than the UK.[12] This relative lack of interest is reflected domestically. While UK universities seek to attract ever more students from overseas, a high proportion of them from Asia, the number of UK universities offering language degrees is in decline and anecdotal evidence suggests a similar decline in area studies programmes, including those specifically focused on North East Asian countries.[13]

This apparent complacency may not matter if the UK remains an attractive destination for North East Asia, be it for investment, trade, tourism or studies. Those arguing in the UK for a complete break from the EU claim that as the UK runs a merchandise trade deficit with most of the rest of the world, other countries will be keen to negotiate new bilateral trade agreements to mutual benefit. The argument lost some credibility in spring 2016 when, faced with a very real risk that the entire UK steel industry would close down as a result of a flood of cheap Chinese steel imports, it was revealed that the UK government, after trying to blame the EU for the crisis, had in fact blocked EU efforts to impose emergency duties on steel imports.[14] On the other hand, initial reaction in Korea to the result of the referendum seemed to support the protagonists' case, as the government immediately considered plans for a $17bn stimulus amidst fears about the impact on the country's exports. Reaction in other countries in the region was milder.[15]

Examination of the trade figures of each country helps explain why. The proportion of their overall exports to the EU going to the UK is very similar for all four North East Asian countries. Korean worries notwithstanding, of the four it is arguably the least dependent on the UK market. As Table 3.1 shows, in 2015, 16.16% of its exports to the EU went there—down from over 21% in 2000. For Japan, the proportion of its EU exports going to the UK has fallen steadily from just under 20% in 1995 to 16.2% in 2015, while in dollar terms the decline has been even more marked—from $14.1bn in 1995 to $10.7bn in 2015. Only China has seen the UK take a consistently increasing share of its overall exports to the EU but at 16.73% in 2015, the proportion was in line with those of Korea and Japan.

Table 3.1 Exports from North East Asian countries to United Kingdom and the EU

Exports from	*Year*				
	1995	*2000*	*2005*	*2010*	*2015*
(a) Japan to UK	14.1	14.8	15.2	14.2	10.7
(b) Japan to all EU	71.2	80.1	87.1	87.1	66.0
(a) As percent of (b)	19.8	18.5	17.45	16.3	16.2
(c) China to UK	2.79	6.31	18.98	38.78	59.66
(d) China to all EU	20.5	41.1	146.24	237.6	356.6
(c) As percent of (d)	13.61	15.35	12.98	16.32	16.73
(e) Korea to UK	2.87	5.38	5.34	5.55	7.85
(f) Korea to all EU	17.89	24.93	44.44	53.66	48.58
(e) As percent of (f)	16.06	21.58	12.02	10.34	16.16

Figures are in US $bn and the EU refers to exports to all current 28 members, irrespective of the year. Due to the way the figures are presented at source, it is not possible to give figures for Taiwan's exports on the same basis.

Source: Direction of Trade Statistics, International Monetary Fund

(In 2014 the UK overtook Germany to become Korea's main market within the EU but while this was also the case in 2015, it remains to be seen whether this is a long-term change following the EU-RoK FTA or a short-term blip.) The proportion is highest for Taiwan, at 17.1% in 2015, but in echoes of Japan's position, in dollar terms its exports were lower in 2015 than 15 years earlier.[16]

In all cases the figures suggest that while the UK is a significant export market, its importance falls some way short of being critical. For China, it is the seventh largest market in its own right, after Korea and ahead of Russia, while Korea's exports to the UK are just over half the level of those to Singapore, its fifth most important market. Overall, this would suggest that should the UK indeed exit the Single Market as expected, new bilateral trade agreements with it are unlikely to be the top priorities in trade policy for any of the countries concerned. A possible exception might be Taiwan, for whom a bilateral FTA would be attractive for political reasons. But the UK is most unlikely to risk possible displeasure on the part of China by agreeing to early negotiations with Taiwan, while for the latter the EU's willingness to consider a comprehensive investment agreement is a much more attractive prize. It also seems reasonable to assume from these figures that some tough negotiations will be involved to reach any new agreements. It is hard to see why China would be willing to negotiate a bilateral FTA with the UK on any more favourable terms than it would have done so with the EU, for example.

Investment: The Real Pillar of the Relationship

The investment picture is very different. FDI is more important to the UK than any comparable economy. In 2014, it was equivalent to 58.3% of GDP against an EU average of 43.6% and a world average of 31.8%. The figure for China was just 10.4%.[17] If anything, these figures understate the actual impact of FDI on the economy. An independent report on the likely impact of 'Brexit' on FDI calculated that foreign-owned companies account for approximately 30% of UK Gross Value Added, half of all UK manufacturing investment and one-third of employment in UK manufacturing.[18]

This is very much a legacy of Margaret Thatcher. In 1995, two years after the Single Market came into being, FDI in the UK was equivalent to a far more modest 16.1% of GDP, broadly in line with the then overall EU figure of 13.2%. Its steady rise since has been a consequence of the foundations she laid in terms of domestic reforms, enticing Asian companies, from Japan in particular, to invest in the economy and benefit from the access to the whole of the Single Market made possible by such investment.

FDI from the USA, Germany and France exceeds that from Asian companies but the latter is still very significant for the UK economy. Almost 54% of Taiwan's stock of FDI in the EU is in the UK. The figure for Japan is almost as high. More than 300 Korean companies are reported to have invested in the UK. Chinese companies are fast catching up: there was a reported $12.1bn of green field investment by Chinese companies in the UK in the first nine months of 2016, more than double the spending by Chinese companies on mergers and acquisitions in the UK.[19]

As the letter Prime Minister Abe handed to Mrs May at the G20 meeting in Hangzhou states clearly, the bulk of these investment decisions were made in the expectation of continued access to the European Single Market. It is impossible to imagine that foreign investment in the motor industry, for example, would have taken place on anything like the scale it has if it was only to supply the UK domestic market, even less so if foreign manufacturers were able to take advantage of the sort of generous bilateral FTAs some of the Leave campaigners have proposed and export to the UK from their home markets.

In terms of its broader international relations therefore, certainly as far as North East Asia is concerned, the key issue the UK government needs to be addressing as it considers its future relationship with the EU is less trading arrangements and more ensuring that the UK remains an open and attractive destination for inward investors. On this, Prime Minister Abe's memorandum could not have been clearer:

> *Since Europe including the UK is a major trading partner and investment destination for other countries in Asia as well as of Japan, it is in the common interest of all Asian countries as a whole that they continue to have access to the free market of Europe, including the UK. It is of great importance that the UK and the EU maintain market integrity and remain attractive destinations for businesses where free trade, unfettered investment and smooth financial transactions are ensured. In light of the fact that a number of Japanese businesses, invited by the Government in some cases, have invested actively to the UK, which was seen to be a gateway to Europe, and have established value-chains across Europe, we strongly request that the UK will consider this fact seriously and respond in a responsible manner to minimise any harmful effects on these businesses.*[20]

In short, access to the Single Market is what has made the UK such an attractive place for Asian investors and if that access disappears, or becomes less straightforward, much of the appeal of the UK as a country in which to invest will disappear.

Two industries demonstrate the importance of this especially clearly. The first is the automobile manufacturing sector, now completely foreign-owned in the UK apart from a few niche or craft companies. In 2016 Japanese-owned plants accounted for 48% of UK output in the sector.[21] But the biggest selling brand of cars in the UK for most of the last 40 years has been Ford, which no longer makes cars in the country. It remains a significant manufacturer in the UK but of engines and transmissions, which are shipped to plants elsewhere in Europe for installation in vehicles. Ford's production methods (it also maintains a significant R&D division in the UK) highlight the way in which modern manufacturing has responded to globalisation, with components being moved around the world, possibly several times, before final assembly. Within the EU the Single Market made this especially easy, largely eliminating the need for cross-border paperwork. Designing a new customs agreement that allows European or global supply chains to continue to function unhindered will be far from easy. As a further example, Ford currently exports diesel engines made in the UK to its plant in Turkey for assembly into vans which are then re-exported to the EU, including the UK. So, the UK will have to negotiate new agreements not only with the EU but also Turkey and all other countries with similar processes in place.

The second industry is financial services. As Sam Beatson observes in Chap. 4, the UK, specifically London, is the world's largest foreign exchange market by trading volume but the growth of its business has been due in large measure to the freedom the financial sector has had to conduct business unrestricted throughout the rest of the EU. The UK government is fully aware of the importance of the sector to its own coffers as it contributes an estimated 11% (£66.5bn) of the government's total tax income.[22] Other European cities would dearly love to capture a share of this business for themselves. The details of future trading agreements for the sector will therefore almost certainly be one of the key areas of negotiations. On their outcome will depend not only whether Japanese, Chinese and other Asian banks maintain or expand a presence in London but also whether or not currency trades and other financial business will be channelled through London in the future or through Paris, Frankfurt or elsewhere.

What the actual impact of the eventual settlement will be is hard to calculate at this stage. Inevitably all will depend on the details, how long they take to be agreed and what if any transitional arrangements may be put in place. The report cited at the start of this section suggested that FDI from China is likely to remain strong as it is mainly focused on the domestic market and stimulated by the relative decline of asset prices in the UK. But it concluded that not staying in the Single Market would certainly have a negative impact on most Japanese investors, while FDI from Korea was thought to be at serious risk, with major Korean companies already relocating operations out of the UK and new investments being postponed or eliminating the UK as a location option. There is also anecdotal evidence of some Taiwanese companies already deciding to move out of the UK.[23]

For Japanese, Korean and Taiwanese companies therefore, if not Chinese ones, the key to maintaining investments in the UK appears to be access to the Single Market. But Mrs May has ruled out continued membership of it, saying instead that she is seeking a 'bespoke' relationship between the UK and EU built around a new customs agreement.[24] The extent to which she can achieve this remains to be seen: the all- important details of an agreement, which will be key to companies deciding whether to remain in the UK, will not be known until after progress has been made in the negotiations underway between the UK and EU. Mrs May's weak parliamentary position as of mid-2017 may yet force her to modify her negotiating objectives. But it seems safe to conclude from the currently available evidence that the UK's continued attractiveness to North East Asian countries will depend in large measure on the degree of tariff and regulation-free access to the EU that it retains under the terms of its break. The higher the level of continued access, the less will be the disruption to the UK's commercial relations with North East Asian countries.

UK Diplomatic Influence and East Asia

While Leave campaigners' nostalgic views of the UK's impact on world history may have been overstated and outdated, this history has still been of relevance to the UK in its relations with the rest of the world, East Asia included. Until the handover of Hong Kong in 1997 it had at least maintained a semblance of a commitment to regional security, with troops and a naval presence there and a garrison in Brunei. Until 1992 it also maintained a token troop presence in the UN Command in Korea. It remains a member of the Five Power Defence Arrangements (FPDA) covering

Singapore and Malaysia, although these days even visits to the region by Royal Navy ships are unusual.[25] Although its physical presence may be vestigial, the UK has used the influence and knowledge it has acquired through this history to good effect within the EU, where it has played a leading role in the formation of policy to the region, a role recognised within Asia.

It was the leading proponent within the EU of the latter's hard-line approach to the military regime in Burma/Myanmar in the first decade of this century, for example, resisting efforts by its partners to 'engage' with the regime instead. It was also the first European country to remove visa requirements for Taiwanese, an outdated political imposition that had become an irrelevant irritant. Not being a party to the Schengen Agreement allowed the UK to do this unilaterally but it was a move taken in full discussion with EU partners, who were kept informed and followed suit soon afterwards.

But the clearest example in recent years of the UK's influence on the EU's East Asian policy was its lead in preparing and getting EU member states to agree in 2006 common guidelines *designed to provide a broad orientation for the EU's approach to East Asia, across the full range of its activities.* The background was a move in 2005 led by France and Germany to push for the EU to lift its Arms Embargo against China. This had been introduced following the crushing of the Tiananmen Square protests in 1989 and the move to lift it was motivated almost certainly by commercial reasons. It sparked alarm in the USA, Japan and elsewhere and almost prompted a crisis in both EU-US and EU-Japan relations before it was dropped. That matters reached this stage was widely seen as a reflection of the EU's lack of strategic interest in or understanding of North East Asia, most of its member states seeing the region only through the prism of commercial opportunity. Arguably the UK was more sensitive not only to views within East Asia but also crucially within Washington, and pushed for the guidelines as an attempt to reassure the USA, at least as much as East Asian countries, about EU behaviour and actions in the region. Last updated in 2012, the guidelines explicitly recognise the role of the USA in providing security commitments to East Asia and say that *it is important that the EU remains sensitive to this.*[26]

Self-evidently, a UK outside the EU would have been unable to do this. But any thoughts that an EU without the UK might thereby be more attractive to North East Asian countries were quickly dispelled, ironically given the background to the guidelines, by China itself. In a characteristically trenchant commentary, the *Global Times* described the outcome of the 'Brexit' referendum as 'a lose-lose situation' for the UK and the EU, seeing it as reflecting the general decline of Europe and crucially from China's perspective, making it easier for the USA to influence Europe.[27]

China's neighbours may see the possible increase of US influence on Europe in a more positive light but European reaction to remarks made by Donald Trump both in his election campaign and more especially following his inauguration as US President suggest there must be a question mark over the likelihood of this happening. What is not in doubt is that without the UK as a member, the EU will lose an important source of knowledge and experience in working with Asia generally. While the UK will clearly be far less able to influence EU policy, it is also likely to find that, as suggested by the *Global Times'* editorial, for North East Asian countries the value of their relationship with it is inevitably influenced by its own membership of the EU. Remove that and the influence the UK can bring to bear along with it and it is a considerably less attractive interlocutor.

This does not mean that the UK will be able to take a back seat on issues of international concern or significance. It remains a Permanent Member of the UN Security Council and as one will be expected to take positions on such issues. It is still required to present a twice-yearly report to Parliament on Hong Kong matters. These and other expectations could expose it in ways it might rather avoid. In the report to Parliament on Hong Kong in February 2016, the then Foreign Secretary Philip Hammond described China's abduction of a Hong Kong bookseller who was also a British passport holder as a 'serious breach of the Sino-British Joint Declaration' (on Hong Kong), the first time the UK had accused China of such a breach. But the statement came over a month after the EU had already said the disappearance of the bookseller was 'extremely worrying' and called on China to investigate.[28] So however unwelcome Hammond's statement may have been to the Chinese government, it can hardly have been a surprise. The UK could also claim that its position simply reflected wider EU policy. Once outside the EU it will no longer be able to hide behind such policy, or wait for the EU's External Action Service High Representative to make a statement first on issues on which it might feel uncomfortable in taking a lead. On the other hand, regular failure to make statements on potentially uncomfortable positions may lead other UN members to question its continuing status on the Security Council. This could prove particularly challenging for the UK in its bilateral relations with China.

There will also be uncomfortable, albeit lesser, questions over the nature of the UK's future involvement in regional multilateral groupings. It will presumably remain a member of ASEM (Asia-Europe Meetings) as this is a national matter but this group has never been of major importance for the UK, whose prime ministers have as often as not failed to attend its biennial summit.[29] UK diplomats and academics alike have paid more attention to the ASEAN Regional Forum, a more focused body than the disparate ASEM and which concentrates on regional security issues. The EU is a member but a bid by the UK in the 1990s for a seat of its own was rebuffed. Whether ASEAN will be willing to consider another bid by a UK outside the EU remains to be seen. The UK's seat on the Security Council gives it a good case but Asian members will presumably expect more from membership than simply turning up to meetings. If the UK is to keep engaged and on the region's radar it will therefore have to increase its current level of commitment and engagement but is likely to struggle to find the energy, resources and expertise necessary to do so.

Conclusion

The referendum on the UK's membership of the EU was fought overwhelmingly on domestic issues and perceptions. That is the nature of politics. But the consequence was that the way in which the UK's relationship with the rest of the world has benefited from its membership of the EU, and the accompanying benefits to the UK economy, above all foreign investment in the Single Market, was largely overlooked or ignored. Insofar as wider relationships did feature in the debate, they did so primarily in the context of trade.

Only when the final divorce agreement has been signed will we be able to say with real confidence what it will mean for the UK's relations with the countries of North East Asia. Even then, the full impact may not be known for some time longer, just as it took decades for the full effect of the Single Market and domestic de-regulation to become clear.

But for the countries of North East Asia bilateral trade with the UK, while important, is unlikely to be seriously affected by the latter's departure from the EU. On the other hand, they have valued and welcomed the UK's membership of the EU as an attractive location in which to invest to benefit from the European Single Market and as a voice of experience and moderation within the EU on wider issues. On its own, shorn of EU membership, the UK is unable to offer anything comparable or as attractive. North East Asian countries will look for alternatives—other investment locations that still give them access to the Single Market and alternative interlocutors within the EU.

Whatever the eventual outcome of the exit negotiations therefore, the future standing of the UK in the world is unlikely to be anywhere near as rosy as some Leave campaigners claim. This will be particularly true of its relations with North East Asia. No dramatic change in these is likely, rather a steady reduction over time, in much the same way that the trading relationship has been reducing in importance over the last two decades. In their current form these ties are very much part of Margaret Thatcher's legacy in which the UK was in the vanguard of globalisation. It was a policy which benefited both the UK and the countries of East Asia but a policy which her own avowed disciples now seem set on reversing. As one German business leader put it: 'They have buried Margaret Thatcher in the deepest grave possible.'[30]

Notes

1. Much of this background comes from my time as a UK civil servant, including as the desk officer responsible for G7 Summit policy from 1984 to 1986 and a dinner conversation with Baroness Thatcher in Seoul in September 1992. For Thatcher's views on her own philosophy and on Europe, see *Speech to the College of Europe*, Bruges, 20 September 1988, http://www.margaretthatcher.org/document/107332, retrieved 8 November 2016, and *Speech in Korea (The Principles of Thatcherism)*, 3 September 1992, http://www.margaretthatcher.org/document/108302, retrieved 12 November 2016. Probably the most famous example of tabloid abuse of Delors was *The Sun* newspaper's headline of 1 November 1990, *Up Yours Delors*.
2. Treaty establishing the European Economic Community, Title 1, http://www.cvce.eu/obj/treaty_establishing_the_european_economic_community_rome_25_march_1957-en-cca6ba28-0bf3-4ce6-8a76-6b0b3252696e.html, retrieved 27 January 2017.
3. Society of Motor Manufacturers and Traders, press release 21 January 2016, https://www.smmt.co.uk/2016/01/best-year-in-a-decade-for-british-car-manufacturing-as-exports-reach-record-high/, retrieved 12 November 2016; *Britain cannot easily dismiss Japanese Brexit warning letter*, The Guardian, 4 September 2016, https://www.theguardian.com/politics/2016/sep/04/britain-japanese-brexit-letter-eu, retrieved 10 November 2016.
4. Thatcher, *Speech to the College of Europe*, op.cit.

5. *Nissan delays Sunderland investment plans,* Financial Times 30 September 2016, https://www.ft.com/content/53bc5cec-8660-11e6-a29c-6e7d9515ad15, retrieved 9 November 2016; *Brexit makes Theresa May centre of attention at G20 summit,* Financial Times 5 September 2016, https://www.ft.com/content/ed63b37c-7364-11e6-b60a-de4532d5ea35, retrieved 9 November 2016.
6. *May assures Nissan of shield against Brexit tariffs,* Financial Times, 15 October 2016, https://www.ft.com/content/68c12fbe-920e-11e6-8df8-d3778b55a923, retrieved 9 November 2016.
7. *Theresa May's speech means the Brexit phony war may be ending,* Financial Times 17 January 2017, https://www.ft.com/content/a7fdb5b3-a0d9-36ee-ba47-9efa7808f43f?emailid=56b08ef56fee900300791f37&segmentId=2f40f9e8-c8d5-af4c-ecdd-78ad0b93926b, retrieved 27 January 2017.
8. *'Opportunities are ENORMOUS' Liam Fox launches trade talks with India, China, Singapore,* The Tap Blog 11 September 2016, http://tapnewswire.com/2016/09/opportunities-are-enormous-liam-fox-launches-trade-talks-with-india-china-and-singapore/, retrieved 9 November 2016.
9. Daniel Hannan, '*Free Britain to trade with the world,*' Financial Times 21 June 2016, https://www.ft.com/content/6d4a444a-36f5-11e6-a780-b48ed7b6126f, retrieved 9 November 2016.
10. *Theresa May seeks meeting with Trump before inauguration,* Financial Times, 15 November 2016, https://www.ft.com/content/d320139a-aa62-11e6-a0bb-97f42551dbf4?emailid=56b08ef56fee900300791f37&segmentId=2f40f9e8-c8d5-af4c-ecdd-78ad0b93926b, retrieved 16 November 2016.
11. Speech delivered by International Trade Secretary Liam Fox at the Manchester Town Hall on 29 September 2016, https://www.gov.uk/government/speeches/liam-foxs-free-trade-speech, retrieved 9 November 2016; International Monetary Fund, *Direction of Trade Statistics.*
12. European Economic and Trade Office Taipei, *EU–Taiwan Factfile 2016*; Bureau of Exit-Entry Administration Shanghai Municipal Public Security Bureau, *Resident Foreigners in Shanghai in Main Years* (via Wikipedia).
13. A 2013 newspaper investigation claimed that 'more than one-third' of UK universities had stopped offering specialist European language degrees over the previous 15 years—*European language degree courses abandoned by many UK universities,* The Guardian, 7 October 2013, https://www.theguardian.com/education/2013/oct/07/european-language-degree-courses-abandoned-universities, retrieved 16 November 2016.
14. *Tata steel crisis: Cameron defends blocking tariffs as Javid faces workers' anger*, The Guardian, 2 April 2016, https://www.theguardian.com/business/2016/apr/01/cameron-defends-blocking-steel-tariffs-as-javid-faces-workers-anger, retrieved 9 November 2016.

15. *South Korea- when Brexit is worth $17bn,* Financial Times, 28 June 2016, http://www.ft.com/fastft/2016/06/28/south-korea-when-brexit-is-worth-17bn/, retrieved 10 November 2016.
16. International Monetary Fund, *Direction of Trade Statistics.*
17. Investment Commission, Ministry of Economic Affairs, Republic of China (Taiwan); UNCTAD, *World Investment Report 2016.*
18. *The Impact of Brexit on foreign direct investment into the UK: Recommendations for Investment Promotion Strategy,* WAVTEQ, http://www.wavteq.com/brexit/, retrieved 12 November 2016.
19. *Lustre of 'golden era' wears thin for UK and China,* Financial Times, 11 November 2016, https://www.ft.com/content/b65c52ca-a75e-11e6-8b69-02899e8bd9d1?emailid=56b08ef56fee900300791f37&segmentId=2f40f9e8-c8d5-af4c-ecdd-78ad0b93926b, retrieved 12 November 2016.
20. Ministry of Foreign Affairs, Tokyo, *Japan's Message to the United Kingdom and the European Union,* http://www.mofa.go.jp/files/000185466.pdf, retrieved 10 November 2016.
21. *17 year high for British car manufacturing as global demand hits record levels,* https://www.smmt.co.uk/2017/01/17-year-high-british-car-manufacturing-global-demand-hits-record-levels/, retrieved 27 January 2017.
22. City of London Corporation, *Total Tax Contribution of UK Financial Services, Eighth Edition,* 2015 https://www.cityoflondon.gov.uk/business/economic-research-and-information/research-publications/Documents/Research-2015/Total-Tax-2015-OnlineFinal.pdf, retrieved 27 January 2017.
23. *The Impact of Brexit on foreign direct investment into the UK,* op.cit.
24. *UK trade minister faces questions over his role,* Financial Times, 29 July 2016, https://www.ft.com/content/a082b37a-54bd-11e6-9664-e0bdc13c3bef, retrieved 11 November 2016; *Theresa May's speech means the Brexit phony war may be ending,* Financial Times, 17 January 2017, op.cit.
25. The Five Power Defence Arrangements were established in 1971 between Malaysia, Singapore, the UK, Australia and New Zealand. They are not a formal defence treaty or commitment but the powers undertake to consult among themselves should Malaysia or Singapore come under attack.
26. *Guidelines on the EU's Foreign and Security Policy in East Asia,* http://www.consilium.europa.eu/ueDocs/cms_Data/docs/pressdata/en/misc/97842.pdf, retrieved 13 July 2016.
27. *Britain steps backward as EU faces decline,* Global Times 25 June 2016, http://www.globaltimes.cn/content/990440.shtml, retrieved 11 November 2016.
28. *UK challenges China over missing Hong Kong bookseller Lee Bo,* BBC News 12 February 2016, http://www.bbc.com/news/world-asia-china-35557226,

retrieved 12 November 2016, *Statement by the Spokesperson on the disappearance of individuals associated with the Mighty Current publishing house in Hong Kong*, EEAS Brussels, 7 January 2016, https://eeas.europa.eu/headquarters/headquarters-homepage/4962/statement-by-the-spokesperson-on-the-disappearance-of-individuals-associated-with-the-mighty-current-publishing-house-in-hong-kong_en, retrieved 12 November 2016.

29. There have been 11 such summit meetings since the first in Bangkok in 1996. The UK Prime Minister has attended six at most, and some of those for only part of the time.
30. Financial Times, 7 October 2016, in a round-up of reactions to speeches at the Conservative Party Conference.

CHAPTER 4

Era of Realignments: Britain and Its Relations with China Post-Brexit

Sam Beatson

Introduction: The Brexit Decision and the Triggering of Article 50

On 23 June 2016, despite both Scotland and Northern Ireland voting to remain, 52% of British people overall voted to exit the European Union (EU), precipitating the greatest change in British foreign policy since the Second World War. Then Prime Minister David Cameron announced his resignation live on television as soon as the result became clear. His political career was finished only a few weeks later with a cloud of disapproval and ignominy hanging over his head. The lack of domestic certainty that followed has made it very difficult to spell out clearly what Britain's existence outside the Union might look like in any detail. Core issues remain unresolved more than a year after the vote and almost six months into a two-year limit for negotiations around leaving the EU after Theresa May triggered the Article 50 plan from the 2009 Lisbon Treaty on 28 March 2017. If an agreement is not ratified or there is no agreed extension period, trade rules between the UK and remaining EU countries could then default to being based on World Trade Organisation (WTO) tariffs.

S. Beatson (✉)
St John's College, The University of Hong Kong,
Hong Kong, Hong Kong

D. W. F. Huang, M. Reilly (eds.), *The Implications of Brexit for East Asia*, https://doi.org/10.1007/978-981-13-0185-8_4

No agreement on the 'divorce' aspects is likely until late 2017 and probably later, including financial settlement costs the UK may have to bear for Brexit. The bill will likely cover budget commitments for multi-year projects, pension contributions for EU officials, existing contingent liabilities based on outstanding loans to EU member states and costs of relocation of EU research and agency sites, offset partially by budget, rebate and asset share receipts. Moreover, there have been highly visible internal splits at cabinet level around what Brexit ought to look like in respect of broader issues.

Hypothetical scenarios have arisen despite Theresa May rejecting the idea of an 'off the shelf option'—a possible 'hard Brexit', a 'soft Brexit' and what I will term a 'malleable Brexit' (see Table 4.1). The UK government seems at present to acknowledge the complexities of the issues involved and seeks to address transitional arrangements as the discussions evolve, while factionalism in the cabinet indicates there is a clear 'hard Brexit' leader in International Trade Secretary Liam Fox and 'soft Brexit' proponent in Chancellor Philip Hammond. The key indicator for the hard Brexit would be a tough and unrelenting stance by the UK government on immigration—both a very important concern of Brexit voters and one of the four essential movement 'freedoms' of EU membership—people, capital, goods and services. EU leaders have repeatedly relayed the mantra that the four freedoms are non-negotiable.[1] The 'soft Brexit' seeks an approach that keeps existing arrangements on trade and labour aligned with current measures under EU membership but under a non-membership framework. The 'malleable' stance presented here mitigates exiting the EU Customs Union by negotiated bilateral agreements and access to public and service contracts without necessarily the commitment to the extent of free movement opposed so strongly by 'Brexiteers' and offers flexibility in transitional arrangements.

Adoption of any of the models or some variant in the end does still mean that the only outcome for the UK will be to leave a group it had at least some influence and power in and to sit outside it, forced to accept its diktats and unable to offer any responses. This seems a somewhat perverse outcome to a referendum for which those promoting leave had made, as their mantra, the words 'take back control'. Control would be precisely what the UK would be losing.

Most accept now that leaving the Union and the Single Market is the most likely outcome of the referendum and Theresa May's public commitments to Brexit have done little to change this prognostic conjecture.

Table 4.1 Hypothetical hard, soft and malleable Brexits

Mode of Brexit	*Advantages*	*Disadvantages*	*Example country*
Hard Brexit	Control over immigration Freedom to arrange trade deals No payments to Brussels	No longer a member of the Customs Union No longer a represented member of the political union Loss of tax revenues Predicted 10% lower GFP Tariffs may be applied to British goods and services	Brazil, Russia
Soft Brexit	Free trade agreements (FTAs) can be tabled with other countries if not custom union member Substantial access to the single market Predicted to be the least economically harmful Potentially tariff free, with financial services 'passporting' rights retained	Incomplete access to the single market Some of the arrangements (e.g. Norway, Turkey) require making EU budget contributions EU leaders are demanding commitment to freedom of movement	Norway, Switzerland, Turkey, Iceland, Lichtenstein
Malleable Brexit	No need to commit to freedom of movement rules Negotiated bilateral trade agreement (e.g. reduced tariffs) Access to public contracts and market for services IP protection Transitional flexibility	Access to single market on less favourable terms, for example, tariffs need to be negotiated WTO membership may need to be renegotiated	Canada

Sources: IBTimes.co.uk (Silvera, Ian. 2016. "Learn the difference between a hard Brexit and a soft Brexit in just four minutes." *International Business Times.* 11 October. Accessed 01 10, 2017. http://www.ibtimes.co.uk/learn-difference-between-hard-brexit-soft-brexit-just-four-minutes-1585795) and BBC News (BBC News. 2016. "Politics." *Brexit—What are the options?* 16 December. Accessed 01 11, 2017. http://www.bbc.co.uk/news/uk-politics-37507129)

However, voters on 23 June 2016 probably did not think much about the diplomatic consequences of the vote were it to favour leaving the EU. As in most polities, international relations figure rarely, if at all, in the calculations of people voting. Domestic issues, economic growth in particular, are foremost. And despite the almost universal support by economists and experts that leaving the EU was not in the UK's interests, this had little impact on the end result at the ballot box. Brexit has left the British government in a unique position: possession of a clear instruction by the British people to do something, which they themselves do not quite know how to do, and, in many cases, are very reluctant to do.

Since 2014, Britain under the then Chancellor of the Exchequer George Osborne has been pursuing a zealously transactional relationship with China, largely predicated on increasing Chinese investment into the UK and ensuring that London is placed at the forefront of Chinese plans about the development of its finance sector and internationalisation of the renminbi (RMB). The direct consequence of this was to have a state visit by Xi Jinping in October 2015, the unilateral decision by the UK to be a founder member of the Chinese instigated Asian Infrastructure Investment Bank (AIIB) in March 2015 and support for Chinese investment in a nuclear power station at Hinkley Point, Somerset, confirmed after a delay to investigate security implications in September 2016. Each of these carries risks, in some cases viewed as substantial security risks, and each has been seen as jogging UK-China relations in directions they have never gone in before.

What are the implications of Brexit on the UK-China relationship? This chapter examines it, beginning with a very brief foray into the historical relationship between Britain and China, then looks at contemporary trade ties (imports and exports), foreign direct investment (FDI), financial markets, including the internationalisation of the RMB, free trade agreements (FTAs) of China and security and diplomacy. These sections are followed by a concluding set of remarks.

The UK-China Relationship

The Historical Relationship

The UK-China relationship is a long established one. Of all European nations, Britain has perhaps the longest and deepest engagement with China. It sent trade missions to the Qing Court in the late eighteenth century. From the middle of the nineteenth century, it engaged in the infamous Sino-British Wars, gaining rights over Hong Kong, a territory it maintained sovereignty over until 1997. There were few areas in China where Great Britain did not seek some interest and benefit. Through the 1913 Simla Convention, Britain even managed to have an influence on the remote region of Tibet.

This history may have led to mutual awareness and interest, but it also created a fair amount of baggage. In the post-1997 era, after the handback of Hong Kong, a process which had been long and often fraught, the UK decided to simplify things by entering an era of 'engagement'. This meant, in the immortal words of the then Prime Minister Tony Blair, that the UK would 'discuss difficult issues, but in a context where both sides were polite, respectful, and still carried on their other business'. That other business meant, in short, trade. From the 2000s, trade was accompanied by investment, and by increasingly large flows of students. Trade, investment and students are the three prongs of the relationship to this day. They have been added to by intellectual partnership and finance.

Post-Brexit, therefore, the most likely scenario is for the UK, either in or out of the Single Market, to seek a better quality of relationship with the People's Republic. If one looks at the current situation, in terms of trade, investment and finance flows, while things have increased markedly in the last few years, they are still suboptimal.

Comparative Analysis of Trade and Investment

Imports and Exports

Total trade flows between the UK and China from 2005 show obviously large deficits. The UK and China deficits are somewhat larger in percentage terms than the negative trade balance between the EU and China as a whole (Fig. 4.1). The trade deficit between the UK and China has ranged from about 20 billion euros to 25 billion euros from 2005 to 2015 (Fig. 4.2). While UK exports to China have increased, particularly over the last few years, so have imports, so little progress has been made on aggregate in closing the gap, in fact the difference between exports and imports hit a new record in 2015. At the same time, the amount of trade between the UK and the EU in 2015 accounted for around 21% of the EU's total trade with China. The UK is therefore a strong player considering all the other countries in the EU.

The UK is the EU's second largest economy by gross domestic product (GDP) and Germany is the largest. Nevertheless, Germany's overall trade with China was closer to the 140 billion euro mark in 2015 according to the data, whereas the UK's as can be seen was just over half of that. Germany has managed to balance trade flows with China and even operated at a surplus for several recent years (Fig. 4.3). Germany's manufacturing sector

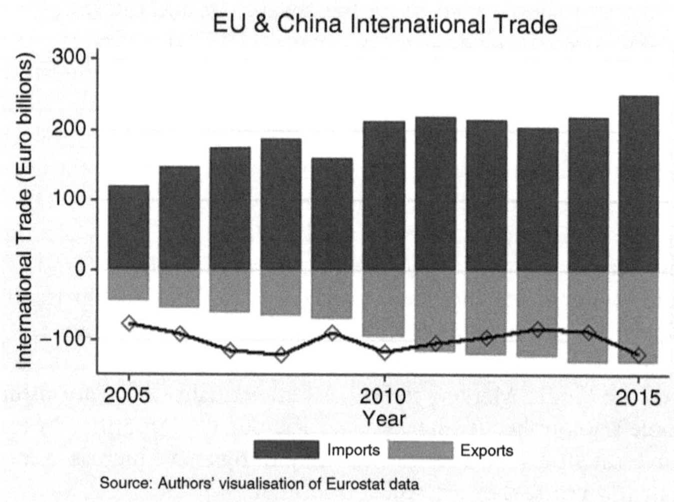

Fig. 4.1 Graph of import and export statistics, with trade balance, between China and the EU

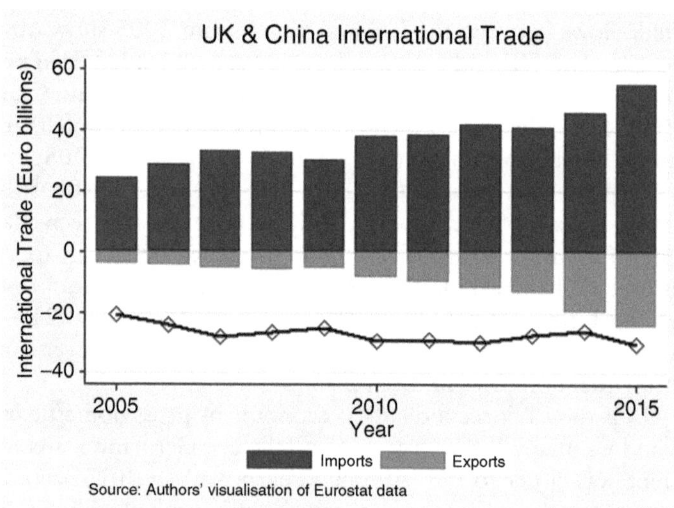

Fig. 4.2 Graph of import and export statistics, with trade balance, between China and the UK

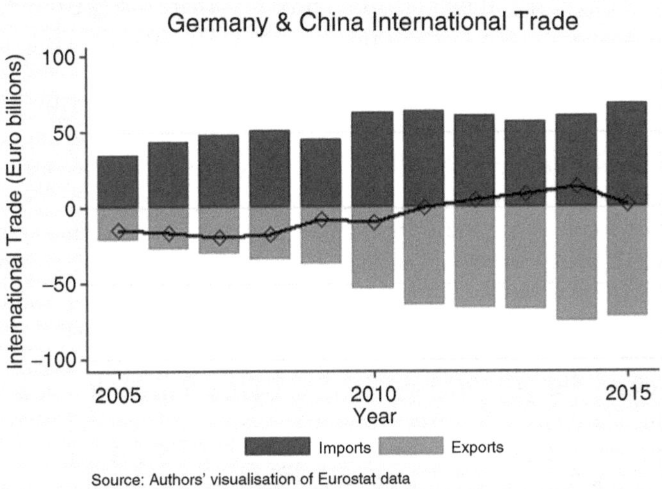

Fig. 4.3 Graph of import and export statistics between Germany and China

contributes 23% of its GDP vs. 11% in the UK.[2] Greater links between Germany and China in terms of imports and exports are not terribly surprising due to Germany offering a more prolific and diverse array of manufactures and China being a manufacturing economy, whereas the UK's service sector is particularly well known, accounting for 80% of the economy. EU services have traded at a surplus with China compared to the exchange of goods over the same period examined. However, overall trade in services accounted for only around 11.8% of overall EU trade with China in 2015,[3] the latter which, as has been shown, is at a deficit, with the UK's sustained deficit a contributor to that.

The 11% of GDP that manufactures contribute to the UK economy, combined with the UK government's 'export drive'—see the corporate report by UK Trade and Investment entitled '2020 Export Drive'[4]—in addition to the collapse of the pound after Brexit ought together to offer scope for reducing the trade deficit. This is important to note as it demonstrates how the actively trading foreign exchange market participants perceive UK economic prospects in the event of a hard Brexit—and the outlook is overwhelmingly bleak by this metric, even though UK stocks have reached an all-time high.

China has been pushing for domestic consumption, including by lowering import tariffs on certain consumer products, to try to stem the amount of direct spending abroad on products that could be purchased in China if it were not for higher prices due to tariffs, and thus to reduce its trade surplus.[5]

It seems as though the ingredients are there, but Germany has been doing something that the UK has not which has enabled a more stable economic relationship with China. John Benedetto[6] argues quite convincingly that the German model, particularly selling into China mechanical parts for production stages, for example, luxury cars, is difficult to replicate given the export profile of the USA, for example. At the same time, the Chinese reforms towards encouraging consumer spending in China on imports seem to offer an opportunity to capture markets that were previously considered unattainable in China.[7] The landscape seems to be changing, however, the clear strategy for the UK in China both politically and economically seems big on the ideas but lacking on real deficit-reducing detail after the Brexit vote. In some ways the forex markets could have offered a blessing in disguise via the decimation of sterling, which has failed to recover its losses, even after court decisions in the UK temporarily delayed the triggering of Article 50 by the government.

Foreign Direct Investment

The discrepancies in the FDI story are even more pronounced, in part due to China's foreign exchange policy. China has been the world champion FDI recipient since the 1990s, at which time China had had 20 years to reform experimentally towards implementing market mechanisms and began opening up of special economic zones in southern and eastern regions to encourage FDI and exports by lowering tariffs and a host of other policies. The UK accounts for less than 10% of EU FDI stocks in China, with almost 9 billion euros of FDI invested assets in China by 2012. And yet FDI by China into the whole of the EU equated to only around 40 billion euros by 2012, compared to three times that amount by the EU into China. Chinese FDI more than doubled in the UK between 2011 and 2012, possibly as a result of hot money flows.

The figures for FDI stock from both the EU and the UK into the USA dwarf those into China for obvious long-term historical reasons, while UK FDI stock held in Taiwan by 2012 was only about a quarter that into China. Reflecting historical, political and business ties between the two, the UK has around 43 billion euros in FDI stock in Hong Kong. It could be that Hong Kong records flow figures whose ultimate destination from the UK is mainland China; however, this is less likely to show up in the FDI stock numbers, which ought to be a more static and less volatile representation of FDI into the recipient economy. Nevertheless, both stock and flow (around four times higher in 2012) from the UK into Hong Kong speak volumes about the UK's trusted relationship with the entrepôt and its continued importance as the gateway to Asia for UK international trade. It is worth noting the fractious quasi-diplomatic relationship between the mainland and Taiwan, and that official mainland Chinese FDI, treated with great suspicion, was only permitted through government-mandated investment programmes after 2010, reflected by the figures.

RMB Internationalisation and Financial Cooperation

The importance of the service industries to the UK has been highlighted. It is certainly worth mentioning the internationalisation of the RMB at this juncture. RMB trade through London has reached a zenith, although still nowhere near as much trading of RMB is done in London as Hong Kong. International trade necessitates exchange of funds and ultimately, repatriation of profits, yet the Chinese capital account was very much closed 25 years ago and still so in the early 2000s. For instance, it was impossible in 2002 for foreign portfolio (share and bond) investors to purchase shares on the Shanghai and Shenzhen stock exchanges because of the inconvertibility of the RMB. Only since the advent of various schemes since 2002 have such investors been able to gain exposure to Chinese securities in these markets through the qualified foreign institutional investor (QFII) and foreign strategic investor (FSI) programmes, and this with strict limits on qualification, quotas, industries and sectors invested in and the length of time for an investment to be held, for instance. Moreover, the Chinese stock market's performance has been lacklustre compared to developed countries' stock markets since 2008, after the worldwide sell-off following the financial crisis.

In part due to a slow economy, and in part due to Brexit, the pound sterling has depreciated vis-à-vis the RMB. Figure 4.4 shows the performance of the sterling (GBP)/offshore *yuan* (GBPCNH—CNY denotes the domestic *yuan*) cross currency pair from November 2015 to November 2016. The y axis shows the number of offshore *yuan* to £1 at the end of trading on a given day. Depreciation of the pound against the *yuan* of about 15% can be clearly seen between 2011 and 2017.

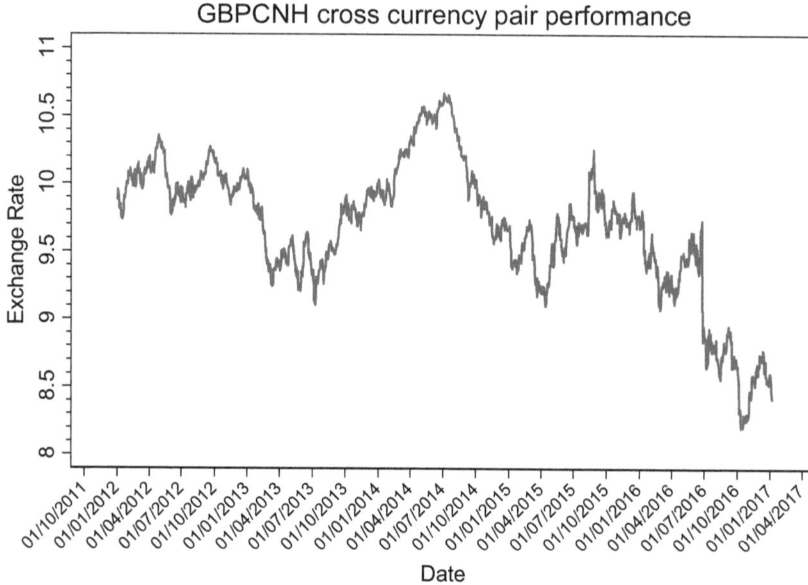

Fig. 4.4 Performance of the GBP vs. the offshore Chinese *yuan*. (Source: Authors' visualisation of Pepperstone Pty Ltd data)

The pound has lost ground to the Chinese *yuan*, and markedly so. This supports the notion that Brexit should improve the trade balance numbers with China; however, this is not as a result of Brexit itself, rather the response of the market in frank disdain for the pound and the decision of the British people in light of the outcome of the vote, in addition to devaluation of the RMB against the US dollar, for which President Trump blames China under the 'currency manipulator' rhetoric. A more fundamental view would be that the Chinese economy is weakening and the weakening *yuan* results from that (less demand plus speculative selling).

The internationalisation of the RMB more broadly refers to the currency becoming a worldwide currency in trade settlement, it has been said ambitiously even a reserve currency for Asia and the world. The head of the People's Bank of China lobbied the International Monetary Fund (IMF) hard to gain acceptance of the RMB as a special drawing rights (SDR) currency, meaning that countries can receive RMB as a part of IMF loans.[8] The mechanism for internationalisation has been one of attempting to maintain control of the mainland capital account, while utilising Hong Kong's position as a world financial centre to segregate offshore and onshore trade of the currency.

Where the UK comes into this picture is firstly through its relationship with Hong Kong as a financial centre. Thus, for example, HSBC in London has had a small team dedicated to trading the Chinese currency since 2010 and the advent of the offshore RMB (CNH). However, knowing there is considerable RMB settlement business going on in Asia, what the UK has vied to do is become a clearing *centre*, and it has actually overtaken Singapore as the regional alternative during 2016.

In terms of RMB trade, Hong Kong still vastly overshadows the UK (72.5% of RMB trade vis-à-vis 6.3% of trade in the UK and 4.6% in Singapore)[9] but the UK has clearly impressed China with its financial services experience and capabilities. For example, China chose London as the first sovereign RMB bond issuing centre outside of China during May 2016, a deal sealed by the then Chancellor of the Exchequer, George Osborne, corporate bonds already having experimented with issuance, such as the ICBC.

Stock markets have been mentioned briefly. In 2014, the Hong Kong-Shanghai Stock Connect scheme was announced, followed by a Hong Kong Shenzhen Stock Connect in 2016. London wishes to follow suit and a feasibility study was launched in 2015.[10] It looked like progress on this would follow a proposed merger between the Deutsche-Bourse and London Stock Exchange (LSE) which would also most likely have facilitated greater access to Chinese security-based products, such as index following exchange traded funds, for UK and other European investors. Although the merger with Deutsche-Bourse was blocked by the European Commission in March 2017 on competition grounds, the LSE is likely to move ahead with the stock connect scheme anyway. In November 2016, following the UK-China Eighth Economic and Financial Dialogue, Philip Hammond, the Chancellor of the Exchequer (Finance Secretary), announced that the programme would move to the next stage, with reciprocal promises of further openness to UK ownership in Chinese listed companies, including the insurance sector, alliances in the FinTech arena and other initiatives.[11]

Collaboration in financial markets is needed if China is to make the most of these markets in its nuanced way, their lacklustre performance and drastic volatility indicate. Compared to the returns offered by UK and US stocks since the financial crisis, China's stock market has left an awful lot to be desired. One way scholars argue that China can improve the efficiency and stability of stock markets is to allow greater liberalisation. Forming co-operative agreements with the UK like those mentioned above is a step in this direction, building on successes of previous liberalisation schemes like the QFII and FSI programmes, which have either aimed or been shown to improve market stability and/or corporate governance of the Chinese enterprises.[12] However, some argue that China has become so concerned with Brexit as to have backed away from the idea of a Golden Age relationship, not only in finance but trade more broadly.[13]

Summing Up the Trade Relationship Between the UK and China

The trade relationship between the UK and China, as ever, remains rather lopsided, and highly service oriented from UK to China and export goods oriented from China to the UK. Mutual ground has been gained through a desire to trade and to leverage the UK's position as a leading world financial centre, particularly when it comes to trade and settlement of currency instruments. The position of the UK government in terms of Brexit seems to be that the UK will remain as open as ever to international trade and forging ties with trade partners further afield will be a natural and spontaneous follow on from exiting the EU. It is unclear whether the trends in international investment and FDI numbers support the success of this notion with China. What is clear is that the UK has run a deficit that is relatively larger than the overall EU trade deficit with China, and that Germany has run a surplus.

It is also clear that China has not exactly been the UK's darling of FDI lately, even though over the last 30 years it has been the most successful attractor of FDI in the world, barring none, including developing economies also competing for FDI such as Brazil, India and Russia. UK FDI stocks in Japan were approximately equal to those in China in 2012, so in some sense China has done well to attract some FDI from the UK. Then again, Chinese FDI in itself, while it tends to be 'shouted from the rooftops' seems to be rather modest in nature when looking at the long-term relationships regions have built up over decades, if not centuries in investing in one another, for example, the UK in the USA and Hong Kong. This is perhaps why the UK has received Chinese investment rather more welcomingly than, say, Australia: to encourage that outward spending that China has missed out on through its long interregnum in staunchly Soviet style communist territory, the legacy of which very much lives on. Such investments are considered more below.[14]

This all shows that while the UK and China are developing relations, there is a long way to go. It also raises questions about just how far China could ever possibly figure as heavily in the UK's real economic future as the EU currently does. The standard response of politicians supportive of leaving the EU at the moment in the UK is that it will figure as a moment of liberation, leaving Britain to pursue unilateral deals with what is euphemistically called 'high growth markets', of which China is the largest and the one ostensibly with the most potential.

Free Trade Agreements

China does have the appetite for FTAs. Its attempts to agree one with the EU have been stymied, however, by the refusal of the Union to grant Market Economy Status (MES). In theory, once the UK does eventually leave the EU it can engage quickly in a trade deal with China (before it does so, it cannot legally discuss any trade agreements with other non-EU partners). To expect things to be fair sailing however would be obtuse. China's agreements with other partners so far have been largely in its interests. Its deal with Switzerland only granted the Swiss entry to its market 15 years after signature. With Australia and New Zealand, the deals were relatively straightforward, focussing on agribusiness, resources and some services. The same applies to the bilateral FTA with Iceland.

Table 4.2 is from the Chinese Ministry of Finance and Commerce (MOFCOM) website and shows the FTAs that China has signed and implemented with regions and countries, when this took place, along with those which are under construction and the most recent press release on the site.

There needs to be clarity about what in the end an FTA is. As an inspection of the Australia-China FTA shows, it is no more than a mutually agreed set of rules for how to engage with each other. But having rules of engagement still means one needs companies to enter into a relationship, and then be able to undertake business. There is no clear stipulation of a winner in this process. And on the whole, China has proved during the last decade that it is adept at reaching deals which are in its own interests, and where there is a clear need for knowledgeable and qualified local companies which can then go forward and engage with potential opportunities. In the end, China has an asset that no one else apart from the EU and USA has, a vast internal market and a huge economy. So, the UK would engage with China in negotiations on an FTA on a highly asymmetrical

Table 4.2 Chinese free trade agreements

Name of FTA	*Signed and implemented*	*Recent announcement date*	*Event*
China-India regional trade arrangement joint feasibility study	Under consideration	16/01/2008	Trade and investment summit co-op
China-Fiji FTA joint feasibility study	Under consideration	17/11/2009	Deputy Minister of Commerce visits Fiji on trade and investment promotion visit
China-Norway	Under negotiation	16/09/2010	Eighth round of negotiations in Norway
China-Costa Rica	August, 2011	08/08/2011	FTA entered into force
China-Peru	March, 2010	30/10/2012	Peru's coffee producers look to Chinese market
Asia-Pacific Preferential TA (previously the Bangkok Agreement)	July, 1975	09/05/2014	China mulls a 'mega' FTA as host of APEC ministers responsible for trade meeting in Qingdao
China-Iceland	July, 2014	10/07/2014	Chinese and Icelandic trade ministers announce effect of bilateral FTA
China-Switzerland	July, 2014	10/07/2014	Assistant Minister of Commerce publishes article on implementation of FTA
China-ASEAN	November, 2002	29/09/2014	Upgrading negotiations at sixth meeting of joint committee in Hanoi
China-Singapore	October, 2008	26/01/2015	Fifth meeting of FTA commission in Singapore
China-Maldives	Under negotiation	11/02/2015	Feasibility study launched by working group in Male
China-New Zealand	April, 2008	30/03/2015	Joint committee sixth conference in Wellington
China-Taiwan service trade agreement	June, 2013	08/04/2015	Cross-strait agreement on trade and goods tenth negotiation in Beijing
China-Japan-Korea	November, 2012	14/05/2015	Chief negotiators seventh round conference
China-Chile	November, 2005	28/05/2015	Upgrade MOU signed
China-Pakistan	November, 2006	17/11/2015	Banking business services protocol takes effect

(*continued*)

Table 4.2 (continued)

Name of FTA	*Signed and implemented*	*Recent announcement date*	*Event*
Mainland and Macau closer economic partnership arrangement	December, 2006	07/12/2015	Trade and services CEP signed in Macao, implementation 1/6/2016
Mainland and Hong Kong closer economic partnership arrangement	September, 2003	07/12/2015	Trade and services CEP signed in Macao, implementation 1/6/2016
China-Korea	December, 2015	11/12/2015	Announced to take effect on 20/12/2015
China-Australia	December, 2015	11/12/2015	Announced to take effect on 20/12/2015
China-Nepal FTA joint feasibility study	Under consideration	25/03/2016	Study launched, MOU signed
China-Sri Lanka	Under negotiation	11/08/2016	Third round of FT zone negotiations in Sri Lanka
China-Georgia	Under negotiation	09/10/2016	Substantial negotiations concluded in Georgia
China GCC (Gulf Cooperation Council)	Under negotiation	26/10/2016	Eighth round of negotiations in Beijing
Regional Comprehensive Economic Partnership (RCEP)	Under negotiation	07/11/2016	Ministerial conference in the Philippines
China-Mauritius FTA joint feasibility study	Under consideration	07/11/2016	Study launched, MOU signed
China-Columbia FTA joint feasibility study	Under consideration	n/a	n/a
China-Moldova FTA joint feasibility study	Under consideration	n/a	n/a

Source: http://fta.mofcom.gov.cn/english/

basis. Within the EU at least it has a level of protection, and is part of a massive bloc which matters to the Chinese. Alone, it becomes a second rank player, and one which is in a relatively weak position.

In terms of finance, as was illustrated above, the UK does have a current importance to China—something stressed during the 2015 Xi Jinping visit. The levels of RMB trade through London and the numbers of

Chinese banks moving there in the last few years have been striking. Even so, as a proportion of present overall currency settlement and trading, the Chinese *yuan* is still tiny. It is important because of its potential. And the growth of that potential is highly reliant on London being a European centre, not just a British one. Preservation of passporting rights as any part of the final exit-EU deal is important. As part of the Union, the UK financial sector has the freedom to undertake business unfettered across the EU's other 27 member states. But without that its attractiveness is likely to diminish. It is not certain yet whether the UK will be able to preserve this.

Security and Diplomacy

While at least on the trade front there are tangible benefits to the UK that might result from exiting the EU, on the security and diplomatic front things are inevitably much more complex. In security terms, the UK's principal partnerships remain with the USA, within NATO and with the EU. It has the largest military expenditure within the EU, and is among the most advanced in terms of its military capacity. Leaving the EU does not mean leaving NATO. But it does mean a more complex relationship with European partners. The UK has recently opted to become involved with the USA in military training exercises in South Korea and also with Japan. But it has no direct security role in the region beyond its alliances with the USA.

In many ways, even the symbolism of exiting the EU carries negative connotations for the UK in North East Asia, and particularly in China. China has consistently proved that it is keen to join multilateral organisations even while preserving its own sovereignty. This makes its very low key expressions of support for the UK remaining part of the EU before the referendum even more striking. It felt that it was in the interests of the UK to be part of this alliance system, and to try to engage with reform from within it. Exiting the EU has largely been regarded by Chinese leaders and officials as surprising. It has also been interpreted as signs that the UK is a diminished partner, one whose role in the world is less than even two decades ago.[15]

In terms of the values and human rights dialogue between the two countries, the post-Brexit scenario is bleakest of all. While opportunities in trade and investment might increase, Chinese officials have made clear over the last four years that they have zero tolerance of hearing British lectures on human rights or rule of law. China has been brutal in its handling of most other countries on this issue. But at least as part of the EU, the UK had leverage and a level of protection. It was often able through the EU to address thorny issues like the treatment of dissidents or the jailing of rights lawyers, things that have increased markedly in recent years. Outside of this EU zone of collegiality and comfort, the UK stands very exposed. It has already had some intimations of how fierce the Chinese return fire can be when it gets involved, in, for instance, Tibet or Hong Kong. On the former, when the British Prime Minister Cameron met the Dalai Lama, Tibet's exiled spiritual leader, in 2012 there was a cancellation of all high-level political visits for almost 18 months. On Hong Kong, a group of British parliamentarians were unable to gain access to the territory in late 2014 due to sensitivities over the Occupy Central movement then. The bottom line is that China is now willing and able to dictate to the UK in ways which were never so obvious in the past. And being outside of the EU means that the UK is even more vulnerable.[16]

Chinese Outward Investment in the UK

The UK of course does remain of interest to China as a place of outward investment, and it is perhaps in this area where the most interesting things could happen. Chinese listed enterprises during the 2000s went on an asset accumulation spree. China has been increasing its outward FDI into developed economies, particularly since the global financial crisis, where opportunities were seen to be more readily available given slowing economies, with their lowering employment and need for investment. Investing in developed countries also shows China's desire to move up the value chain.[17] Motivations can include, for example, credibility of European suppliers in the food market. Brightfood, a mainland company, bought 60% of Weetabix from Lion Group when it was valued at £1.2 billion and in early 2015 announced plans to buy the remainder of the company. This kind of purchase by a Chinese agri-food conglomerate is synonymous with outward Chinese spending. At the same time, as Peter Nolan points out, top 500 global asset managers control $64 trillion vs. $3.3 trillion Chinese foreign exchange reserves (Black Rock has $3.3 trillion alone in disposable funds), and total FDI of China was less than $300 billion cf. Netherlands

$1500 billion (see also the earlier figures).[18] China has a long way to go with the outside world but the outside world also has a long way to go with China.

Perhaps a similarly surreptitious Chinese investment in the UK, but one which has had security implications, was that of Huawei technology group. Huawei, after investigations by the UK government concluded that its operations were not going to be a security threat, has a special supervisory board consisting of UK government members, UK business people and Chinese executives working for Huawei, which reports back to government as a mitigation measure against possible clandestine Chinese involvement, presumably in spying and threatening behaviour towards UK mobile telecommunications infrastructure through Huawei.[19]

Even more so than the above has been the recent debate around the Hinkley Point nuclear power plant project, part of the Osborne-Cameron-Xi showcase of the new 'Golden Era' relationship, but then stalled by Theresa May's government before finally being given the green light. Serious consideration has been given towards allowing a Chinese state-owned company to have a major role in building a nuclear power part in the UK, and to have one third ownership in the project. The ultimate decision to approve the project demonstrates that the UK is open for business—though some analysts would argue that it could hardly be more open, short perhaps of allowing an armaments or drone factory staffed and supervised by the People's Liberation Army. At the same time, concerns about security need to be put in context, both for the potential xenophobia involved and the recent failings of the industry outside of China. For instance, Toshiba, a Japanese company, acquired the French NuGen and won the tender to build the 3.8 gigawatt Moorside nuclear plant in Cumbria. Security issues seem to have been less a concern with this project as viability of the sector, which has faced failure to complete projects and massive losses.[20] Toshiba has been looking for partners to buy out its share of the project recently, with China General Nuclear a bidder in the process.[21] Moreover, the Hinkley Point project will provide thousands of jobs over its lifetime. Aside from the downturns for the nuclear industry in the developed nations of the world, these factors help explain the desire that the UK government has to engage with China on this project at this juncture. The interpretation of this is that it is perhaps not only for the direct gains of the project, but to promote trust and crucially to facilitate UK business in China itself, but not without taking precautionary measures.

Conclusion

The Brexit vote confused the Chinese as much as it did many voters and officials alike. The UK government has made clear attempts to vocalise the message that not only is the UK open to business, it is very much open to furthering international networks, business and political ties beyond the EU. At the same time, both China and the UK have further to go in terms of balance of trade and for the UK to compete with its former colony, Hong Kong as the premier RMB trading centre; even though the UK has already become the number one clearing centre outside the East and South East Asian region. Brexit itself seemed to be correlated with a stall but insofar as the present time has not precluded the latest large investment deal, that being Hinkley Point. The leadership transition in the UK has seemed to indicate that the new relationship between the UK and China—one which seeks to promote trade, openness and cooperation in business dealings—has bred some caution that was not there with the very accommodating stances adopted by Osborne and Cameron in what turned out to be their final days in high-level and high-visibility politics.

Time will tell how China responds to Brexit, although it is clearly not impressed by the outcome of allowing a Brexit vote or the process which is incompatible with 'Chinese democracy'. The path will be dependent, of course, on how Brexit proceeds along dimensions of time, negotiations and the careful management and re-building where necessary of diplomatic relationships between the UK and other European players in the political union. Trust has been breached with European counterparties whose familiarity with the union political system was smashed by a small percentage over half of the UK voting populace who turned out on the day of the referendum. It would be logical for China to have questioned therefore the UK's level of commitment to political ties and relationships more widely (i.e. with China itself) and China will also have considered how relations could potentially break down, even after long periods building political understanding, agreement and business ties.

Concurrently, the UK government has tried to distance itself from any notion of business-not-as-usual with international partners—an attempt to provide reassurance on current and future business deals and for partners dependent on accommodationism. The UK surely is seen by China and the outside world as a country that is publicly open to serious Chinese investment and will act independently to receive it if necessary, even in risky strategic areas—note that Australia only recently turned down the *Ausgrid* deal and has effectively vetoed even a minority stake investment by a Chinese firm in an Australian company looking to buy up a swathe of Australian farmland.

Brexit has rattled the cages of Chinese officials, just as it did British and European ones, but particularly around the UK's ability to stabilise and maintain embedded political ties. How markets react to the ongoing negotiations will be important to the trade outcomes. If the pound still fails to recover, this will provide further highly attractive propositions potentially for more Chinese deals in the UK. The downside of this will be similar to the political concerns of the Australians, for instance property in the most desirable areas becoming unaffordable to the country's citizens and a sense of being sold out to foreign acquirers.

The challenge with a hard Brexit scenario is that it will make things more fractious between colleagues in the UK and EU at the negotiating and leadership tables. China will undoubtedly pick up on this and already sees the UK as becoming less relevant. It is therefore very important that the relationship between the UK and China is fostered and nurtured effectively during this period, regardless of the precise Brexit model. Grand plans such as the London-Shanghai stock market connect should not be left to wither for long. A soft Brexit might soften the sense of political disunion and fallout between the UK and EU, but the act of the democratic process of Brexit and its outcome, especially given the circumstances, for example, of misinformation and maligned campaign intents on the part of Brexit campaigners, will have already made the UK look foolish in the eyes of the Chinese, although this would not be communicated directly, of course. What I have suggested as a 'malleable Brexit' model in the introduction, perhaps following a route like Canada, could open the door to an FTA with China because the UK would not be bound by EU rules on FTAs, while continuing much of the access to benefits of the EU, not necessarily including the immigration issue which seems to be a deal-breaker for both sides at present, but offering a gradual transition from that if it smoothes the process. All this would require skillful planning and negotiation.

On the plus side for the UK, continuing or even furthering good relations between the UK and China post-Brexit keeps the vision of London financial services centrality in Chinese international trade on track while greasing the cogs for a deepening of British business in mainland China. If the UK seeks to further its desire to engage in a trade-centric relationship, this necessitates engaging with a political-centric approach from the Beijing side.

Notes

1. David Conolly. 2017. "Merkel: No single market without free movement for EU citizens." *Sky News*. 10 January. Accessed 01 10, 2017. http://news.sky.com/story/merkel-no-single-market-without-free-movement-for-eu-citizens-10723535
2. Larry Elliot. "The UK could learn a lot from Germany's long-term industrial strategy." 30 March 2016. Accessed 19 11, 2016. https://www.theguardian.com/global/2016/mar/30/the-uk-could-learn-a-lot-from-germanys-long-term-industrial-strategy
3. Kerry Brown and Sam Beatson. 2016. "The European Union and China: the need for a more politicised relationship." *Asia & the Pacific Policy Studies* 3 (3): 412–419.
4. UK Trade & Investment. "Corporate Report: 2020 Export Drive." 19 December 2014. Accessed 19 11, 2016. https://www.gov.uk/government/publications/2020-export-drive/2020-export-drive
5. Duncan Hewitt. "China reduces tariffs on imported consumer goods to promote domestic demand." 29 April 2015. Accessed 19 11, 2016 http://www.ibtimes.com/china-reduces-tariffs-imported-consumer-goods-promote-domestic-demand-190
6. John Benedetto. 2011. "Can we apply lessons from German trade balance with China to the United States." *Journal of International Commerce and Economics*.
7. Jim Coke and Sam Beatson. 2016. "Don't carry coals to Newcastle, sell tea in China." *Forthcoming*.
8. Nathaniel Taplin. "China's yuan joins elite club of IMF reserve currencies." 1 October 2016. Accessed 20 11, 2016. http://www.reuters.com/article/us-china-currency-imf-idUSKCN1212WC
9. Hudson Lockett. "UK becomes second-largest offshore RMB clearing centre." 28 April 2016. Accessed 20 11, 2016. https://www.ft.com/content/d552173a-6030-3c83-b4f7-9efc1819bb30
10. HM Treasury & George Osborne. "China Chooses London for its first ever sovereign renminbi (RMB) bond issues outside of China." 26 May 2016. Accessed 20 11, 2016. https://www.gov.uk/government/news/china-chooses-london-for-its-first-ever-sovereign-renminbi-rmb-bond-issued-outside-of-china

11. Enoch Yiu. "London-Shanghai stock connect will address time zone difference." 17 November 2016. Accessed 20 11, 2016. http://www.scmp.com/business/companies/article/2046540/london-shanghai-stock-connect-will-address-time-zone-difference; HM Treasury & Philip Hammond. "UK-China 8th Economic and Financial Dialogue: financial services." 10 November 2016. Accessed 20 11, 2016. https://www.gov.uk/government/news/uk-china-8th-economic-and-financial-dialogue-financial-services
12. Samuel Beatson and Jian Chen. 2017—forthcoming. "Foreign Investment, Corporate Governance & Performance in the Chinese Listed A Share Companies." *Journal of Chinese Business & Economic Studies*. Doi: https://doi.org/10.1080/14765284.2017.1346931
13. Jonathan Ford and James Kynge. "Beijing signals end of China-UK 'golden age'." *Financial Times—China Business*. 06 January 2017. Accessed 11 01, 2017. https://www.ft.com/content/4ab22b66-d42d-11e6-9341-7393bb2e1b51
14. Samuel Beatson. "Mainland firms can exploit HK's advantages." 24 August 2016. Accessed 20 11, 2016. http://www.chinadaily.com.cn/hkedition/2016-08/24/content_26576534.htm
15. Tim Summers. 2017. Brexit: Implications for EU-China Relations. Chatham House. The Royal Institute for International Affairs. https://www.chathamhouse.org/sites/files/chathamhouse/publications/research/2017-05-11-brexit-eu-china-summers-final.pdf on 26 September, 2017.Kerry Brown. 2016. What China Thinks About Brexit. The Diplomat (online). 25 June, 2016. Accessed from http://thediplomat.com/2016/06/what-china-thinks-about-brexit/ 26 September, 2017.
16. Chen-shen J. Yen, Sovereignty, Human Rights and China's National Interest: A Non-Zero Sum Game (2011), Foreign Policy Research Institute E-Notes, February, 2011. Accessed from https://www.fpri.org/docs/media/201102.yen_.china_.pdf on 26 September, 2017.

    Sceats, Sonya and Breslin, Shaun, China and the International Human Rights System. 2012. Chatham House. The Royal Institute for International Affairs. Accessed from https://www.chathamhouse.org/sites/files/chathamhouse/public/Research/International%20Law/r1012_sceatsbreslin.pdf on 26 September, 2017.
17. Sophie Meunier. 2014. "'Beggars Can't Be Choosers': The European Crisis and Chinese Direct Investment in the European Union." *Journal of European Integration* 36 (3).
18. Peter Nolan. 2013. *Is China Buying the World?* Cambridge: Polity Press.
19. Huawei Cyber Security Evaluation Centre (HCSEC) Oversight Board (2017). Annual Report 2017. Online via https://www.gov.uk/government/uploads/system/uploads/attachment_data/file/626110/20170413_HCSEC_Oversight_Board_Report_2017_-_FINAL.pdf accessed 26 September, 2017.

20. Jillian Ambrose. 2017. Toshiba's $8.8bn loss reignites fears over Cumbria nuclear project. For The Telegraph, 10 August, 2017. http://www.telegraph.co.uk/business/2017/08/10/toshibas-88bn-loss-reignites-fears-cumbria-nuclear-project/; Tom Hals and Flitter, Emily. 2017. How two cutting edge US nuclear projects bankrupted Westinghouse. For Reuters, 2 May, 2017. Accessed from https://www.reuters.com/article/us-toshiba-accounting-westinghouse-nucle/how-two-cutting-edge-u-s-nuclear-projects-bankrupted-westinghouse-idUSKBN17Y0CQ on 26 September, 2017.
21. Lucy Hornby and Archie Zhang. 2017. China's CGN seeks stake in Toshiba-led nuclear project. Financial Times, 19 September, 2017. Accessed from https://www.ft.com/content/432ce6f4-4dd4-353b-a14b-43520e98d935 on 26 September, 2017.

CHAPTER 5

EU-China Relations After Brexit

Wai Ting

Introduction

The glorious reception offered by the British government to President Xi Jinping of the People's Republic of China (PRC) in October 2015 during his state visit to the UK marked the beginning of the so-called Golden Era in Sino-British relations. The two nations signed numerous investment and cooperation agreements valued at £40bn sterling. Beijing aspires to see a closer relationship with the European Union (EU) via the UK, as London is the major financial and services centre in the EU. With Brexit and the resulting departure of Premier David Cameron and Chancellor of Exchequer George Osborne, the new Premier Theresa May seems to be sceptical of the intimate partnership with China. She decided to postpone the signature of the tripartite agreement with France and China allowing Beijing's nuclear company to invest in the new nuclear power plant to be built in Hinkley Point, Somerset. Premier May seems to be concerned with the national security of the UK and the political-strategic implications of the rising China, apart from continuing economic cooperation with China in order to benefit from the lucrative Chinese market.

W. Ting (✉)
Department of Government and International Studies, Hong Kong Baptist University, Kowloon Tong, Hong Kong
e-mail: tingwai@hkbu.edu.hk

D. W. F. Huang, M. Reilly (eds.), *The Implications of Brexit for East Asia*, https://doi.org/10.1007/978-981-13-0185-8_5

Eventually she approved the nuclear reactor project at the end of September 2016, by adding a number of additional conditions.

Brexit happens in the rather gloomy context of global development, when the economies of the advanced capitalist countries are in deep crisis, and the new growth engines of emerging economies like Brazil, Russia, India, China and South Africa, or the 'BRICS', also find themselves in trouble. Anti-globalization movements, together with the rise of populism and nationalism in Europe as well as in other parts of the world, can be considered as a major setback to the optimistic development of globalization since the mid-1990s. With globalization, it is alleged that transnational flows of human beings, capital, products and information render the primacy of states and sovereignty "outdated". Although the UK has been a member of the EU since 1973, now more than half of the British ask for tighter control of their borders, better usage of their taxation and protecting the British identity! Many Asian scholars see the development of the post-modernist normative power, the EU, as the best model for solving the difficult relationships among East Asian countries. Yet now the British have chosen to return to the pre-EU stage, when sovereignty of a nation-state is sacrosanct. Anti-globalization forces can be regarded as the reactions of the masses, especially the youngsters who got depressed with their lives, against the "upgrade" of global capitalism after the end of Cold War. Anti-establishment sentiments and the rise of nationalism and populism are evident in Brexit as well as Donald Trump's advent to power in the USA.

This chapter aims to study two major questions. First, taking into consideration the likely political and economic order in the EU after Brexit, especially that the EU has already been encountering difficult problems such as the Eurozone crisis, democratic deficit, immigration, unemployment, nationalism and populism, how does the EU strike a balance between a value-based and an interest-based diplomacy vis-à-vis China? Second, how do we evaluate the prospects of Sino-British and EU-China relations after Brexit? It is often argued that Beijing's leaders are adept in dealing with various European states by driving a wedge in their divergences. The UK was the first Western country to join the China-initiated Asian Infrastructure Investment Bank (AIIB). This shocked its close ally, the USA. Beijing originally hoped that by establishing a "privileged" relationship with the UK, it would be able to enjoy closer economic relations with other EU members, overriding human rights and geopolitical concerns. Now with the UK leaving the EU, what would the PRC government's policy responses be in reaction to the future challenges arising from the UK leaving the Single European Market? This chapter aims to study how the leaders of rising China perceive and act upon this volatile situation in Europe, with the EU and the UK both weakened, in considering the positioning of China on the global stage.

Values Versus Interests in EU Diplomacy Towards China

Since 2010, China's Gross Domestic Product (GDP) has risen to second in the world. In parallel with this is the Chinese government's "over self-confidence", and the increasing assertiveness in its foreign policies. In recent years, some European analysts posit that value-based diplomacy launched by the EU as a "normative soft power" has not been successful in fostering social and political transformation in China. Instead, it has undermined the goodwill and mutual trust between the two. They argue that genuine respect of China's values and ideology should be the foundation for the future EU-China relationship, which means that the EU should not continue to play its role as "missionary" anymore in preaching Western values. Interactions and linkages between the two continents should be constructed on mutual interests, rather than on the transformation of the Chinese social and political system that eventually conforms to Western values.

Prof. Ewa Latoszek of the Warsaw School of Economics and also President of EUSA-Poland emphasizes the view that trying to change the other countries' values and ideology is detrimental to the construction of a healthy bilateral relationship.[1] If one cannot change the beliefs of the Islamic people, by the same token, it is not possible to impose the values of democracy, human rights and rule of law on China. The Chinese model has its own merits, and economic development under one-party dictatorship has truly facilitated tremendous success. Future EU-China relations can only be built on mutual interests, while the EU's efforts in exporting its values as a soft power will be doomed to fail.

A PhD thesis entitled "Socialization in EU-China Human Rights Diplomacy: from the Diplomacy of Values to the Values of Diplomacy" presented by a German student at the University of Hong Kong revealed some astonishing findings.[2] The EU has been unsuccessful in "socializing" China during the past 20 years of "human rights diplomacy", but the opposite now seems to be true. Beijing has succeeded in recent years in "socializing" Europe by modifying the agenda of the Human Rights

Dialogue, a regular encounter of high officials from the European Commission and the Chinese Ministry of Foreign Affairs, that remains fruitless in ameliorating the human rights conditions in China. Therefore, the EU has to change its fundamental focus from promoting human rights to promoting trade and investment for both parties' benefits. The same idea is shared by other scholars, such as British scholar Paul Crookes, who insists that the EU's value-based diplomacy vis-à-vis China risks damaging the bilateral relationship.[3] Similarly, British scholar Richard Higgott is of the view that the institutions and values and even the Chinese currency, the renminbi (RMB), demonstrate China's strong power, contrary to scholars such as David Shambaugh who believe that China is weak in soft power. Western ideas are no longer universal, and Europeans have to learn how to play with rising China in participating in the great international game.[4]

However, other scholars criticize the EU on its inconsistency in shifting between values and interests. The EU is caught in a dilemma in trying to secure economic benefits from China, while at the same time fostering changes inside China by "socializing" her with the European norms and values. American scholar Ayse Kaya maintains that the EU has not tried to link up the two, by utilizing its multifarious economic cooperation with Beijing in order to promote transformation inside China and guide her towards respect of human rights and the rule of law. Kaya stresses the EU's highly significant normative power as its *raison d'être*, but now vis-à-vis China the EU seems to ignore its identity: "Although China has successfully resisted the EU's efforts to link human rights and economic issues, the EU's reactions to China's rise are also to blame. Instead of using its internal market as a tool to extract change in China's policies, the EU has been in the spell of China's market potential."[5]

The crucial question to be answered is this: what would be the impact of this rising power, China, on the EU as a global actor? Before we answer this question, it may be useful to look at how British diplomacy under ex-Premier Cameron treated Beijing. Former Chancellor of Exchequer Osborne over-shadowed the Foreign Office in searching for a more privileged position in the relationship with China among Western countries. Not only was the UK the first Western state to join the AIIB, but Xi Jinping's visit to the UK started the so-called Golden Era in Sino-British relations. The UK under Cameron seemed to be the first major power in the EU to shift its diplomatic focus to an "interests above all" approach. Beijing is keen and adept at using economic benefits to attract the West (and the rest of the world). Through attracting the UK, and shifting the focus to mutual interests and downplaying the preponderance of values, Beijing aspires to extend this "new model" of relationship to other members of the EU.

According to Chinese analysts, the British government has attempted "repositioning" and "rebalancing" in its diplomacy. Instead of the traditional approach of focusing on the Commonwealth, the USA and the EU, it is now paying attention to newly emerging countries, particularly China and India. The moral obligation of promoting "value diplomacy" is to be continued, but Britain is paying more attention to credible and practical methods. Otherwise, the confusion and disorders caused by the Western "maladroit" management of diplomacy such as what has happened in Iraq, Libya and Syria would be detrimental to British national interests and security.[6] Indeed, Western nations' perceptions of China becoming a great power (or global power) have led to reassessments of their diplomacy regarding the positioning of China in the global order, whether they should adapt to the rising China, or whether they should continue to "remodel" her. Not only has Cameron's government policy of tilting towards Beijing really aroused the interest of Chinese strategic analysts, but it has also stimulated a kind of wishful thinking among Chinese analysts that a closer political relationship between at least some of the Western powers and China would foster changes in Washington's thinking and policies. However, this Chinese thinking appears to be premature, especially since Brexit has obliged both the EU and the UK to think about the future of European integration, the role and positioning of both the EU as a global civil power and the UK as a crucial power on the global stage, in addition to the rising scepticism among Western powers towards Chinese aggressiveness in geopolitical issues and economic investments.

The 16 + 1 framework with the participation of 11 members of the EU coming from Central and Eastern Europe (CEE) plus five other non-EU members is seen by Chinese analysts as a new way of cooperation between the PRC and a subregion. The underdeveloped infrastructure in those CEE countries and their lack of financial capital render Beijing's proposal to treat this part of Europe as the "end" part of the One Belt One Road (OBOR) initiative particularly attractive. The European Commission has consistently stressed that any cooperation between CEE and China must be under the scrutiny of EU rules and regulations, as prescribed by the recent Communication of the European Commission to the European Parliament and the Council: "It is in the EU's interest to work with China to ensure that any Chinese involvement in the EU's Eastern and Southern neighbourhoods helps reinforce rules-based governance and regional security…Member states should reinforce agreed EU positions in their bilateral relations with China."[7] However, the CEE's heartfelt welcome of Chinese loans, used to secure Chinese companies providing construction services, technologies, materials and even labour power, demonstrates Beijing's success in driving a wedge between the Western and Eastern EU member countries. The 16 + 1 framework has been lauded as "mini-lateralism" by Chinese scholars. Though it is classified as somewhere in between bilateralism and multilateralism, the cooperation between China and the CEE is primarily a kind of bilateral cooperation in a multilateral framework.[8] The overwhelming control of CEE financial institutions by Western European banks is considered the major reason for CEE members of EU to secure financial funding from other sources.[9]

What the EU worries about is the extension of Chinese political and economic influence in the southeastern part of the European continent, and its ability to weaken the EU's influence and power of discourse.[10] China's improved bilateral relationship with individual member states would override the relationship between China and the EU, thus contributing to the expansion of the Chinese government's discourse power in its relationship with the EU. It has been indicated that "China does not negotiate with a group of countries but uses an annual conference to create a competitive environment in which these countries put in bids for Chinese investments. However, EU member states would have a lot more bargaining capacity collectively than as individual actors."[11]

It goes without saying that the Chinese leaders are delighted to have had both the UK under Premier Cameron and the CEE 16 going in the direction that Beijing wanted, that is, emphasizing trade and welcoming investment from China, while putting aside the political-normative aspects, especially the export of values by the West.

On the other hand, there is no shortage of warnings cautioning against the Chinese strategy in attracting the CEE countries by its "charm offensive". This is even regarded as a kind of "divide and rule" tactic trying to extend her influence in the CEE, who are keen to attract investments for manufacturing and infrastructure development while remaining reticent on the human rights conditions in China, as they think there is no possibility for them to foster any meaningful domestic changes in China facing the long history of Chinese civilization and the sheer size of the nation. In any case, as a result of China's charm offensive towards CEE, the recent document of the European Commission on EU-China relations stresses the significance of "EU cohesion and effectiveness" in dealing with China.[12] The emphasis is clear: unity within Europe is above all, and China's collaboration with CEE in the 16 + 1 framework must abide by the rules, regulations and policies of the European Commission.

Implications of Brexit for Sino-British Relations

If both the UK and the CEE 16 opt for the interest-based approach towards China regarding EU diplomacy, Brexit naturally means that a major power of the EU that puts interests above values in the EU's external relations would be unable to extend its influence within the EU. Brussels without Britain would continue to adopt a more balanced approach: enhancing economic cooperation but encouraging China towards accepting those universal values, as constantly stipulated in various documents of the European Commission, and championed by the European Parliament.[13]

Brexit can be considered as a "lose-lose" situation for both the UK and EU. On the one hand, as Chinese scholar Feng Zhongping rightly points out, "UK loses an important platform (EU) to exert its influence on global economic affairs, thus weaken[ing] UK's international standing."[14] More than 44% of the UK's goods and services are exported to the EU. Would London, after losing its "hinterland", the EU, be able to sustain its position as the most important international financial centre in Europe, or would it have to cede its place to other major European financial centres like Paris and Frankfurt?

London as an international financial centre within the EU plays a particularly significant role for the Chinese economy as it has become the first Western offshore trading hub for the RMB. It started in November 2013 when the Industrial and Commercial Bank of China issued a bond of RMB 2bn in London.[15] Since March 2016, London has become the biggest clearing centre for the RMB. Moreover, "London is the world's biggest centre for clearing euro derivatives, handling three-quarters of all transactions."[16] However, the European Commission is considering imposing legal change to relocate euro-clearing to the Eurozone area.[17] If London loses its role as the euro's main trading centre, Chinese analysts will be concerned that the EU's withdrawal of euros from London will affect China's euro-financing channels there. The internationalization of the RMB would also be affected.[18] Thus Brexit seems to have negative consequences not only for the global financial markets, but also for the external economic actions and financial arrangements of China.

Chinese analysts used to think that the UK played a particularly significant role in Chinese investments in Europe, serving as a "bridge". With Brexit, the UK's importance in this respect may be decreased in China's eyes, as China "loses UK as the gateway for EU investments".[19] Chinese companies will have to move their regional headquarters from London to other members of the EU. In reality, China's economic relationship with other major countries like France and Germany has been equally well developed and there is no need for China to rely on the UK as a gateway to enter the EU. So, it is true that the UK would appear to be less important in the eyes of Chinese firms. This is further exacerbated by the possible economic downturn effectuated in both the UK and EU, which will be detrimental to China's exports, as Chinese analysis points out. The volatility and uncertainties in the European economy would pose more difficulties for China which has been suffering herself from economic downturn as well, in addition to her crucial need for structural economic reform. The volatile financial market caused by the devaluation of the pound sterling and the appreciation of US dollars certainly affect China's capital flows and exchange rate.

Despite the possible downgrading of the international status of the UK after Brexit, PRC scholars are still optimistic about the UK's future relations with China. With the UK no longer part of the EU, Chinese companies will treat the UK as a close partner in its own right and for what the UK itself can offer, without thinking about the potential spillover effects towards the EU market when dealing with British companies or market. China will treat the UK as a great power politically, just as it treats the USA, Russia and Japan. This Chinese attitude towards the UK is reflected by the UK's likely desire to forge a closer relationship with China, to tap into its market potential, as evidenced by Premier May's positioning of the UK post-Brexit as "global Britain", which builds strong relationships with other countries.[20] The weakened UK and its enterprises would depend more on the Chinese market and pay more attention to Beijing, in an interest-based approach to diplomacy. In the absence of institutional constraints imposed by the EU, Westminster hopefully would be more flexible and creative in considering offering Market Economy Status (MES) to China as well as a bilateral free trade agreement (FTA) between the two states.[21] The UK, which has always favoured granting MES to China but was restrained by the EU's opposition, will now be able to do so after

Brexit. Such post-Brexit changes would correspond with the logic of Premier Cameron's policies vis-à-vis China, which hinged on maximizing benefits from her economic prowess and the momentum of her development. The UK and China will both seize opportunities to work with each other, through tapping into China's "OBOR" and the UK's Northern Powerhouse initiatives.

Some Chinese analysts are optimistic about the possible lifting by the UK of the arms embargo originally imposed by the West after 1989. However, there is no reason to mix up the economic-financial aspect of Sino-British relations with the political-strategic aspect. The enthusiasm of Cameron towards the Chinese market was driven by pragmatism and "opportunism" as explained by a French scholar, Philippe le Corre.[22] Exporting weapons to China was not in his consideration, as the continual opposition from its ally, the USA, is the fundamental factor why the arms embargo could not be lifted.

In any case, the future of Sino-British relations will also depend on what relationship model the UK and the EU mutually reach. Premier May confirmed on 17 January 2017 that she opted for "hard" Brexit.[23] However, voices for "soft" Brexit, that would mean the UK staying within the Single European Market, have been propagated by many including the opposition Labour Party.

"Hard" Brexit is defined "in terms of UK's relationship with the EU Single Market".[24] It means the complete separation of the UK from the Single European Market, and only an FTA, like the one signed between Canada and the EU, can be considered. A hard Brexit would certainly lead to the decrease of consumer power of both the UK and the Eurozone, leading to a decrease of exports from China. A consequent devaluation of sterling would also result in the loss for China of some financial assets. The international exchange market would be destabilized, causing negative impacts towards the exchange rate of the RMB, which in turn would lead to capital outflow from China. The Beijing authorities had strengthened the control on capital outflows even before the referendum on Brexit. In order to stabilize the RMB, even more stringent monitoring of capital movements has been exercised by Beijing since the referendum.

However, China sees Brexit as an opportunity as she is keen to conclude a bilateral FTA with the EU. On the one hand, Beijing thinks that if the EU wants to avoid further economic recession after "losing" the UK, China might be regarded as a "safety boat". On the other hand, the UK after Brexit can resume its independence in determining its external economic policies. If the UK loses the EU Single Market, and if trade barriers will be established between the two, for the sake of the UK's economy, London would be more interested in the emerging markets. If an FTA with both the EU and the UK could be achieved, Chinese analysts are optimistic of China's enhancing role as a newcomer in determining the rules of the games of international economy and commerce.

A "hard Brexit" means the re-establishment of trade barriers between the UK and EU. Though this may be eliminated in the future if they succeed in achieving an FTA, the negotiation process might be long and difficult. There will be a transitional process, and China thinks that she could benefit from the effects of "trade transition" during the time lag, as her production structure is complementary to the UK and other advanced economies within the EU.[25]

Moreover, Chinese analysts opine that after Brexit, if the international capital is not optimistic with the market future of both the EU and the UK, this would provide a great opportunity for China to attract further investment. The UK ranks third in attracting foreign direct investment (FDI), after the USA and China, and nearly half of its FDI comes from member countries of the EU. It is predicted that after Brexit, not only will London be separated from the EU market, it will also lose its attractiveness to foreign capital. And with the EU losing the UK, the confidence of foreign capital towards the EU would also be weakened. All these factors might contribute to an increase of FDI to China. The economic instability of both the EU and the UK that leads to shrinkage of property prices and asset values might also provide great opportunities for Chinese entrepreneurs to invest in the European market. In parallel with the Chinese OBOR initiative and the increasing Chinese investments in the CEE, Brexit provides an opportunity for Beijing in promoting the internationalization of RMB, through settling international accounts by using RMB.

A "soft Brexit" means the continual linkage with the Single European Market, which could be done through obtaining membership of the European Economic Area (EEA).[26] The non-EU EEA states accept all the four freedoms of movements—people, goods, services and capital—and they need to contribute to the budget of the EU. They allow the European Court of Justice to play a significant role in the formulation of national laws. Non-EEA states, such as Switzerland, may have preferential agreements with the Single Market. A non-EU state could participate in the customs union for some categories of goods, that is, it can benefit from free trade within the EU, but it has to apply the EU's common external tariff or other barriers in its commercial relationship with third countries.[27] The UK may leave the Single Market, but choose to stay within the customs union. There will be no tariff imposed on UK goods and no customs inspection needed, but London will have no role to play in determining trade agreements.[28]

If the UK stays within the Single European Market, it is possible for Chinese entrepreneurs to ship their products from the UK to other parts of the EU. Establishing an FTA between the UK and China would thus be largely beneficial to China.[29] However, if the EU sets up a strict restriction on the issue of country of origin regarding trading of goods between EU and the UK, this would obstruct the Chinese products entering the EU market via the UK "rear" door. On the other hand, the principal British exports to China are vehicles, including motorcycles and cars, which constitute 35.2% of total UK exports. If the UK and China succeed in signing an FTA, China's import tariff of 25% will be largely reduced. If the UK remains inside the Single Market, this will be detrimental to the competitiveness of other EU member countries in the car industry. The same is true for internal combustion engines, for which the UK accounts for 44.8% of EU's total exports, while Germany constitutes 40.1%. A Sino-British FTA would largely benefit the UK to the detriment of Germany.[30] So, if London signs an FTA with Beijing before the EU and the UK succeed in building the final model of their future relationship, this would pose a significant impact on the negotiation process between Brussels and London. In any case, the Chinese government would pay particular attention as to whether the UK will stay within the Single European Market, while Chinese entrepreneurs will start to think about moving their investments from the UK to other members of EU, a crucial move to rearrange their supply chain in order to avoid damage.

The "hard Brexit" approach is more in line with the pro-economic nationalism ideas of the "Leave" camp. German Chancellor Merkel has made it very clear that the "rules of the single market (the four freedoms of movement) are indivisible",[31] but the Brexiters are steadfast in controlling immigration. The crucial question which would affect the UK's relationship with countries such as China is whether the UK could still maintain free trade and economic liberalism after leaving the EU?[32] Would government policy, as well as public opinion, still be in favour of a high degree of economic liberalism and participating in the global value chains?

Once Premier May initiated the Brexit process by invoking Article 50 in March 2017, the difficult negotiations between the UK and EU were meant to take two years at most. The complicated process has to solve the problem of the exit bill and achieve consensus on principles for the future relationship, that is delineating the conditions for the divorce. According to Michel Barnier, the EU negotiator for Brexit, only after the divorce can the EU negotiate with the UK the terms and conditions for a future trade deal. The discussion on the future trade deal is of a different legal nature and it will take a long time.[33] This is at odds with what the British government wants: to "complete a trade deal in short order with the EU, or at least have clarity on transition arrangements within the first year of Brexit negotiations, so businesses have time to prepare". The uncertainty about the timing of trade deal negotiations would cause an outflow of companies and banks, including the Chinese ones, to move from the UK to the EU, especially during the two years of negotiations when the future UK-EU partnership is still uncertain.

Implications of Brexit for EU-China Relations

China has long remained the biggest source of the EU's imports (351bn euros in 2015), 20.3% of the EU's total. China is the second largest export market of the EU, valued at 170bn euros in 2015, 9.5% of the EU's total. However, this is only slightly larger than the third largest export market, Switzerland, which receives 8.4% of the EU's exports.[34] FDI from China to the EU amounted to US$5.48bn in 2015, which accounted for 3.8% of China's total, while FDI from EU to China reached US$6.51bn in 2015, 5.2% of the total FDI in China.[35] The UK is the second largest recipient of Chinese capital within the EU.

After Brexit, Chinese officials and scholars have emphasized on different occasions that China continues to support European integration and the EU's common policies as well as *acquis communautaire* already achieved, including the European currency, the euro. The EU maintaining its role as a global power is beneficial to China. Nevertheless, the weakened EU is obliged to reflect on how to achieve solidarity among the vast number of members, and strengthen its external actions to continually exert its influence on the global stage. The EU is losing a major power, the UK, whose GDP is one-sixth of the total GDP of the EU. The UK is a nuclear power, a permanent member of the UN Security Council, who enjoys a special relationship with the USA and plays an important role in some global governance frameworks like the G7 and G20. The EU as a normative power is influential in various international institutions, and the role of the UK is significant. Although it is too early to judge Brexit's impact in diminishing the power and prowess of the EU, what is at stake apart from economic matters during the negotiations of the UK with the EU in the future is the relationship between British policies and the Common Foreign and Security Policy (CFSP) and the related Common Security and Defence Policy (CSDP). The key question, as expressed by a British scholar, is "the extent to which the UK may seek autonomy or even divergence from existing EU policies and also the extent to which UK detachment from the EU...may diminish the foreign policy and defence capabilities of the remaining EU."[36]

In the 1990s, one of the EU's major strategic objectives was to integrate China into the international community by "socializing" her to adopt international norms. This has been subjected to change lately, as now the EU considers China as a major partner in global governance, that is, sharing responsibility and participating in global governance in order to encounter global challenges.[37] Good governance means the establishment and operation of mechanisms, which implies setting up clear rules of the games, norms and regulations. According to Chinese analysts, when the EU is becoming more pragmatic in looking for concrete cooperation with China on global governance, their competition with China in values and interests would possibly be aggravated. The Europeans are afraid that Chinese interests, ideas and proposals would pose a challenge to the EU's idea of global governance. Thus, among the BRICS countries, two groups are discerned by the Europeans, with India, Brazil and South Africa belonging to one group, whose positions are considered to be somewhat closer to the EU, while Russia and China belong to the other. Would a weakened EU, after Brexit, make it more "conciliatory" towards the Chinese attitude and position? This is unlikely, as the value-based approach is still very much the fundamental course taken by EU leaders.

The EU-China differences over norms, values and principles lead to the great divergence in the *Weltanschauung* (world view) of Europe and China. The politics of engagement promoted by the EU aiming to induce political and social change in China through the "soft" method of Human Rights Dialogue is generally deemed to be a failure. When China was relatively weak, Beijing already insisted that it had to search for its own model of development, though it would always learn from the West. With China's rise, she has become even more confident of her own path of development, and deeply believes that the "trial and error" method practised under the guidance of one-party dictatorship has already yielded remarkable achievements. Former Premier Wen Jiabao made a big step forward in recognizing that values such as democracy and human rights, though originating in the West, are universal. However, he stressed that the actual practice of these values in China should be different from the West, as the "national characteristics" are radically different. However, China under Xi Jinping's leadership has led to a big step backwards. He has reiterated regularly the "four confidences" during his first five years in power—confidence in institutions, theories, road (path of development) and culture. If the Chinese model is "correct" and suitable to China, why should China accept those Western values?

What will be the prospects of EU-China relations, when one is weakened due to Brexit while the other is more confident of its institutions, values and path of development?

First, China perceives that the EU will become unstable after Brexit, due to the rise of Euroscepticism, populism and economic protectionism. Brexit would lead to the strengthening of Euroscepticism and extremism, leading to the rise of extreme right-wing parties and challenging the EU identity and consensus. Chinese analysts are concerned with whether economic liberalism would be weakened within the EU after Brexit, so that the EU becomes more conservative and protectionist, thus affecting Chinese investments in and exports to the EU. Brexit would probably lead to the shrinking of the economy of scale within the EU Single Market, thus decreasing economic growth of the region. The immediate effect on China is the decrease in imports from it. Brexit by all means will incur a great decrease in the overall budget of the EU, as the UK used to be a major contributor. The potential change in tax regimes, stricter control of tax evasion and stronger measures in collecting taxes are considered as outcomes that would increase the pressure on the cost of business of Chinese entrepreneurs.

Second, Chinese scholar Shi Zhiqin observes that the weakening of the EU, and the UK's closer relationship with the USA due to Brexit, would strengthen the USA's relative position in the global order. This would stimulate further strategic collaboration between the USA and China.[38] He believes that the EU without the UK would become more independent from the USA, and thus the EU would probably be less restricted by the USA on contentious issues between the EU and China, such as the arms embargo and high-technology exports to China. However, there is no reason to believe that the arms embargo will be lifted. The relationship between the EU and the USA will not be weakened as a result of Brexit, as other great powers within the EU such as France, Germany and Italy are equally important allies of Washington. If the USA will consistently oppose it, there is no reason to believe that the EU would lift the arms embargo. Moreover, as Richard Maher rightly points out, "the embargo today is largely symbolic and its impact limited. It has not stopped the export of 'dual-use' equipment and technologies with military applications from European firms to China, and China has emerged over the past decade as a major arms producer and exporter in its own right."[39] But it is in the Chinese government's interest to see the arms embargo lifted, as it is seen as a kind of humiliation and pressure from Europe in response to Beijing's crackdown of student movements in 1989.

Third, Chinese scholars generally believe that the leadership role of Germany in the EU will further be strengthened with Brexit. With the loss of influence of France following the Eurozone crisis, the Franco-German axis seems to be nonexistent. How to achieve equilibrium especially among the stronger powers is considered as a crucial problem in EU's future.[40] China is not willing to see an inward-looking EU that is losing confidence and strategically tilted towards the USA. Chinese analysts believe that pragmatism prevails in Germany's policies towards China. Berlin emphasizes more on economic benefits, but not identifying China as a "strategic partner". Berlin stresses that the EU should be more proactive in Asia-Pacific security matters, and it adopts a very clear position. Merkel insists on sharing democratic values with Asian countries, examines the relationship with Asia-Pacific countries from the framework of the Atlantic Alliance and even supported Obama's "Pivot to Asia" strategy. This is considered as a challenge to China's security interests by Beijing's leaders.

Fourth, China would definitely strengthen the 16 + 1 mechanism and support the CEE to join the OBOR as a result of Brexit. This can be considered as a grand strategy in engaging the less developed EU members.

Fifth, the human rights dialogues between the European Commission and the PRC have been deemed to be a failure. It is difficult to imagine how the human rights situation in China could be ameliorated by a regular meeting of senior officials from the European Commission and the Chinese Ministry of Foreign Affairs. Apart from the rather high-profile reactions of the European Parliament in criticizing the human rights conditions in China, it is worthwhile to note the changing attitude of some European countries in tilting towards the interest-based approach and ignoring the value-based approach.

Sixth, the EU was due to offer the MES to China after 11 December 2016, 15 years after Beijing acceded to the World Trade Organisation (WTO). In contrast to the UK, which is in favour of granting MES, the EU as a whole opposes this, as Beijing has fulfilled only one criterion out of five.[41] China has now lodged a legal challenge against the EU at the WTO, but the EU is likely to continue with its stance of not granting MES to China. While the EU is still searching for a solution to this problem, it is almost sure that other trade defence instruments will certainly be in force to replace the anti-dumping measures through using the "surrogate country" method. The EU may consider whether to label a country as a market economy or not, but if it considers the export behaviour of a certain country as twisting the market, the EU can determine whether it is engaging in dumping behaviour according to international prices, irrespective of whether China is granted MES or not.[42]

Seventh, optimism prevails among Chinese analysts who claim that the weakened EU would compromise on issues like an FTA and bilateral investment agreement (BIA). Regarding the BIA, the EU and China have been negotiating an EU-wide agreement, which should supersede the 27 bilateral investment agreements signed between individual EU member states and Beijing. This is a rather draconian task as the 27 agreements are quite different from each other, and the new comprehensive agreement should incorporate all those conditions and benefits covered by individual agreements. Chinese investments in Europe have been increasing tremendously, and most of them belong to the merger and acquisition category, as Chinese enterprises are looking for European brand names which are appealing in the domestic market, and the acquisition of high technologies from Europe is highly urgent on the agenda of the Chinese companies. Chinese investments hit a historical high in 2015. The total FDI in the EU plus Norway and Switzerland reached US$23bn, up 28% from the $18bn in 2014.[43] Analysis from the approach of political economy might shed new light on the behaviour of the investments of Chinese state-owned enterprises in Europe. They are not so transparent in their economic transactions, and they may carry political functions as well. European analysts are thus keen on emphasizing the importance of transparency, as "more transparency would counter the notion that China uses its business as a foreign policy instrument and highlight those non-market policies that give Chinese exports an unfair competitive advantage."[44]

For European investments in China, two major problems persist. First, the Beijing government encourages investment in environment, energy, high technology and health care, but restricts it in heavy industries, raw materials, banking and insurance and domestic sectors, which are deemed to be key industries in the eyes of Chinese leaders. However, 77% of the European investments in China suffer from intellectual property rights (IPR) problems. Since preferential treatment is given to state-owned enterprises in China, foreign companies face many difficulties.[45] IPR is a long-term, unsolved issue that is becoming even more serious, as cyber theft by Chinese companies to obtain high technologies from Western companies is popular. This has aroused the serious concern of both the US government and the EU. The European Commission has proposed that the EU "should seek with China on combatting cyber-enabled theft of IPR and trade secrets".[46]

The second problem is the Western nations' scepticism and suspicions of Chinese state enterprises' acquisitions of Western manufacturers which are deemed to have strategic significance. It seems that the EU, as well as countries like Australia and the USA, are increasingly concerned with Chinese acquisition of their companies in unique technology. The German government has rejected a Fujian company's offer to acquire Aixtron, a German chip-producing company. Former Vice-Chancellor and Minister of Economics Sigmar Gabriel has designed proposals to enable the government to block Chinese acquisitions of German technology companies. Fifty-one of 99 recent Chinese deals in Germany are related to key industries, as Beijing's plan "Made in China 2025" reveals.[47] While this is criticized as discrimination by China, it seems that at least the German leaders are willing to share the burden of playing a more significant role in upholding the principles of the EU as well as the Western-led liberal world order.

The influence of Brexit on Hong Kong's economic growth is limited. Both the UK and other countries of the EU participate in the Hong Kong economy through investments and trade and help maintain Hong Kong's status as a trading centre, transport hub, international financial centre and the gateway to mainland China. The UK leaving the EU would not affect its investments in Hong Kong, and most British as well as other European companies are still using Hong Kong as their regional headquarters, as the Special Administrative Region is still strong in its rule of law, freedom of movements of people and capital and a robust banking system. Nevertheless, there may be some adjustments to the Hong Kong-UK bilateral economic relationship. In 2015, 631 British companies used Hong Kong as their regional headquarters. The UK is Hong Kong's ninth largest export destination and also third largest destination for service exports, as well as Hong Kong's fifth largest foreign direct investment destination. If Brexit affects British companies, and causes sterling's devaluation, this would have an impact on British companies' businesses in Hong Kong, as well as Hong Kong's trade with and investment in the UK.[48]

Concluding Remarks

A major obstacle can be discerned in the development of the EU-China relationship. It is related to the role and positioning of the EU as a global actor that would try to extend her influence to the proper functioning of the global system through disseminating her ideas and soft power.

The EU's *raison d'être* is to exist as a normative and civilian power, different from a sovereign state. The EU opts for a so-called new sovereignty that calls for a violable sovereignty and that interference in other states' domestic affairs is allowed if human rights are infringed upon. This is contrary to the so-called traditional sovereignty upheld by China.[49] The EU has always tried to balance two competing items in its agendas vis-à-vis China: promoting its values and norms, while pursuing interests at the same time. Now with the continual growth of power of China, there are more and stronger voices asking the EU to put aside the export of its values and principles, since this has been proven as a fruitless attempt. Instead, the EU should benefit from China's rise and rethink about the relative positions of Europe and China in the "grand chessboard".

The answer to this question might illuminate the choice of European leaders: is China a reformist or revisionist power? How would the answer to this question influence the relationship between the EU and China? Though it is true that China today is "neither interested in nor capable of providing a coherent alternative to the liberal, rule-based (global) order",[50] and she has really benefitted from this Western-dominated order in the last four decades since the death of Mao, the potential resurgence of the Middle Kingdom mentality, as depicted from the growing self-confidence and assertiveness of Beijing, has aroused serious concerns of the scholars who study the role of this rising power in the global political and economic order. This question is epitomized by the positions of China regarding her role in international institutions or regime.

The Chinese ideas regarding the PRC's relationship with the international institutions or international regimes are related to the crucial problem of the rules of the games inherent in these international institutions. In the late 1990s when Jiang Zemin was still in power, Chinese analysts created the term *daguo waijiao* (great power diplomacy) in anticipation of China's ascension to a great power. Since then, the Chinese literature revealed that Beijing sought to join all those international institutions so as to prove that she was "joining the world". But the PRC's second objective is even more significant: it is only after joining these international regimes that the Chinese government is able to modify the rules of the games, or international norms, of these international institutions in the interests of China. The third objective of the PRC is that even if the rules of the games suit Chinese national interests, and that there is no need to transform them for the time being, for the future formulation of the new rules of the games, Beijing should be in a position to exercise its influence, due to its sheer size and increasing power. The fourth objective of China is to construct new kinds of international institutions by her own efforts, such as the Shanghai Cooperation Organization that incorporates the Chinese ideas of "cooperative security", and the AIIB, which offers loans to the OBOR countries based on different conditions, or with no political conditions attached. The AIIB is clearly in competition with the World Bank, International Monetary Fund (IMF) and Asian Development Bank, which are all financial institutions created by the USA aiming to offer assistance to developing countries but inducing sociopolitical changes with Western favour.

It will be difficult for an EU that continues to propagate its ideas and values as a normative civilian power, facing a fast-growing China that aspires to modify the rules of the games of the international system. This is especially the case as Beijing is adept and capable of managing bilateral relationships with individual states. A critical observer rightly points out the "tactics" of China in dealing with individual states bilaterally, as she is always in a stronger position and thus easier to engage the partner for the benefit of China. "China prefers to deal with national capitals rather than the EU as a whole, provoking and encouraging political division in Europe and openly pursuing a divide-and-rule strategy. In many ways China reveals the limitation of the EU as a strategic actor in world politics."[51]

It seems that, post-Brexit, facing a weaker EU and a weakened UK outside the EU, China might even strengthen its position in influencing the formulation of international norms.

Notes

1. Discussion with the author during the Annual Jean Monnet Conference held by the European Commission, Brussels, 17–18 October 2016.
2. The PhD thesis of Thomas Stiegler from the School of Modern Languages and Cultures, University of Hong Kong, defended in October 2016.

3. P. I. Crookes, "Resetting EU-China Relations from a Values-based to an Interests-based Engagement", *International Politics*, 50:5, 2013, pp. 639–663.
4. Presentation given by Professor Richard Higgott, University of Warwick, at the seminar on "Brexit and the Future of EU-China Relations", European Institute for Asian Studies, Brussels, 5 October 2016.
5. See Ayse Kaya, "The EU's China Problem: a Battle over Norms", *International Politics*, 51:2, 2014, p. 224.
6. See Zhou Xinyu, "UK's New thinking on China Policy", *Guoji Wenti Yanjiu* (International Studies), 171, No. 1, 2016, pp. 63–76.
7. See High Representative of the Union for Foreign Affairs and Security Policy, Joint Communication to the European Parliament and the Council, *Elements for a New EU Strategy on China*, JOIN (2016) 30 final, Brussels, 22 June 2016, pp. 11, 17.
8. See Bu Shaohua, "Sino-European 'Sub-regional Cooperation': Dynamics and future Directions", *Guoji Wenti Yanjiu* (International Studies), 172, No. 2, 2016, pp. 29–39.
9. According to Chinese analysts, 76.5% of Polish banks, 88.5% of the Czech bank, more than 80% of Hungarian's banks and 99.2% of Slovakia's banks are controlled by capital from Western Europe. Ibid., p. 33.
10. Ibid., p. 39.
11. See Benjamin Barth, "China's Re-emergence as a Global Economic Power: How should Europe Respond?", *European View*, 13, 2014, pp. 233–241.
12. High Representative of the Union for Foreign Affairs and Security Policy, Joint Communication to the European Parliament and the Council, *Elements for a New EU Strategy on China*, JOIN (2016) 30 final, Brussels, 22 June 2016, p. 17.
13. See Zhang Lei, "The European Parliament in China-EU Relations", *Guoji Wenti Yanjiu* (International Studies), 174, No. 4, 2014, pp. 37–49.
14. See Feng Zhongping, "Brexit and its Influence to China", *Xiandai Guoji Guanxi* (Contemporary International Relations), No. 7, 2016.
15. See *Financial Times*, 13 November 2013, https://www.ft.com/content/f9a4a22c-4bbc-11e3-8203-00144feabdc0
16. Ibid.
17. See Alex Barker & Jim Brunsden, "Brussels Readies Rule Change to Target UK Euro Clearing", *Financial Times*, 16 December 2016, p. 4.
18. Angela Stanzel, "Brexit: An Opportunity for China?", *China Analysis*, European Council on Foreign Relations, September 2016, p. 3.
19. Ibid.
20. See George Parker & Alex Barker, "May eases Brexit fears but warns UK will walk away from 'bad deal'", *Financial Times*, 18 January 2017, p. 1.
21. See Jin Ling, "UK leaving EU: Background, Impacts and Prospects", *Guoji Wenti Yanjiu* (International Studies), 174, No. 4, 2014, pp. 24–36.

22. See the interview of Philippe le Corre in *Ta Kung Pao*, 29 September 2016, p. A12.
23. See George Parker & Alex Barker, "May eases Brexit fears but warns UK will walk away from 'bad deal'", *Financial Times*, 18 January 2017, p. 1.
24. See Anand Menon & Brigid Fowler, "Hard or Soft? The Politics of Brexit", *National Institute Economic Review*, No. 238, November 2016, pp. R4–R12.
25. See Wang Yuanxue, Xu Zhiyu & Zhang Xiaolei, "The Influence of Brexit towards Sino-British and Sino-EU Trade and Investment", *Guoji Jingji Hezuo* (Journal of International Economic Cooperation), 12, December 2016, p. 8.
26. Norway, Iceland and Liechtenstein belong to the EEA.
27. See Anand Menon & Brigid Fowler, p. R8.
28. See *Ta Kung Pao*, 14 June 2017, p. A18.
29. See Xu Jianwei, Alicia Garcia-Herrero & Zhang Jiawei, "Would Brexit Affect Trade Relations between China and Europe?" *Guoji Jingji Pinglun* (International Economic Review), 3, 2017, p. 48.
30. Ibid., pp. 53–55.
31. See Philip Stephens, "How Brexit may not Mean Brexit", *Financial Times*, 16 December 2016, p. 11.
32. See Philip Stephens, "A Hard Brexit Heralds a Closed Britain", *Financial Times*, 21 October 2016, p. 11.
33. See Alex Barker & Jim Brunsden, "Barnier Calls for UK Realism on Brexit", *Financial Times*, 1 December 2016, p. 2.
34. *European Union, Trade in Goods with China*, DG for Trade, European Commission, 4 Nov 2016.
35. Wang Yuanxue, Xu Zhiyu & Zhang Xiaolei, "The Influence of Brexit towards Sino-British and Sino-EU Trade and Investment", *Guoji Jingji Hezuo* (Journal of International Economic Cooperation), 12, December 2016, p. 5.
36. Jagjit S. Chadha, "UK and Europe: What Next? Introduction", *National Institute Economic Review*, No. 238, November 2016, p. R2.
37. See Jin Ling, "EU's New Thoughts on Global Governance and its Implications to Sino-EU Relations", *Guoji Wenti Yanjiu* (International Studies), 154, No. 2, 2013, pp. 59–71.
38. Shi Zhiqin, "The influence of Brexit on Sino-European and Sino-British relations", Tsinghua-Carnegie Global Policy Centre, Tsinghua University, 10 August 2016, http://carnegietsinghua.org/2016/08/10/zh-pub-64625
39. See Richard Maher, "The Elusive EU-China Strategic Partnership", *International Affairs*, 92:4, 2016, p. 965.
40. See Zhao Ke & Li Gang, "The Strategic Risk that Brexit brings to Sino-EU Relations", *Guoji Shiye* (International Horizon), No. 8, 2016, p. 58.

41. The five criteria include: (a) absence of state intervention on allocation of resources, production costs and prices, (b) absence of state intervention in enterprises linked to privatization and the absence of non-market forms of exchange, (c) a company law in practice, including modern accounting standard, (d) businesses subject to bankruptcy and intellectual property laws, (e) financial sector independent from the state. See *Commission Staff Working Document on Progress by the People's Republic of China towards Graduation to Market Economy Status in Trade Defence Investigations*, European Commission, SEC(2008) 2503 final, Brussels, 19/09/2008. China only fulfills condition (b). See also "Status of market Economy to China: What Political answers can be Given to this Legal Straitjacket?" *European Issues*, No. 389, 18 April 2016.
42. See Feng Zhongping, "Brexit's Influence to EU and Sino-EU Relations", *Ouzhou Yanjiu* (European Studies), No. 4, 2016, p. 8.
43. "Chinese investment in Europe hits $23bn record", *Financial Times*, 9 May 2016.
44. See Benjamin Barth, "China's Re-emergence as a Global Economic Power: How should Europe Respond?", *European View*, 13, 2014, p. 236.
45. Francois Godement & Angela Stanzel, "The European Interest in an Investment Treaty with China", European Council on Foreign Relations, *Policy Brief*, February 2015, p. 6.
46. See High Representative of the Union for Foreign Affairs and Security Policy, Joint Communication to the European Parliament and the Council, *Elements for a New EU Strategy on China*, JOIN (2016) 30 final, Brussels, 22 June 2016, p. 9.
47. Guy Chazin, "China not Amused by Berlin Blockade", *Financial Times*, 4 November 2016, p. 4.
48. E. Zhihuan, Dai Daohua & Choi Wing Hung. *Zhongying Caijing Suping* (Financial and Economic Insight), Economics and Strategic Planning Department, Bank of China, No. 70, 24 June 2016, http://www.bochk.com/dam/investment/fininsight/EI2016070.pdf
49. See Ayse Kaya, "The EU's China Problem: a Battle over Norms", *International Politics*, 51:2, 2014, pp. 214–233.
50. See R, Maher, p. 975.
51. See Richard Maher, p. 976.

CHAPTER 6

Is the Western Alliance Crumbling? A Japanese Perspective on Brexit

Daisuke Ikemoto

Introduction

For Japan, the UK has long been a gateway to Europe. The Japanese government regards itself as one of the three pillars of the Western Alliance alongside the USA and the EU—and Britain as its closest partner in Europe. The UK accounts for nearly two-fifths of Japanese direct investment in the EU, and many Japanese companies use their British subsidiaries and branches as a base for their commercial activities throughout the continent. It is natural, therefore, that both the Japanese government and business community found the outcome of the Brexit Referendum an unpleasant surprise. This chapter will first argue that Japan's response to Brexit is influenced not only by its economic interests but also by its political considerations. Indeed, the Japanese government sees Brexit as a potential threat to the solidarity of the Western Alliance. Next, it will examine how Brexit might affect future relations between Japan and the EU. Finally, it will discuss how both Brexit and the election of Donald Trump as President of the USA have influenced Japan's perspective on the desirability of regional integration in Asia based on the European model.

D. Ikemoto (✉)
Faculty of Law, Meiji Gakuin University, Tokyo, Japan
e-mail: ikemoto@mail1.meijigakuin.ac.jp

D. W. F. Huang, M. Reilly (eds.), *The Implications of Brexit for East Asia*, https://doi.org/10.1007/978-981-13-0185-8_6

Brexit as a Potential Threat to the Solidarity of the Western Alliance

From the Japanese perspective, Britain's exit from the EU could not have come at more inconvenient moment: since the global financial crisis of 2007–8, the US has become increasingly inward-looking and is no longer willing to play the same role of the world's policeman.[1] Needless to say, for America's allies—such as Japan and the EU—this has caused real security concerns. Japan is worried about China's territorial ambitions on the islands in the South and East China Sea, while the EU is facing potential threats in the form of Russia's military interventions first in Ukraine and then in Syria. These, which are a part of President Putin's attempt to restore Russia's international influence and status, are particularly worrisome for member states in Eastern Europe.

A shared sense of insecurity led Japan and the EU to strengthen their economic and political ties in order to reinforce the solidarity of the Western Alliance.[2] In 2011 both sides declared their intention to conclude a strategic partnership and a free trade agreement (FTA). However, these diplomatic efforts could be undermined by the result of the UK's referendum. Not least because following Brexit the UK may no longer be able to work as Japan's gateway to Europe. The UK will certainly continue to support the North Atlantic Treaty Organization (NATO), and remain a permanent member of the UN Security Council. Yet its political and economic ties with the EU may well be weakened after Brexit.[3] This will diminish the UK's international influence and standing.[4] It might, for instance, no longer be able to act as a deal broker between the US, Europe, and Japan in multilateral forums such as the G7.

It is in this context that we should interpret the response of the Japanese government to Brexit. The Japanese position was most clearly articulated in the memorandum titled 'Japan's Message to the United Kingdom and the European Union', which listed its requests for the future economic relationship between the UK and the rest of the EU. The paper was dispatched by the Japanese government to British Prime Minister Theresa May on the eve of the G20 meeting in September 2016, and then published on the website of the Ministry of Foreign Affairs of Japan.

> In the international community today, where the global order is beset with challenges, the presence of a strong, united Europe is essential. Japan hopes to further cooperate with Europe with a view to maintaining the rule-based

> global order in the international community, including Asia. It enjoys strong partnerships with the UK and the EU in the major areas of politics, the economy and security on the basis of our shared fundamental values and the global perspective that underpins our contribution to the international community. Japan expects to continue cooperating and collaborating closely with the UK and the EU for international peace, stability and prosperity.[5]

One can, of course, question the paper's formula for the solidarity of a law-abiding and value-sharing alliance between Europe and Japan. First of all, for the EU, China is a more important economic partner than Japan.[6] Secondly, the implicit contrast between the rule-following Japan and the rule-breaking China is misleading, not least because Japan failed to obey the ruling of the International Court of Justice (ICJ) on its whaling for scientific research.[7] Last but not least, the strategic interests of both sides sometimes prevent cooperation based on shared values. For instance, the EU considers that Japan's stance on Russia's aggression in Ukraine was too lenient, while Japan believes the EU has not been critical enough of China's strategy in the South China Sea. With these provisos in mind, the next section analyses the Japanese perception of the economic and political fallout from Brexit.

The Economic and Political Impacts of Brexit on Japan

The Japanese government is primarily concerned with the issue of whether and to what extent Brexit will impair the activities of Japanese companies that use British subsidiaries to gain access to the EU's Single Market. Japan's direct investment in the UK is estimated to value US$ 89,228 million—making the UK the fourth most important destination for Japanese foreign investment (Japan is the ninth biggest foreign investor for the UK).[8] Japanese manufacturing companies such as Nissan and Hitachi can currently export the products of their factories in the UK to countries within the single European market without tariffs. Likewise, Japanese financial institutions in London—including Nomura and Daiwa—can offer their services throughout the Single Market, thanks to the so-called financial 'passport'. They can also conduct financial transactions in the euro. As such, the Ministry of Foreign Affairs of Japan made it clear that the Japanese government desires the UK to stay in both the Single Market and the Customs Union even after it leaves the EU.[9]

By contrast, there was initially little talk in Japan about a possible trade deal with the UK after Brexit. This is not surprising given the fact that if the UK stays in the Customs Union, as the Japanese wish, it cannot conclude an individual trade deal with countries outside the EU. However, there is heated controversy in the UK over whether the country should stay in the Single Market after Brexit, in other words, whether to pursue a 'soft' or 'hard' Brexit.[10] The supporters of the latter option argue that the UK will be able to have a better commercial relationship with the rest of the world if it leaves both the EU's Single Market and Customs Union. In contrast, it seems that those sections of the British government that are backing a soft Brexit coordinated with Japan's Ministry of Foreign Affairs on their call for the retention of strong ties.[11] From a diplomatic perspective, the Japanese government risks being seen as interfering with the UK's domestic politics by supporting the 'soft' Brexiters.[12] The fact that the Japanese government is willing to take such risks cannot be explained simply by economic considerations. Rather, it probably reflects the concern that a hard Brexit could severely damage the relationship between the UK and the EU, and thereby undermine the solidarity of the Western Alliance.

In any case, how Brexit affects the UK-based Japanese companies depends on the type of economic relationship the British government negotiates with the rest of the EU. There are three possible models.

1. The European Economic Area (EEA): The Norwegian model.

   Norway is not a member of the EU (full membership was rejected twice by national referenda in 1972 and 1994). However, it is a part of the Single Market—though not the Customs Union—through its membership of the EEA. In exchange for Single Market membership Norway makes financial contributions to the EU budget and accepts the free movement of people.
2. Bilateral agreement: The Swiss and the Canadian models.

   Switzerland negotiated sector-by-sector agreements with the EU in order to gain access to the Single Market. However, Swiss banks do not have the financial passport, nor can they engage in settlement business conducted in euros (these are the reasons why they have established subsidiaries in the City of London).[13] Even so, Switzerland still has to make small financial contributions to the EU. It also accepted the free movement of people as a part of the deal. However, the Swiss government unilaterally suspended it following the 2014 referendum vote to cap immigration, and the agreement is now under dispute between the two sides.

Canada recently concluded an FTA with the EU. Once ratified by both sides, the pact will abolish most tariffs on manufactured goods. Yet it does not cover the service sector, which accounts for around 90% of the UK's GDP.

3. The World Trade Organization (WTO) rules.

   If the UK fails to strike a deal with the EU, international trade will be based on the WTO rules. This means that the EU will impose common external tariffs on British exports.

The Japanese government recently commissioned a very detailed survey on the economic impact of Brexit (Table 6.1).[14] Of the three alternatives mentioned above, the Norwegian model will have the least effect on Japanese companies located in the UK and the Japanese economy more generally. By contrast, if—after Brexit—the WTO rules are applied to the UK/EU trade relationship, it will inflict considerable damage on Japan's exports to both the UK and the EU. Between these two extreme possibilities lies the bilateral model, which would allow Japanese companies to export their goods to the EU without tariffs. Even in this case, though, the Japanese government fears there will be significant negative impacts. They are particularly nervous that the UK and the EU might not reach an agreement swiftly, that cheap labour from Eastern Europe could become unavailable, and that the UK will opt out of the EU's safety standards.[15]

One interesting dimension of the Japanese memorandum is that it is very detailed about the impact of Brexit on the manufacturing sector. Indeed, one European journalist tweeted that 'the Japanese government

Table 6.1 The possible economic impacts of Brexit

	The UK's GDP (%)	*Japan's export to the UK (%)*	*Japan's export to the EU (%)*
EEA	−3.8	−8.7	−5.7
Bilateral agreement	−6.2	−10.4	−6.2
WTO rules	−11.3	−11.3	−6.5

Deloitte Tohmatsu consulting, 'Reports on the prospects of Japan-UK and Japan-EU Relationships', pp. 9, 11 has done a more thorough analysis of Brexit than the UK government has'.[16] The British debates, by contrast, tend to pay more attention to the future of the financial sector. This difference in emphasis probably reflects the relative importance of each sector for the British and Japanese economies.[17] Still, the lack of interest in industry among British politicians and media is surprising; given the fact that some of the strongest support for Brexit was in England's old industrial heartlands.[18] Instead, it is the Japanese government and companies like Nissan that are fighting hard to defend the interests of the manufacturing sector in the UK.

Before the Brexit referendum in June 2016, Nissan Motor issued a warning that it might be forced to relocate outside of the UK if the British people decided to leave the EU.[19] However, the company subsequently announced that it will produce two new models at its Sunderland plant. Nissan is satisfied with the guarantees obtained from the British government, including that it will seek a free trade deal with the EU for the automotive industry.[20] This episode suggests that the British government is willing to pay a price in order to ensure that the country remains an attractive investment destination for multinational companies. If the UK leaves the Single Market, the EU's competition law, which bans state aid distorting competition, will not be applied to the UK, thus giving the British government more leeway to attract foreign investors.

The British government will also face tough challenges in protecting the UK's financial sector, since most FTAs do not cover trade in services. It remains to be seen whether the UK-based institutions can maintain their financial passports in the EU—this would be difficult if the British government continues to insist on the right to control immigration. Nonetheless, it is widely expected that the City of London will maintain its status as the centre of international finance, though it might lose its euro-clearing business after Brexit.[21]

Although it is often said that it was the people that felt left out by globalization that voted for Brexit, in reality the Brexit camp is composed of very diverse socio-economic groups.[22] Many Conservative Brexit supporters dislike the EU because of its relatively strict regulations on issues including workers' rights and environmental protection. In other words, they want the UK to become a de-regulated and globalized economy outside of the EU. If they have their way—despite the economic turbulence expected during any transitional period—the UK will remain or become even more business-friendly after Brexit.

How Brexit Affects Future Relationships Between Japan and the EU

How will Brexit affect future relationships between Japan and the EU? Although both Japan and Western Europe belong to the Western Alliance, economic and political ties between the two sides remain weaker than the relationship between the US and Japan or even the relationship between the US and Europe. During the Cold War, the flooding of European markets with Japanese exports sometimes created friction. This experience, combined with the establishment of the Single Market, led Japanese companies to increase direct investment in the EU—rather than exporting their products from Japan (ironically it was then British Prime Minister Margaret Thatcher who supported this initiative). Political cooperation was also limited to multilateral frameworks such as G7 and the bilateral relationship remained relatively weak. However, since the end of the Cold War, the economic relationship between Japan and the EU has grown and matured. In 1991 the two sides issued The Hague Declaration, which strengthened their political and economic ties.

Meanwhile, since the 1990s, Japan has lagged behind in the global race to conclude bilateral and regional FTAs.[23] This was partly because the Japanese government preferred global trade liberalization through the General Agreement on Tariffs and Trade (GATT) and the WTO. Strong domestic opposition from the agricultural sector also prevented the government from reaching an agreement with food-exporting countries. South Korea's success in negotiating FTAs—first with the USA and then with the EU—changed the situation, however, as Korean companies now enjoy competitive advantages against their Japanese counterparts in the two largest and most developed markets in the world. Negotiations for an FTA between Japan and the EU began in 2013, and were going rather smoothly before Brexit, despite initial reservations on the European side.[24]

Brexit could have two contradictory effects on the outcome of the negotiations. On the one hand, Brexit might make the EU more economically inward-looking by changing the balance of opinion within the institution. In the EU, while both the UK and Germany supported free trade with the outside world, the French have taken a more protectionist stance. If the latter gains the upper hand as a result of Brexit, this certainly would not help the successful conclusion of a trade deal between Japan and the EU. On the other hand, as the EU is beset by a series of crises, including Brexit, it needs positive achievements desperately. For Japan, whether the USA will ever ratify the Trans-Pacific Partnership (TPP) has become unclear upon the election of Trump as the US President. In these circumstances, Brexit and the Trump regime might give both the EU and Japan renewed political impetus to make a compromise and conclude an FTA swiftly.

The announcement in July 2017—on the eve of the G20 meeting in Hamburg—that Japan and the EU have reached outline agreement on an economic partnership agreement suggests that the second consideration prevailed over the first.[25]

Will Brexit and the Trump Presidency Change Japan's Attitudes Towards Regional Integration in East Asia?

This section will investigate whether Brexit and the election of Trump as the US President will change the way in which Japan evaluates the possibility of regional integration in Asia.

During the Cold War the Japanese government regarded the maintenance of the Japan-US alliance as its top priority. This stance worked to limit Japan's relationship with neighbouring countries in East Asia—particularly those countries within the 'Eastern camp', such as China and the USSR. While Western Europe witnessed the proliferation of multilateral organizations such as the European Community and NATO, in East Asia the relationships between the US and its allies were based on bilateral networks that centred on the US. Therefore, regional ties remained relatively weak, even among the countries aligned with the US, such as Japan, South Korea, Taiwan, and the Philippines.

The situation began to change gradually in the 1980s.[26] After the Plaza agreement of 1985, Japanese companies began to move their production to other Asian countries so that they could capitalize on cheaper labour costs. As a result, economic interdependence deepened between Japan and its East Asian neighbours. Next, the end of the Cold War meant US interest in the region was diminished—though it remained hostile to the emergence of a closed regional bloc. It was against this backdrop that Japan played a leading role in the early stages of regional integration both in Asia-Pacific and East Asia.[27] In the Asia-Pacific region, Asia-Pacific Economic Cooperation (APEC) was established in 1989 as a joint initiative between Japan and Australia. The 1997 Asian financial crisis further spurred regional integration in East Asia. The proposal of the Japanese government to establish the Asian Monetary Fund (AMF) was aborted by US opposition. Nonetheless, Japanese Finance Minister Kiichi Miyazawa offered 30 billion dollars as medium- and long-term assistance to the Asian countries affected by the crisis. In 2000, the financial ministers from the Association of Southeast Asian Nations (ASEAN), Japan, China, and South Korea agreed to establish bilateral networks of currency swaps in order to prepare for a future financial crisis. This has come to be known as the Chiang Mai Initiative. In the course of these negotiations rival frameworks for regional integration emerged in East Asia, including the ASEAN+3 (adding Japan, China, and South Korea to ASEAN) and the ASEAN+6 (adding Australia, New Zealand, and India to the ASEAN+3). China preferred the former, while Japan—fearing that ASEAN+3 could eventually become dominated by China—supported the latter.[28] Politically, ASEAN and the other six nations held the first meeting of the EAS (East Asian Summit) in 2005 (the US and Russia also became members in 2011). In the economic sphere, negotiations for the Regional Comprehensive Economic Partnership (RCEP) were formally launched by the member states of the ASEAN+6 in 2011. Japan also concluded its first multilateral FTA with ASEAN in 2008.

Japan's policy towards regional integration was based on the following three principles.[29] First of all, the Japanese government has an aversion to legalistic models of regional integration similar to the EU, and prefers a functional approach. In this sense, one cannot say that Brexit discredited the EU as a model of regional integration in the eyes of the Japanese. Even before Brexit, Japan did not regard the EU as an attractive model. Secondly, Japan holds the position that regional organization should not be an exclusive club and should be open to the influence of outside countries, especially the USA. Indeed, Japan will be a part of it only if it remains compatible with Japan's close relationship with the US. Last but not least, the Japanese government has insisted that regional integration in East Asia should be based on universal values, such as human rights and democracy.

To conclude, one cannot say that Japan was ever very enthusiastic about regional integration, even during this period. Maintaining its good relationship with the USA remained a top priority for Japanese diplomacy. Although Japan proposed to turn the ASEAN+6 into a free trade area, fierce opposition by the agricultural sector prevented it from concluding an economic partnership agreement with Australia until recently.[30] Still, it is noteworthy that Japan played a positive and constructive role in promoting regional integration both in Asia-Pacific and East Asia until the mid-2000s.[31]

However, the situation has changed since then as China's economic growth has altered the balance of power in the region. Japan has begun to regard China as a serious threat to its security.[32] With the rise of Beijing's influence, Japan became less willing to join a regional framework in East Asia. Instead, it has emphasized the importance of cooperation across Asia-Pacific. Japan turned its back on regional cooperation with its East Asian neighbours during the first Premiership of Shinzo Abe.[33] Prime Minister Yukio Hatoyama—who took office in 2009 after his Democratic Party of Japan beat the Liberal Democratic Party (LDP) in the general election—might be seen to have swung the pendulum in the opposite direction. He advocated the idea of an East Asian Community, but his proposal remained very ambiguous.[34] When viewed alongside his negative stance towards the US military base in Okinawa, it tended to be regarded as an anti-American move both inside and outside Japan. Meanwhile, Japan's territorial disputes with China over the Senkaku Islands have intensified: a Chinese fishing vessel crashed into Japan's patrol boat in 2010, and the Chinese government halted the export of rare earth minerals to Japan temporarily in order to negotiate the release of the arrested ship's captain.[35] Both countries went head to head again in 2012 over the nationalization of these islands by the Japanese government. Critics of the government in Japan argued that China had taken provocative actions because Hatoyama's policy was damaging Japan's relationship with the USA. It was proposed that Japan should strengthen its military alliance with the USA. The LDP returned to power in 2012 and Abe became the Prime Minister again. The major decisions taken recently by his administration should be viewed in this light.[36] Key examples include the re-interpretation of the Japanese constitution, which now allows Japan to exercise right to collective self-defence, and participation in the TPP negotiations. By contrast, less effort was made to improve the relationship with China.

One remaining question is whether the recent election of Trump as the US President will change the direction of Japanese diplomacy. After entering the White House, Trump withdrew the USA from the TPP.[37] On international trade issues he seems to prefer bilateral negotiations over multilateral frameworks such as the WTO, the TPP, and the North Atlantic Free Trade Area (NAFTA).[38] Under his presidency Washington will surely ask Japan to shoulder a much heavier burden in exchange for US security guarantees.

Theoretically, Japan could use a regional framework of cooperation in East Asia as a tool to check the rise of China, and regard it as a supplement or even an alternative to the now fracturing alliance with the USA. My prediction, however, is that the Japanese government will not choose this course; instead, it is more likely to do whatever it takes in order to maintain its military alliance with the USA. In other words, although the Western Alliance might be crumbling, Japan is still clinging to it. Even if a future Japanese government is more inclined to take a positive stance towards regional integration in East Asia, at least two conditions have to be met before doing so. First of all, Japan must accept that China will play a leading role in the process, given the current balance of power between the two countries. Secondly, the Japanese government needs to persuade a sceptical public of the merits of such an endeavour.

In this context, it is important to assess the possibility that Japan's decisions might give rise to populist opposition to regional economic integration, similar to that seen during Brexit and the Trump campaign. How people perceive the effect of globalization and regional integration depends on their economic position. From a transnational perspective, it is the Chinese and Indian middle classes who have seen their incomes increase most rapidly during the last 20 years (1988–2008).[39] The wealthiest 1% of the world also did quite well during the same period. By contrast, though, throughout the developed world people in the bottom half of income distribution have seen their incomes stagnate. It was their political dissatisfaction that was mobilized in Brexit's Vote Leave campaign and in the election of President Trump.[40] Japan still records one of the highest GDPs per capita among East Asian countries, but the country's average household income has declined by nearly 20% during the last 20 years. It has fallen from 664.2 million yen in 1994 to just 541.9 million yen in 2014.[41] Japan also records a relatively high level of income inequality and poverty: among OECD countries its Gini coefficient (0.33) ranks 15th and its poverty rate (0.161) 7th.[42] Viewed through this lens, it is possible that Japan has become more susceptible than other Asian countries to a political backlash against economic globalization.

At the same time, it should be emphasized that Japan has so far witnessed only a limited rise in populism. Populism is often identified with an anti-elitist or anti-establishment movement. However, Jan-Werner Müller contends that the essence of populism is, in fact, anti-pluralism.[43] According to Müller, the hallmark of populists is their claim that they are the only representatives of the 'real people' (liberal elites and ethnic minorities are excluded from this category). In the light of this definition, there are certainly populist tendencies in Japan. Japan has now plunged to 72nd in the World Press Freedom Index,[44] while hate speech against ethnic Koreans and other minorities is becoming a social and political problem. 'Initiatives from Osaka'—a political party widely regarded as populist—holds 15 parliamentary seats in the House of Representatives. However, Toru Hashimoto, its leader, is critical of hate speech. Therefore, it is debatable whether we can call 'Initiatives from Osaka' populist in Müller's sense of the word. One might be able to explain the relative weakness of populism in Japanese politics as a result of Japan not having accepted as many immigrants as either the USA or some European countries. Japan remains a relatively homogenous society and therefore to attack ethnic minorities and immigrants is not an effective way to gain political support. In any case, it remains to be seen whether populism in Japan will become more widespread if the government concludes a free trade deal with the EU and/or RCEP.

Conclusion

To conclude, Japan made it clear that it wanted the UK and the EU to maintain as close a relationship as possible after Brexit. The Japanese government has successfully reached an outline agreement on free trade deals with the EU and is striving to maintain its military alliance with the USA. Yet, with the rise of China, it has become increasingly reluctant to participate in the process of regional integration in East Asia. All of this suggests that the Japanese government still prefers to see itself as one of the three pillars of the Western Alliance alongside the USA and Europe, rather than as a truly equal partner with its Asian neighbours. Meanwhile, Japanese politics has so far witnessed only a limited rise in populism despite the economic malaise in the country during the last two decades. This more than likely comes down to Japan's comparatively low levels of immigration, which has ensured that it remains a relatively homogenous society.

Notes

1. 'Obama Says U.S. Will No Longer Be the World's Policeman', *Foreign Policy*, 28 May 2014.
2. For an overview of EU-Japan relationship, see Paul Bacon, Hartmut Mayer and Hidetoshi Nakamura (eds.), *The European Union and Japan: A New Chapter in Civilian Power Cooperation?* (Surrey: Ashgate, 2015).

3. LSE Commission on the Future of Britain in Europe, *Britain as a Global Actor after Brexit* (2016).
4. John Nilsson-Wright and Kiichi Fujiwara, *Brexit and Its Consequences: Anglo-Japanese Relations in a Post-EU Referendum World* (London: Royal Institute of International Affairs, 2016).
5. Ministry of Foreign Affairs of Japan, 'Japan's Message to the United Kingdom and the European Union', 2. http://www.mofa.go.jp/files/000185466.pdf (accessed on 22 November 2016).
6. China ranks as the EU's second trading partner in 2015. Japan is only the seventh.
7. The Guardian, 28 November 2015. https://www.theguardian.com/environment/2015/nov/29/australia-slams-japans-decision-to-resume-antarctic-whaling (accessed on 22 November 2016).
8. JETRO, direct investment statistics. https://www.jetro.go.jp/world/japan/stats/fdi/ (accessed on 19 January 2017).
9. Ministry of Foreign Affairs of Japan, 'Japan's Message'.
10. BBC news, 7 July 2016. http://www.bbc.com/news/uk-politics-36723220 (accessed on 19 January 2017).
11. This was confirmed to the author of this article by a Japanese diplomat. See also Daily Telegraph, 5 September 2016. http://www.telegraph.co.uk/business/2016/09/05/japans-demand-for-seamless-brexit-is-a-timely-warning-against-hu/ (accesses on 22 November 2016).
12. For example, Sky news described the Japanese memorandum as an 'unprecedented warning'. http://news.sky.com/story/japans-unprecedented warning-to-uk-over-brexit-10564585 (accessed on 19 January 2017).
13. Financial Times, 19 August 2016. https://www.ft.com/content/5cebe746-655a-11e6-8310-ecf0bddad227 (accessed on 19 January 2017).
14. Deloitte Tohmatsu Consulting, 'Report on the Prospects of Japan-UK and Japan-EU Relationships after Brexit', March 2017. https://www.mofa.go.jp/mofaj/files/000243120.pdf (accessed on 14 September 2017).
15. Ministry of Foreign Affairs of Japan, 'Japan's Message'.
16. https://twitter.com/AlbertoNardelli/status/772841114512531456
17. The GDP share of manufacturing is 19% for Japan and 10% for the UK in 2014. The data is from the World Bank. http://data.worldbank.org/indicator/NV.IND.MANF.ZS (accessed on 19 January 2017).
18. BBC news, 24 June 2016. http://www.bbc.com/news/uk-politics-36616028 (accessed on 19 January 2017).
19. BBC news, 8 November 2013. http://www.bbc.com/news/business-24859486 (accessed on 19 January 2017).
20. BBC news, 30 October 2016. http://www.bbc.com/news/uk-politics-37815864?SThisFB (accessed on 22 November 2016).

21. Scott Lavery, Adam Barber, Sean McDaniel and Davide Schmid, 'Frankfurt, Paris and Dublin: Post-Brexit Rivals to the City of London?' (SPERI Global Political Economy Brief No. 6, 2017).
22. John Curtice, 'Brexit: Behind the Referendum', *Political Insight*, September 2016, 4–7.
23. Satoshi Oyane and Yutaka Onishi (eds.), *The Politics of FTAs and the TPP: Securitization of Trade Policy?* (Tokyo: Yuhikaku, 2016, in Japanese).
24. Frederik Ponjaert, 'The Political and Institutional Significance of an EU-Japan Trade and Partnership Agreement', in Bacon, Mayer and Nakamura (eds.), *The European Union and Japan*, 85–114.
25. BBC news, 6 July 2017. http://www.bbc.co.uk/news/business-40520218 (accessed on 14 September 2017).
26. Mie Oba, *Asia as a Multi-layered Region: In Search for Co-existence in Conflicts* (Tokyo: Yuhikaku, 2014, in Japanese). See also Mie Oba, 'Sino-Japanese Competition over Regional Institutions in Asia', in Jeffrey Reeves, Jeffrey Hornung, and Kerry Lynn Nankivell (eds.), *Chinese-Japanese Competition and the East-Asian Security Complex: Vying for Influence* (Abingdon: Routledge, 2017), chapter 3.
27. Both East Asia and Asia-Pacific are a socially constructed concept, and the exact scope of each region is hotly contested. In this chapter, Asia-Pacific refers to a region which is larger than East Asia and includes countries such as the US and Russia.
28. Oba, *Asia as a Multi-layered Region*, 162–3, 239.
29. Ministry of Foreign Affairs of Japan, 'Japan's View on the Construction of an East Asian Community' (2006). http://www.mofa.go.jp/mofaj/area/eas/pdfs/eas_02.pdf (accessed on 16 January 2017).
30. ABC news, 8 April 2014. http://www.abc.net.au/news/2014-04-07/australia-japan-free-trade-deal/5372242 (accessed on 19 January 2017).
31. It is worth noting that, from a historical perspective, Japan's position in Asia is somewhat similar to that of the UK in Europe. Both are island nations and separated from the continent. Arguably, they were confined to the periphery of the civilizations they belonged to. However, both countries achieved industrialization and modernization more rapidly than their neighbours, which allowed them to build the empires, and acquire a sense of superiority – or individuality – in the process. Perhaps these past experiences make it difficult for both countries to participate in a framework of regional integration on an equal footing with other members. Compare Linda Colley, *Acts of Union and Disunion: What has held the UK together and what is dividing it?* (London: Profile Books, 2014) with Glenn Hook, 'Japan and the Construction of Asia-Pacific', in Andrew Gamble and Anthony Paine (eds.), *Regionalism and World Order* (Basingstoke: Macmillan, 1996), 170–1.

32. Taizo Miyagi, *Japanese Diplomacy since the End of the Cold War* (Tokyo: Chuko Shinsho, 2016, in Japanese).
33. Susumu Yamakage, 'Japan's View on Regionalism and the Rise of China', in Mie Oba (ed.), *The Making of East Asia: Order, Integration and Stakeholders* (Tokyo: Chikura Shobo, 2016, in Japanese), chapter 7.
34. Yukio Hatoyama, 'A New Path for Japan', New York Times, 26 August 2009. http://www.nytimes.com/2009/08/27/opinion/27iht-edhatoyama.html (accessed on 16 January 2017).
35. New York Times, 22 September 2010. http://www.nytimes.com/2010/09/23/business/global/23rare.html (accessed on 19 January 2017).
36. Miyagi, *Japanese Diplomacy*, 214–5.
37. BBC news, 24 January 2017. http://www.bbc.co.uk/news/world-us-canada-38721056 (accessed on 14 September 2017).
38. Reuter's news, 13 January 2017. http://www.reuters.com/article/us-usa-trump-trade-adviser-idUSKBN14X1X8 (accessed on 19 January 2017).
39. Branco Milanovic, *Global Inequality: A New Approach for the Age of Globalization* (Cambridge, Mass: Harvard University Press, 2016).
40. Robert Ford and Matthew Goodwin, *Revolt on the Right: Explaining Support for the Radical Right in Britain* (London: Routledge, 2014).
41. Ministry of Health, Labour and Welfare, Comprehensive Survey of Living Conditions, 2014.
42. The data from the website of the OECD. https://data.oecd.org/japan.htm (accessed on 17 January 2017).
43. Jan-Werner Müller, *What is Populism?* (Princeton: Princeton University Press, 2016). See also Cas Mudde and Cristóbal Rovira Kaltwasser, *Populism: A Very Short Introduction* (Oxford: Oxford University Press, 2017).
44. The Word Press Freedom Index is published every year by Reporters without Borders. https://rsf.org/en/ranking (accessed on 19 January 2017).

CHAPTER 7

Lost in Brexit: The Complexities of Negotiating a New Trade Deal Between Korea and the United Kingdom

Sunghoon Park and Michael Reilly

The Current Features of the Korea-EU and Korea-UK Relationships

The Republic of Korea (RoK, Korea) and the then European Economic Community (EEC) established official diplomatic relations as long ago as 1963. Today, Korea is one of the ten strategic partners of the European Union (EU). This partnership is underpinned by three key agreements, all signed within the last decade—the Framework Agreement of 2010, a free trade agreement (FTA) of the following year and the Agreement on Participation in Crisis Management Operations of 2014. The burgeoning partnership has been accompanied by a major expansion of people-to-people, academic and other links.

Under this partnership, the two sides have held annual summit meetings and established several high-level consultation channels, including regular meetings at ministerial or vice-ministerial level on foreign affairs,

S. Park
Graduate School of International Studies, Korea University, Seoul, South Korea

M. Reilly (✉)
Taiwan Studies Program, University of Nottingham, Nottingham, UK

D. W. F. Huang, M. Reilly (eds.), *The Implications of Brexit for East Asia*, https://doi.org/10.1007/978-981-13-0185-8_7

trade and in other areas, as well as high-level policy dialogue in areas such as international development cooperation. The strategic partnership has been instrumental in expanding bilateral cooperation and consultation to other areas, including human rights, cyber security, crisis management, public diplomacy, industrial policy dialogue and next-generation cooperation areas.

But the agreement which receives most attention, both before and after the UK referendum on 'Brexit,' is almost certainly the 2011 FTA. At the time it was signed, this was groundbreaking, extending the scope and extent of FTAs to hitherto untouched areas, especially non-tariff issues such as the mutual recognition of standards and going further in the coverage of services than previous agreements. The speed and relative ease with which it was agreed took many by surprise. Perhaps paradoxically, the absence of any historic security commitments may have made this easier: at least one observer has suggested that precisely because the EU was not considered significant to East Asian geopolitics, the negotiations were not accompanied by 'baggage' and had a much lower profile than the concurrent negotiations between Korea and the USA over a similar agreement.[1]

The UK's relationship with Korea is of long-standing. It was one of the first countries to establish diplomatic relations and provided the second largest contingent of overseas troops to the UN forces fighting there in the Korean War, subsequently maintaining a token military presence through a rotating detachment to the UN Command Honour Guard. Since withdrawal of Honour Guard troops in 1992, however, there is no longer a formal security commitment.

Notwithstanding the lack of any security guarantees, today's relationship is stronger than ever, with a sizeable Korean community living in the UK, frequent direct flights between the two and significant bilateral overseas direct investment. But the modern relationship is driven overwhelmingly by trade, as was made clear by the Korean government's reaction to the result of the referendum, when it immediately considered plans for a major stimulus package to help exporters.[2] Trade will almost inevitably remain the focus of the post-'Brexit' bilateral relationship. In its position papers for the start of formal negotiations over its withdrawal from the EU, the British government affirmed its desire to maintain continuity in its existing trading arrangements, including those covered by EU agreements.[3] This applies to its bilateral trade with Korea as much as any other country: in 2015 Korea was the UK's 11th largest trading partner and since the FTA entered into force, the UK's trade with Korea has moved into surplus for the first time. So, protecting and nurturing this position by means of a new bilateral agreement would seem a high priority for the British government post-'Brexit,' while the Korean government's initial reaction suggests it attaches similar importance to one. This chapter considers the prospects for this. It argues that contrary, perhaps, to expectations, developing a new trade relationship will be far more complex than some British politicians might think and that any new agreement is unlikely to be as beneficial to the UK's interests as the current arrangements.

Changing Policy Environments Following 'Brexit'

Notwithstanding its desire for continuity in existing arrangements, the UK is likely to have to negotiate more than 100 trade agreements upon its withdrawal from the EU.[4] In some cases this should be straightforward and the EU will no doubt likewise hope that its existing agreements will continue unchanged, save for no longer applying to the UK. But the UK's departure from the EU will expose several complexities in the latter's relationship with Korea and it is far from certain that the current FTA can simply be modified to take account of UK withdrawal from the EU and a new bilateral agreement on similar terms extended to the UK.

The British government recognizes that its first priority in international trade post- 'Brexit' will be to maintain as far as possible its current trading relations with the rest of the EU. If only because of geography, this will remain the UK's most important bilateral trading partner by far. In 2015, the EU-27 accounted for 44% and 53% of the UK's total exports and imports respectively and these shares are unlikely to change quickly, however much some politicians may hope.[5] Based on the government's position papers, the next priority will be the preservation of current trading relations with those countries that currently have an FTA with EU, preferably by adopting existing arrangements in their entirety until new bilateral agreements can be negotiated.[6] These countries account for a further 14% or thereabouts of the UK's bilateral trade. This will be followed by other Most Favoured Nation (MFN) trade partners within the WTO's policies. At the bottom of the likely priorities will be least developed countries and the beneficiaries of the UK's generalized system of preferences (GSP). In respect of negotiating new deals as opposed to 'cutting and pasting' existing EU agreements to meet the changed circumstances, the British government's position paper appears to single out China as a priority candidate although International Trade Secretary Liam Fox has said that the first priorities for new bilateral agreements will be the US, Australia and New Zealand, in that order.[7] The US is currently the UK's largest trade partner outside the EU and is not currently the subject of a bilateral trade agreement, so is an obvious priority. The importance given to Australia and New Zealand is less obvious. In 2015, the UK's total trade with both was only 81% of its trade with Korea, suggesting new agreements may have more to do with nostalgic sentiment than modern reality, a view shared by at least one prominent Australian expert.[8] As with the US and unlike Korea, however, neither currently has an FTA with the EU.

In the case of least developed countries and GSP arrangements, there is probably no need for any revisions to current procedures. As for other WTO members, to whom the MFN principle would be applied, matters should also be straightforward once the UK has established itself as a member of the WTO in its own right, rather than as part of the EU. The negotiation of any new agreements with them would be a matter of determining priorities.

Clearly, future arrangements with the EU-27 and countries with whom the EU currently has an FTA will be crucial. The British government appears increasingly cognizant of this, its stance shifting from one of leaving both the Single Market and Customs Union in January 2017, to one in which membership of both could continue during a 'transition period' following formal withdrawal, to be followed by a 'new, deep and special partnership' with the EU, involving a 'new customs arrangement' with the 'most frictionless trade possible' between the UK and EU-27.[9] Whether the final agreement with the EU will be anything like this remains to be seen. The main opposition party in the UK Parliament has called for the country to remain in the Single Market, at least during a transition period but key members in it have gone further, arguing the country should stay in the Customs Union permanently unless a better alternative can be identified.[10] For its part, the EU has made clear that it will not even discuss the shape or scope of the trading relationship until agreement has been reached on core issues including the UK's future financial obligations and the nature of the border between Ireland and Northern Ireland. Inevitably therefore, the detail of future trading arrangements must remain speculative for the time being.

Unfortunately, the UK government does not give any detail as to how its preferred outcome of a 'deep and special partnership' might be applied in practice, speaking only of either 'a highly streamlined customs arrangement' or 'a new customs partnership,' while noting that the ultimate arrangement will depend on the outcome of the negotiations.[11]

If we assume that under such an arrangement, the UK would not be a member of the EU's Customs Union but would in effect maintain the status-quo free-trade relationship with the EU-27, keeping the common external tariff and other non-tariff barriers as some experts have recommended,[12] then the UK would be receiving discriminatory favourable treatment from the EU under WTO rules and both the EU and UK would have to negotiate with the two other groups of countries—FTA partners and other WTO members—for a derogation from WTO rules to get their agreement to this. The UK might be obliged to extend the preferences given to the EU-27 to all other countries in the WTO on an MFN-basis. This would be costly and most probably politically unacceptable within the UK and maybe within the EU too.

One alternative but still consistent with the UK's stated preference might be for it to negotiate a preferential trading partner arrangement with the EU in the way Switzerland has done, again maintaining the current common external tariff and non-tariff barriers. This would probably require the UK formally to join the European Economic Area (EEA). As this is a formal regional trade agreement (RTA) and recognized as such by the WTO, the UK would be permitted to treat non-EU and non-EEA members less favourably. At the time of writing, the British government appears to have ruled out membership of the EEA, so the likelihood of it pursuing this option does not seem high. Should it decide to pursue it, however, then the EU might be expected to seek a high price for doing so in the negotiations. Even in the most favourable circumstances, the negotiations would likely be prolonged.

As the UK's position paper is vague as to the detail of preferred future arrangements, it is also possible that it could decide not to maintain the EU's current common external tariff but to devise its own new trade instruments. It could re-join the European Free Trade Association (EFTA) should it so wish. As a former member, this should be relatively easy. Unless it can join the EEA, however, or decides to remain in the Single Market, its future status as a trading nation will be as a normal WTO member. This would mean it would then have to open negotiations with other WTO members, both the EU's existing FTA partners and others, over new agreements. Given that the position paper speaks of boosting trade relationships 'with both old friends and new allies,' this may be the UK's preferred approach, especially if it is able to roll over existing EU agreements en masse while it pursues such negotiations.[13] Even to start formal negotiations, however, the UK will first need either the acquiescence of the EU to do so, or to have formally separated from the EU's trading arrangements.

Other alternatives are possible but the less obvious the option, the greater the likely degree of complexity. In short, whatever the approach finally adopted by the UK, unless it either remains in the Single Market or Customs Union, or joins an RTA with the EU, it will be required to extend MFN treatment to all WTO members until new bilateral agreements can be negotiated. One obstacle to doing this quickly will be the UK's lack of capacity to conduct negotiations. For more than 40 years its trade policy in general and trade negotiations in particular have been handled on its behalf by the European Commission, so it lacks more than an entire generation of expertise in handling these.

Rolling over of existing EU agreements on a bilateral basis will therefore provide the UK with temporary 'peace clauses' while new negotiations are under way and the government's target countries for new agreements seem to assume this. If not, they suggest a badly misplaced sense of priorities.[14] In turn we may infer that the UK government's aim will be to ensure that the existing FTA with Korea continues to apply to UK businesses for a temporary but unspecified period after it leaves the EU.

Negotiating a New Trade Agreement Between Korea and the United Kingdom

The UK is currently Korea's largest export market in the EU and 12th largest worldwide, its exports more than doubling in dollar terms from \$3.79bn in 2009 to \$7.86bn in 2015. Over the same period Korea's exports to Germany, its second largest EU market, fell from \$8.2bn to \$6.2bn. Bilateral trade is now roughly in balance, imports from the UK being \$6.1bn in 2015, ranking it 3rd as a source of imports from the EU and 17th worldwide.[15] This is a recent phenomenon: prior to the FTA with the EU entering into force, the long-term trend had been for Korea to enjoy a large trade surplus with the UK. Since the FTA came into force in 2011, however, the balance of trade between the EU and Korea generally has shifted markedly in favour of the former. Exports to the Euro area fell from \$41.4bn in 2011 to \$31.8bn in 2015, while imports increased over the same period from \$38.9bn to \$45.7bn.

This shift, and more especially the size and speed of it, took many observers by surprise. Within Europe several lobby groups, notably those representing the automotive industry, had feared the FTA would lead to an influx of Korean imports, while Korean politicians were taken aback by the apparent rapid change in circumstances. Much of the change was due to factors unrelated to the FTA, notably a shift in the terms of trade that made North Sea oil cheaper to import than Middle East oil for example, and prolonged slow growth in the Eurozone following the 2008 financial crisis. But for the FTA, the change may have been even more dramatic. Nevertheless, it has inevitably generated political reactions within Korea and calls for the FTA to be re-negotiated. As a bloc, the EU is a major trading partner for Korea whereas bilateral trade with the UK accounts for only 2–3% of its total trade, so the first consideration is whether Korea will be willing to agree discussing a new bilateral FTA with the UK, even on a 'cut and paste' basis, without first seeking to re-open the EU agreement and whether in turn the EU would be willing to consider this.

On the other hand, there are good reasons for both sides to prioritize a new bilateral agreement. Korea's principal exports to the UK are automobiles and petrochemical products. Very soon after the referendum in June 2016, the *JoongAng Daily* newspaper reported that the business associations for these industries were expected to petition the Korean government to negotiate a new bilateral FTA with the UK, so as to avoid damage to their sales. Just four days later, however, and reflecting wider confusion about the impact of 'Brexit' in the aftermath of the referendum, the same newspaper reported Korean car manufacturers as expecting a competitive boost from 'Brexit,' for while Japanese manufacturers had concentrated their European investment in the UK, their Korean counterparts had opted for Eastern European locations. They were therefore anticipating gaining an advantage within the EU over their Japanese rivals, expecting the latter to be subject to tariffs once the UK left the Single Market.[16]

The two positions are not necessarily contradictory. Presumably, from Korean motor manufacturers' viewpoint, the best possible eventual outcome would be the complete withdrawal of the UK from the Single Market and Customs Union, with no immediate comparable arrangements put in place, accompanied by the rapid agreement of a bilateral FTA between the UK and Korea, so that they would benefit from both access to the Single Market and the UK market, while their UK-based rivals would face tariff walls in the former. If so, there is more than an element of wishful thinking in this. It is highly unlikely that the UK would be able to agree any new FTAs until the future of its trading relationship with the EU had been agreed. In any case, Prime Minister Theresa May moved quickly to assure Japanese manufacturers with UK plants that they would continue to be able to trade with the EU on the same basis as at present, although whether she can deliver this commitment remains to be seen.[17]

Considering the respective strengths and industrial competitiveness of the two countries, the most contentious areas in negotiating a new agreement are likely to be: the services sector generally but especially the provision of professional (legal, accountancy and the like) and financial services, pharmaceuticals, chemicals, automobiles and electronics. For Korea, while car makers may be upbeat about the consequences of 'Brexit,' electronics companies seem much less positive, with at least one major company in the sector reported to be considering moving its European headquarters out of the UK.[18]

Pharmaceuticals are not among the top exports to Korea from the UK. But it is a sector which has often featured on the EU's market access database as facing barriers to exports to Korea and one where only limited removal of barriers was agreed under the FTA with the EU.[19] It is also a sector in which the UK has successful global companies which might be expected to press for improved access under a new bilateral agreement. But for the UK overall, trade in services is of greater importance to the economy than that in manufactured goods. The EU-Korea FTA went considerably further in addressing trade in services than previous FTAs, including improving access to the Korean market, especially for financial and legal services, although education and audio-visual services, also likely to be of interest to UK companies, were excluded from the deal. UK service providers have been quick to take advantage of the improved access. For example, EU law companies are now permitted to open offices in Korea and to provide legal advisory services or to establish joint ventures with Korean counterparts. By the end of 2016, five European law firms had taken advantage of this agreement and all five are British.[20]

Korea's FTA with the EU does not address foreign direct investment in any detail but this has grown considerably between Korea and the UK in recent years and in both directions, so a new bilateral agreement would also be an opportunity to cover issues relating to this, including investor protection and dispute settlement procedures.

There is therefore likely to be pressure on both the British and Korean governments from their respective business interests to ensure that current bilateral trading provisions can continue unchanged, if not enhanced, through a new bilateral agreement. Politicians on both sides seem to recognize this. Shortly after the referendum outcome, the then Korean Foreign Minister Yun Byung-se was reported as saying Korea would be interested in negotiating an FTA with the UK after it left the EU. An accompanying comment suggested Korea badly needed to secure market access for its products so as to revive its economic growth dynamics which had suffered from a slowdown in the Chinese economy.[21] British officials also appear to have seen the attractions of an early trade agreement with Korea post-'Brexit' and the two countries have now established a joint task force to examine trade barriers and ways of reducing them.[22]

The key to success is likely to be the level of ambition acceptable to the two sides in any new agreement. As noted, Liam Fox has already admitted that the UK will not have the capacity to negotiate bespoke new trade agreements, saying that instead Britain wants to adopt existing EU agreements in their entirety until it can update or renegotiate them bilaterally.[23] This certainly seems a logical approach for the UK to take with Korea, given the benefits the country has gained to date from the FTA with the EU. It would be politically attractive domestically, enabling the British government to show that it was able to keep existing markets for its businesses open while concentrating efforts on negotiating new bilateral agreements outside the EU.

Even if both the EU and Korea agree to this approach, however, the complexities of contemporary trade agreements mean that the UK could still end up worse off than at present. This is because of the application of the rules of origin applied in trade agreements to ensure non-parties cannot take unfair advantage of them. The degree of local content permitted and the consequent tariff levels applied vary from product to product.[24] In the case of the EU-Korea FTA, unless the UK remains in the EU Customs Union, or reaches a separate agreement with the EU, as matters stand, cars made in the UK will not have sufficient content to qualify as being made in the EU and will therefore be subject to higher tariffs on export to Korea than, say, cars made in Germany. To avoid this happening, either the UK would have to remain in the Single Market, or at least Customs Union, or the relevant provisions of the agreement would have to be re-negotiated.

Whether Korea would agree to this given the importance of its own automotive industry is far from certain; if it did, it would almost certainly demand concessions from the UK in return. It is by no means an insuperable obstacle but unless the EU agrees a blanket extension of existing agreements, which seems a remote possibility at best, resolving it will require a new bilateral agreement to be negotiated rather than simply rolling over the existing one in a bilateral form. It is also far from obvious that Korea would be content simply to extend the current agreement with the EU on a bilateral basis with the UK. It was very much the junior partner in the negotiations that preceded that agreement and both sides were also negotiating with one eye on concurrent negotiations between Korea and the USA. The EU was determined to secure at least as good a deal from Korea as the USA achieved, while Korea was hoping that the USA would show more flexibility so as not to put its exporters at a disadvantage in Korea against European competitors. And as noted, the agreement has turned out to be controversial in Korea, so any proposals to extend it are likely to be subject to close scrutiny.

In the case of any negotiations with the UK, Korea is in a much stronger position. First, the two countries are much more evenly matched in trade terms. Although Korea's economy is somewhat smaller than the UK's, its total trade (exports plus imports) in 2015 was over 90% that of the UK—$978bn to $1073bn.[25] It will therefore not feel under the same pressure as it did with the USA and EU to conclude a deal on terms with which it may not feel wholly comfortable. Indeed, it may well see negotiations as an opportunity to redress issues which it considers disadvantageous. Secondly, as we have noted, the UK accounts for at most 3% of Korea's bilateral trade; so while an important market, it is hardly critical for Korea, and thirdly, the new importance of access to the Korean market for UK service sector industries gives Korea important leverage in negotiations. It can be reasonably assumed that banks, law firms and others will be pressing the UK government hard to ensure this access is not reduced. They may even hope to go further, but more concessions from Korea are unlikely as under the terms of its FTAs with both the EU and US, any further market opening measures in services offered to third countries would have to be extended to EU and US companies too. So, Korea will have more leverage with the UK than when negotiating with either the EU or USA (not to mention considerably more experienced trade negotiators) and will be under less pressure to reach agreement than the UK may be, especially if domestic pressure groups do not feel it gives Korea sufficient benefit.

Conclusion

Since the outcome of the 'Brexit' referendum, British government ministers have repeatedly spoken of a future in which the UK remains a nation committed to trading freely with the rest of the world. It is still too early to know how the outcome of the UK's negotiations with the EU-27 will affect this vision in practice, much less the outcome of subsequent ones with its current FTA partners and other WTO members. What is clear is that if any politicians in the UK who argued for 'Brexit' thought negotiating new trade agreements would be simple and straightforward, they should now realize that this is not the case. The complexities are considerable and interim agreements appear unavoidable, not simply pending the final outcome of negotiations between the UK and EU but also to minimize disruption to and uncertainty in international trade flows while subsequent replacement agreements are negotiated.

Both Korea and the UK have given positive signals about maintaining the free trade relationship they have been deepening over the past five years. The prospects for a future bilateral FTA between them also seem more promising than between the UK and other East Asian countries: their economies are more evenly matched and in many sectors their bilateral trade is complementary. That Korea already has an FTA with both the EU and EFTA should make it easier to negotiate a new and separate bilateral FTA with the UK, especially if the latter was to consider joining EFTA. This would offer an alternative avenue while also reducing substantially the burden of negotiations.

But the global nature of international trade, supply chains especially, and the often complex nature of trade agreements mean that it would still not be straightforward. In these circumstances, the UK's apparent objective of maintaining the status quo through the current EU FTA is sensible, even if this risks some adverse consequences due to the rules of origin treatment. It is unlikely to be able to negotiate a more favourable agreement with Korea and will want to concentrate its limited negotiating capacity on new agreements with major partners outside existing FTAs. But this approach pre-supposes firstly the agreement of the EU-27 and secondly that of Korea, both of which are subject to further negotiations. What does seem clear is that the UK is most unlikely to be able to negotiate a better bilateral deal with Korea than the one to which it already has access through its membership of the EU.

Notes

1. Y. Kim in James Harrison, ed.: *The EU and South Korea, The Legal framework for Strengthening Trade, Economic and Political Relations,* Edinburgh 2013, p. 50.

2. Michael Reilly, Chap. 3 above, note 15.
3. HM Government: *Future Customs Arrangements, A future partnership paper*, London, 15 August 2017.
4. Emily Lydgate, Jim Rollo and Rorden Wilkinson: *The UK trade landscape after Brexit,* UK Trade Policy Observatory Briefing paper, September 2016.
5. HM Revenue and Customs: Overseas Trade Statistics.
6. HM Government: *Future Customs Arrangements,* op.cit; *Liam Fox: Britain does not have capacity to strike trade deals now,* Politico, 4 September 2017, http://www.politico.eu/article/brexit-trade-negotiations-liam-fox-britain-does-not-have-capacity-to-strike-deals-now/, retrieved 12 September 2017.
7. *Liam Fox: Britain does not have capacity to strike trade deals now,* Politico, 4 September 2017, http://www.politico.eu/article/brexit-trade-negotiations-liam-fox-britain-does-not-have-capacity-to-strike-deals-now/, retrieved 12 September 2017.
8. Geoff Raby: *The fantasy of Commonwealth bonds hinders trade progress,* Financial Times, 9 March 2017, https://www.ft.com/content/f33aa220-04bd-11e7-aa5b-6bb07f5c8e12?segmentId=7d033110-c776-45bf-e9f2-7c3a03d2dd26, retrieved 6 October 2017.
9. HM Government: *Future Customs Arrangements,* op.cit.
10. *Keir Starmer eyes indefinite stay in EU customs union,* Financial Times, 7 September 2017, https://www.ft.com/content/17c896a4-92fa-11e7-a9e6-11d2f0ebb7f0?emailId=59b0ec99768d110004451710&segmentId=2f40f9e8-c8d5-af4c-ecdd-78ad0b93926b, retrieved 6 October 2017.
11. Ibid.
12. Lydgate, Rollo and Wilkinson, *op.cit.*
13. HM Government: *Future Customs Arrangements,* op.cit.
14. Lydgate, Rollo and Wilkinson, *op.cit.*
15. International Monetary Fund: *Direction of Trade Statistics.*
16. *'Brexit' effects here may vary by industry,* Korea JoongAng Daily, 28 June 2016.
17. *May assures Nissan of shield against Brexit tariffs,* Financial Times 15 October 2016—see Chap. 3, note 5.
18. *'Brexit' effects here may vary by industry,* Korea JoongAng Daily, 28 June 2016.
19. Michael Reilly: *Towards an EU-Taiwan Investment Agreement, Prospects and Pitfalls,* 2018.
20. Simon Hix and Hae-Won Jun: *Can 'Global Britain' forge a better trade deal with South Korea? This is why it's unlikely,* http://blogs.lse.ac.uk/brexit/2017/02/07/can-global-britain-forge-a-better-trade-deal-with-south-korea-this-is-why-its-unlikely/, retrieved 11 September 2017.

21. *South Korea's Brexit example,* Wall St Journal 26 June 2016.
22. *Most South Korean firms want to stay in London after Brexit, says senior official,* Daily Telegraph 26 April 2017, http://www.telegraph.co.uk/business/2017/04/26/south-korean-firms-want-stay-london-brexit-says-senior-official/, retrieved 12 September 2017.
23. Ibid.
24. Hix and Jun: *op.cit.*
25. International Monetary Fund: *Direction of Trade Statistics.*

CHAPTER 8

The Lessons from Brexit and Its Impact on Singapore and ASEAN

Lay Hwee Yeo

Introduction

The day after 51.9% of the participating British electorate voted to leave the European Union (EU), the Singapore Deputy Prime Minister, Tharman Shanmugaratnam, was quoted saying that while the economic uncertainties in the UK and EU would hurt the rest of the world including Asia, the more profound questions revolved around politics.[1] He added that it would take some time to draw the full lessons of the Brexit vote, but remarked that there was a new brew in politics around the world, especially in the most mature democracies like the USA, UK and in Europe. The Brexit vote could presage a broader nationalist, anti-establishment and anti-immigration backlash in many of the world's democracies.

The Prime Minister of Singapore, Lee Hsien Loong was similarly quoted saying that "we all live in a globalized, interdependent world, but at the same time, there is a yearning to turn inward, and disengage and take back control. Yet in reality, for many countries, disengaging and turning inwards will only lead to less security, less prosperity and a dimmer future".[2]

L. H. Yeo (✉)
European Union Centre, Singapore, Singapore

Singapore Institute of International Affairs, Singapore, Singapore
e-mail: eucylh@nus.edu.sg

D. W. F. Huang, M. Reilly (eds.), *The Implications of Brexit for East Asia*, https://doi.org/10.1007/978-981-13-0185-8_8

The comments from the two top leaders of Singapore reflected the concerns on how they think Brexit will impact Singapore. It is not only the direct impact on the financial and stock markets, and the economic uncertainties that worry them. It is the longer-term implications of what Brexit portends for the global liberal economic order and the unpredictability in the political dynamics both within the UK and in Europe. If the UK is unable to hold itself together as the United Kingdom (Scotland has threatened to have another independence vote, and the thorny issue for Northern Ireland of its border with the Republic is a major aspect of the Brexit negotiations) and if nationalism and populism gather pace among the EU's member states, there will be a permanent weakening of their economies. These, coupled with other factors such as a sharper slowdown in China and the anti-free trade sentiments in the USA, would have a major impact on the Singapore economy. For a city state which depends on openness, and a rule-based economic and political order, the forces further unleashed by the Brexit vote would have profound impact. Whether the traditional good ties that Singapore enjoyed with the UK because of the colonial past could be harnessed to compensate for the potential economic loss is far from certain. What is clear is that Singapore will be watching and following the developments in Europe and the Brexit negotiations closely in order to make the necessary adjustments.

As for the Association of Southeast Asian Nations (ASEAN), the EU has been a dialogue partner for almost 40 years, and had in 2015 announced its desire to upgrade and enhance its partnership with ASEAN to one with a "strategic purpose".

While it has been said time and before that the European integration model cannot be copied by ASEAN due to the different historical and regional context, the EU nevertheless has been a firm supporter in helping ASEAN build capacity towards achieving an ASEAN Community. Brexit has dealt a severe body blow to the EU's image as a successful, supranational regional entity that delivers on peace and prosperity to its member states. Additionally, the forces of regressive nationalism unleashed by Brexit (and now with the election of Donald Trump as the US president) would spread, making it harder also for ASEAN member states to reconcile their national and collective ASEAN interests.

The reasons that led to the Brexit vote have been analysed at length elsewhere. This chapter will therefore discuss briefly some of the broader implications and lessons that can be drawn, and then zoom in to discuss the implications of Brexit for Singapore and ASEAN.

The Road to Brexit

Much has been written about the reasons behind Brexit. It was a multitude of factors, from a lacklustre "Stay" campaign to a post-truth "Leave" campaign; from the "disgust" with Brussels and desire to "take back control" to real concerns over immigration, housing, health care, jobs and wages.

Margaret Thatcher's tussles with Europe and her battle against what she saw as the excessive powers of Brussels were a reflection of the Euroscepticism within the British political class. Together with the media they often "played an anti-EU game" with stories of the "horrors" of the EU bureaucracy "plastered across the front pages of tabloid newspapers". As pointed out by Alan Riley and Francis Ghiles, "the drip drip effect of 40 years of negative media coverage was difficult to reverse in a four month referendum campaign".[3]

The influx of migrants, particularly from the other EU member states, was also seen as a factor contributing to the stagnation of wages and rising inequality, and increased fears over competition in the job markets coupled with socio-cultural dislocations contributed to the backlash against the EU—itself a symbol of a post-national, globalized world.

The UK also has itself to blame when it comes to the immigration from other EU member states. The decision by the Blair government in 2003 to permit full freedom of movement of people to all EU member states, including the ten accession states from Central and Eastern Europe (CEE) (instead of exercising their Treaty rights to restrict free movement for up to seven years) led to a genuine influx of people moving to the UK from the CEE states. This influx was further fuelled by the Eurozone crisis. As noted by Migration Observatory, "inflows of EU nationals migrating to the UK stood at 268,000 in 2014, up from 201,000 in 2013". And in 2015, this stood at 333,000. This was in contrast to inflows from the EU to the UK for the 1991–2003 period averaging only around 61,000 a year.[4]

Immigration thus became a highly politicized issue associated with issues of job insecurity, wage stagnation, cultural dislocation and most importantly, the sense of the UK's loss of control over its own sovereignty, hence the leave slogan of "Take back control" which proved very effective.

Thus, there were a myriad of different reasons for people voting to leave—from the more general argument that decisions about the UK should be taken in the UK to very specific concerns over the question of immigration; and from those who think that the UK would actually benefit more from being outside the EU to those who are more concerned about enlargement and the future of the EU. Within Theresa May's Cabinet, it appeared that there were differences over what "type" of Brexit, hard or soft, and the terms of the relationship that the UK should have with the EU. There were even differences between the three leading Brexit figures, David Davis, Secretary of State (Minister) responsible for Brexit negotiations; Liam Fox, Secretary for International Trade and Boris Johnson, the Foreign Secretary. This led to concerns that the EU-UK negotiations would be chaotic and acrimonious, creating more uncertainties and damage to the EU and UK.

Lessons from Brexit

For Politics

Immediately after the Brexit vote, both the Prime Minister and Deputy Prime Minister of Singapore, when asked about the impact of Brexit did not focus so much on the economic impact but expressed more concern about the "profound questions revolving around politics". One of the reasons for this focus on politics is perhaps because of Singapore's own development trajectory. In some way, Singapore has been facing its fair share of discontent as a result of a fairly open immigration system and widening inequalities. From 2000 to 2010, the population of Singapore increased by more than a million, from 4.027 million to 5.076 million as a result of immigration. This, together with the stagnation of wages of the lowest 30% of Singaporeans and the rising inequalities (Singapore's Gini coefficient in 2012 was at 0.432—even after government transfers, one of the highest in the developed world), had led to a backlash, losing the government crucial support in the 2011 general election. The government has since taken steps to address the issue of immigration and stagnating wages. Also an issue was the perceived disconnect between the elites and policy makers and the ordinary Singaporeans.

The Brexit vote reinforced the lessons about the need to be mindful of the economic dislocations and the political disconnect between elites and the people. Unfortunately, we live in a world where economics is global, but politics remain local. As the Prime Minister of Singapore lamented "we all live in a globalized, interdependent world, but at the same time there is a yearning to turn inward".[5] However, the reality is that for many countries, disengaging and turning inwards will only lead to less security, less prosperity and a dimmer future. The challenge for political leaders is how to adequately prepare citizens for a globalized world rather than simply trying to protect them from the forces of globalization. There is a need for an honest conversation between leaders and voters, and together forge the fine balance between preparing and protecting the citizens in an ambiguous and fast changing world.

A related lesson to be drawn from this is the importance of getting the politics and the policies right, or in Euro jargon, combining democracy and technocracy. There are some interesting parallels to be drawn between Singapore and the EU in this respect. Singapore has long been seen as an administrative state, depoliticized and with the government seen as comprising technocratic elites who focused on the rational and cost-benefit analysis in setting the policy direction. The leaders tried to "depoliticize" debates and avoid overt political deliberations. Similarly, the EU has been seen as suffering from democratic deficit with decisions taken by a bunch of technocrats in Brussels that are not accountable to anyone. The desire by the Brexiteers to "take back control" in some way reflects this aversion to an elitist, technocratic character of the EU. The dismissal of "expert views" in the Brexit debate further illustrates the importance of using the emotional connection to rally people rather than simply focusing on the quantifiable cost and benefit arguments.

The Brexit vote also brought to the fore the debates on representative and direct democracy. Most modern democracies are formed of a combination of direct and representative processes. However, the assumption that more direct democracy means better accountability and engagement is a fallacy. In particular, the use of a referendum to make key political decisions has several pitfalls. As Chris Patten, the former EU Commissioner for External Relations commented, "a referendum reduces complexity to absurd simplicity".[6] It should therefore not be used to decide complex issues. Referendums can also lead to incoherent policies especially when voters are looking at issues in isolation, for example in voting for higher spending in one referendum and then voting for big tax cuts in another.

The demand for the use of referendums in recent years is in part a reflection of the wider malaise of the alienation of voters and the erosion of trust and support for mainstream parties. Indeed some referendums are called by mainstream politicians to fend off pressure from populists as was the case for the British in/out referendum.

The lesson to be learnt is that while referendums can be a celebration of the democratic process, politics let loose can be the bane of social integration, with the potential to harm social compacts built up over decades. Kenneth Rogoff in his article on "Britain's democratic failure" remarked that the Brexit referendum was actually a failure of democracy.[7] In commenting on the low benchmark that was set for the exit (simple majority and with no provisions on percentage of turnout), Rogoff called it a Russian roulette and not democracy. He added that the idea that somehow any decision reached by a majority is necessarily democratic is a perversion of the term. Modern democracies have evolved systems of checks and balances to protect the interests of minorities and to avoid making uninformed decisions with catastrophic consequences.

The idea that referendums foster engagement is also questionable. It has been noted that as they have proliferated, the median turnout for them is also beginning to fall.

For Regionalism

The Brexiters' slogan "Take back control" reflects the resurgence of nationalism in response to what is perceived as creeping supranationalism and European integration gone too far. Increased EU supranationality was perceived by many as an erosion of British sovereignty. However, what is even more worrying is the rise of a far more xenophobic and regressive nationalism that rejects immigrants and harks back to a nostalgic era of close knit, homogeneous community.

For the ASEAN which has often been compared to the EU, and with the latter seen as a model for emulation, Brexit offers a tale of caution and serves up a few lessons with regard to regionalism and regional community building.

First, Brexit reminds us of the importance of not losing sight of the instrumental nature of regional integration. Regional integration in many instances should not be an end in itself. Instead it is primarily pursued as a means or instrument to achieve something that cannot be achieved by nation-states acting alone, which have become plentiful (from environmental pollution, climate change to pandemics and international terrorism), as the world becomes far more interconnected and globalized. What regional institutions should look like, what norms and procedures should underpin them, and what kind of decision-making structures they should have, will depend on the objectives that the nation-states have agreed on or the type of problems that they wish to solve.

The Treaty of the European Union (also commonly referred to as the Maastricht Treaty) that was signed in 1992, and in its very change of name from European Community to European Union (EU), reflected the heightened aspiration in moving towards ever closer union among the peoples of Europe. Unfortunately, it was rejected by the Danes in a referendum. It was only after the Union agreed to some opt-outs by the Danes that the Treaty was ratified in a second referendum. This was perhaps the first sign that there are people within the EU who felt that integration has gone too far. The French and Dutch rejection of the draft Constitution in 2005 provided further hints that perhaps integration has gone too far for people to embrace wholeheartedly.

The inability of the EU to address effectively the various challenges and crises that erupted from 2010 sows doubts in the minds of many with regard to the "usefulness" of the EU. Several Eurobarometer surveys show that trust in EU institutions has plummeted. Interestingly trust in national institutions also dropped, and the only ones that saw an uptick were local institutions.

This brings me to another lesson that should be learnt—the principle of subsidiarity. The EU in its enthusiasm towards greater integration and ever closer union had overlooked its two fundamental principles—the principle of subsidiarity and the principle of proportionality.

The principle of subsidiarity in the Lisbon Treaty stipulates that "in areas which do not fall within its exclusive competence, the Union shall act only if and in so far as the objectives of the proposed action cannot be sufficiently achieved in the Member States, either at central level or at regional or local level, but can rather, by reason of the scale or effects of the proposed action, be better achieved at Union level". In other words, what it says is that action should be taken at the EU level only when and where there are clear advantages to doing so. Subsidiarity as an organizing principle basically refers to the idea that actions or decisions ought to be taken at the level closest to the people. Additionally, the principle of proportionality says that the EU may only do "what is necessary to achieve the objectives of the Treaties" and no more.

Together these two principles are supposed to guard against the Union overstretching itself and overstepping its authority and to ensure that powers are exercised as close to the citizen as possible.

ASEAN is looking at deepening its cooperation to create an ASEAN Community. However, because of a different historical context, ASEAN has clung to its norms on sovereign equality and the principle of non-interference. Even in its pursuit of deeper economic integration in order to attract more investment into the region and to compete with bigger economies such as China and India, ASEAN has not developed any formal institutions with supranational authority. ASEAN remains inter-governmental in character and decision-making is by consensus and often based on unanimity. In the aftermath of Brexit, ASEAN could distil useful lessons to take a pragmatic, step-by-step approach to regional integration, and it is able to communicate the benefits of integration to its citizens. Ultimately, the key lesson is to keep focus on a few objectives, be aware of the limitations and constraints and design the right framework or build the appropriate institutions that can deliver concrete results. Integration to create a new "community with its own identity" should only be attempted when there is a very high level of trust and possibly only amongst a smaller group of members.[8]

The Impact of Brexit on Singapore/ASEAN

In evaluating the impact of Brexit on Singapore and ASEAN, the immediate short-term fallout may be quite different from the longer-term impact and implications. There is still a lot of uncertainty, not least due to the weakness of the British government's domestic position. Much will depend on how protracted and acrimonious the UK-EU negotiations will be and the final deal coming out of the negotiations.

Before going into the impact, there is a need to examine the state of play of Singapore's relations with the EU.

Singapore is a former colony of the British empire. Historical ties between Singapore and the UK are therefore strong. In view of the relatively peaceful process by which Singapore achieved its independence from the British, there was no strong anti-colonial fervour, and the British maintained a strong presence in Singapore first with naval bases until 1971, and also a strong commercial presence through British companies.

Singapore's engagement with the European Community (the predecessor of the EU) began in 1972 as a founding member of ASEAN, which was concerned about the UK's entry into the Common Market, and how that might affect their access to the UK market. The UK was then the key trading partner in Europe of several of the ASEAN member states. Formal relations between ASEAN and the European Community were established in 1977, and broadly, Singapore's relations with the EU have developed in the context of inter-regional dialogue and cooperation between the EU and ASEAN.

In 1977, the EU officially became one of the dialogue partners of ASEAN. This dialogue partnership was given a boost and a greater political significance with the signing of the ASEAN-EC Cooperation Agreement in 1980 at the Second ASEAN-EC Ministerial Meeting held in Kuala Lumpur. The Cooperation Agreement provided the legal and institutional framework to further develop the inter-regional ties. The main emphasis of the agreement was on economic cooperation and development, extending the Most Favoured Nation (MFN) treatment to the contracting parties.

However, despite these positive developments in general, until the 1980s, ASEAN remained at the bottom of the EC's hierarchy of relations. In the area of development cooperation in particular, more attention was on the African, Caribbean and Pacific (ACP) countries which also received more favourable trade benefits under the Lomé Convention. The ASEAN-EC relationship was also seen very much as a donor-recipient relationship, an unequal relationship in which the ASEAN countries were inevitably in a weaker bargaining position.

In contrast to this unequal economic relationship, political cooperation between ASEAN and the EC in the 1980s was boosted by their common concerns over the expansion of Soviet influence. Specifically, Vietnam's invasion of Cambodia (then known as Kampuchea) in December 1978, and the Soviet Union's invasion of Afghanistan in 1979 provided the impetus for the two regions to work to coordinate their positions and support each other on these two issues in international fora such as the United Nations. These two issues remained on the agenda for political discussions in successive ASEAN-EC Ministerial Meetings (AEMM) until their resolution with the pullout of the Soviet forces from Afghanistan in 1989 and the Paris Peace Accords on Cambodia in 1991.

The end of the Cold War unfortunately ushered in a much more "contentious" phase of relationship as differences over democracy and human rights bubbled to the surface. Without the competition to keep ASEAN in the capitalist Western camp vis-à-vis the communist Soviet bloc, the EU, which witnessed the democratic transition of Central and Eastern European countries, was euphoric about the march of history towards democracy. The emphasis on promoting democracy and a focus on human rights began to dominate the discourse. ASEAN, recognized for the diplomatic role that it played in bringing about the end of the Kampuchean crisis, was also brimming with confidence, and was not about to be pushed by the Europeans into quietly accepting the latter's agenda.

In 1994, following the publication of the EU's New Asia Strategy, a more pragmatic turn to capitalize on the EU-ASEAN partnership for broader economic gains in Asia was reflected in the 11th ASEAN-EU Ministerial Meeting in Karlsruhe in September. The issue over unrest and human rights abuses in East Timor was sidestepped and an EU-ASEAN Eminent Persons Group (EPG) was commissioned to develop a comprehensive EU-ASEAN partnership towards the year 2000 and beyond.

Unfortunately, the recommendations in both the 1996 EPG Report on "A Strategy for a New Partnership" and the Commission's own Communication on "Creating a New Dynamic in EU-ASEAN Relations" did not have a chance to be translated into concrete measures. A series of events and a number of factors, notably the Asian financial crisis, and the enlargement of ASEAN to include Cambodia, Laos and Myanmar, changed the dynamics and further impacted the dialogue between EU and ASEAN. In particular, Myanmar's entry into ASEAN in 1997 brought new tensions and strains in EU-ASEAN relations. Myanmar, with what was seen as an appalling human rights record by the Europeans, became a millstone around ASEAN's neck.

The events of 9/11 and developments in international terrorism, the dramatic rise of China and the "re-invention" of ASEAN in the aftermath of the Asian financial crisis led the EU to adopt a more pragmatic and differentiated approach towards ASEAN and its member states. The Commission's policy paper in 2003 entitled "A New Partnership with Southeast Asia" acknowledged that the EU-ASEAN partnership should not be held hostage by Myanmar as there were strong reasons for the EU to enhance its engagement with ASEAN, including first and foremost the fight against international terrorism, as well as underlying economic imperatives. These must also be seen in the context of ASEAN then in the process of rethinking its regional cooperation model and seeking greater institutionalization as it contemplated building an ASEAN Community by 2015.

From 2003, the EU scaled up efforts to engage ASEAN, in particular in the area of providing support for capacity building towards integration through programmes such as the ASEAN-EU Programme for Regional Integration Support (APRIS) from 2004 to 2010 and the current ASEAN

Regional Integration Support from the EU (ARISE) from 2011 to 2017. The EU also stepped up cooperation in counter-terrorism with several ASEAN member states such as Indonesia and Philippines.

However, despite such efforts, the EU-ASEAN dialogue continued to be plagued by disagreement on how to engage Myanmar, with ASEAN preferring constructive engagement over the EU's imposition of sanctions. It was not until Myanmar's elections in 2011 that set in motion a credible reform process and a number of other factors that the EU truly re-evaluated its relations with ASEAN. What are some of these factors?

First and foremost, the US pivot (or rebalancing) to Asia in 2011 changed the geopolitical undercurrents in the Asia-Pacific region. For the first time, the EU paid serious attention to the political and security dialogue platforms in the region, several of them being "driven" by ASEAN. Second, ASEAN's efforts to build an ASEAN Economic Community (AEC) with a market of over 600 million consumers were making some progress. Despite the low ambitions of the AEC with the key objectives of creating a single production base, and transforming ASEAN into an attractive investment destination, Southeast Asia remains an attractive region with a growing middle class, and good growth potential. The EU's need to search for new growth areas to pluck itself out of economic doldrums makes ASEAN an increasingly attractive economic partner. Taken as a single entity, ASEAN is the EU's third largest trading partner outside of Europe, after USA and China. ASEAN is also the fifth most important location for the EU's outward foreign direct investment (FDI).

In May 2015, the EU issued a Joint Communication on its relations with ASEAN entitled "The EU and ASEAN: A Partnership with a Strategic Purpose". In this Communication, the EU acknowledged that "it has a strategic interest in strengthening its relations with ASEAN" because ASEAN "combines high rates of economic growth as well as economic dynamism" and that it is also "at the heart of the efforts to build a more robust regional security order in the wider Asia Pacific". It added that the EU has a huge stake in the success of ASEAN, and that a united and self-confident ASEAN is in the direct interest of not only the citizens of the region, but also of the EU.[9]

Singapore's relations with the EU thus followed broadly this trajectory. It was from 2003 (after the publication of the Communication's strategy on "A New Partnership with Southeast Asia") that the EU began taking a more pragmatic and differentiated approach towards ASEAN and its constituent states. Relations between Singapore and the EU gained more traction when the EU decided to set up its delegation office in Singapore in 2003. With the suspension of the negotiations for a region-to-region EU-ASEAN Free Trade Agreement (FTA) in 2009, the EU decided on a bilateral approach and picked Singapore as the first Southeast Asian country for the FTA negotiations. The EU-Singapore Free Trade Agreement (EUSFTA), the first for EU in Southeast Asia, was initialled in 2013.

Singapore's status as a regional hub and its dynamic economy has attracted a lot of European investments and many European companies used Singapore as a gateway to Southeast Asia or even the broader Asia-Pacific. Singapore is host to more than 10,000 European companies and the EU is the most significant source of FDI in Singapore accounting for over 25% of total FDI stock in Singapore. This makes Singapore the tenth most important destination for EU investments globally. Conversely, Singapore is the ninth largest investor in the EU globally. It is the largest investor in the EU from ASEAN, and third largest in the whole of Asia, just behind Japan and Hong Kong.

In the area of trade, the figures are also significant. Total EU-Singapore trade in goods reached €48.6 billion in 2015 and trade in services amounted to €36.1 billion. The EU enjoys a trade surplus with Singapore.

Beyond the solid trade and investment ties, Singapore's foreign policy activism in various regional and multilateral forums, its strategic position in the Asia-Pacific and global outlook made Singapore an attractive partner for the EU. The EU views the city state as central to its engagement in Southeast Asia and ASEAN, and has sought to strengthen ties also in the diplomatic and political arena. The Partnership and Cooperation Agreement between the EU and Singapore broke new ground on cooperation in many diverse fields, from education, science and technology to transport and energy and into expanding people-to-people links.

From the above, it is clear that the EU is an important partner, particularly in trade and investments, for Singapore and ASEAN. Singapore thus looked with great concern on the impact of Brexit on the EU.

So far, as pointed out in discussing the broader impact of Brexit, it is not only the economic implications but the broader trends of anti-globalization taking root in the developed world. Trade is Singapore's lifeline, and Singapore's prosperity depends on an open, global economy. As the economic environment becomes more difficult with a Europe marred in slow growth and turning inwards, Singapore would be facing serious headwinds. The backlash against trade has already reared its head resulting in greater scrutiny of trade deals. The protests against the

Transatlantic Trade and Investment Partnership (TTIP), the near torpedo of the EU-Canada Comprehensive Economic and Trade Agreement (CETA) and the opinion of the Advocate General of the Court of Justice of the European Union that the EUSFTA is a mixed agreement are signs to come.

Beyond the economic concerns, there is also the broader strategic implication of the demise of a global liberal world order.

As a small open economy, Singapore's fate is very much tied to an open, rules-based order. The breakdown of a global order based on international law and institutions will make life tougher for small countries like Singapore. Its room for manoeuvre will narrow considerably. Much will depend on the shape of EU-UK relations, and also UK-US relations.

In this volatile and unpredictable world brought about by Brexit and Trump, it is in the interests of ASEAN to cohere and act as one. However, the kind of forces unleashed in retaliation against globalization and openness might also fuel rising nationalistic sentiments within ASEAN. Whether ASEAN could move on with its ongoing economic integration and become more united in facing a dangerous world cannot be taken for granted.

A silver lining with the Brexit vote and the election of Trump as US president is that under such existential threats, the EU has since focused its mind to prevent the breakup of the EU. The double shocks seem to have woken up the Europeans to the dangers of populism. The election of pro-EU Emmanuel Macron as the President of France in May 2017 gave Europe a cause for relief. Running on a clearly pro-EU platform, his victory seemed to put a brake to the rising tides of Euroscepticism. The sustained economic recovery and the slow but gradual decrease in unemployment rates also brought a whiff of hope.

Trump's first visit to the EU and North Atlantic Treaty Organisation (NATO) also did not give much confidence to the Europeans about the future of the transatlantic partnership. Angela Merkel's fiery speech in a Bavaria beer tent a day after the G7 and NATO meetings with Trump was a wake-up call. Merkel called on Europeans "to take destiny in their own hands" adding that Brexit and the Trump presidency have put the western traditional alliance under threat.

If all these signal an EU that will become more engaged internationally, and determined to uphold the multilateral free trade order, it would be good for ASEAN-EU and Singapore-EU trade and investment relations. The EU in signalling its commitment to free trade is busy with free trade negotiations. A political agreement has been reached on an EU-Japan

FTA. During her visit to Southeast Asia in March 2017, the EU Trade Commissioner, Cecilia Malmström proclaimed that "trade is in the DNA of the EU" and said that the EU would look into reviving the bloc-to-bloc EU-ASEAN FTA. ASEAN has welcomed this new interest by the EU in pushing for stronger economic ties.

Summing up, while the mood in the EU has improved in 2017 and Brexit and Trump seem to have given the EU a new lease of life, which would hopefully also translate to better engagement with Asia (and thus also ASEAN and Singapore), there are still some worries on the horizon with regard to the Brexit negotiations.

An acrimonious and bad divorce between the EU and UK may dampen the mood and stall the economic recovery that has just been gaining strength. Increased business costs due to uncertainties and hedging, problems at the Irish border if no agreement is reached on free movement of goods, services and people, and other unintended consequences and unknowns could result in a 'lose-lose' scenario that leaves both the EU and UK exhausted and exasperated. Both the EU and UK are important trading partners for ASEAN and Singapore. None of them wish to see a messy divorce that would result in loss of business confidence, trade barriers and toxic competition between the EU and UK. But the signs from the early negotiations have not been encouraging.

Conclusion

The British vote to leave the EU in itself offers several lessons for political leaders and politicians in other parts of the world. The specific impact that Brexit would have on countries such as Singapore and ASEAN is far less predictable and will in part depend on how smooth or acrimonious the negotiations between the EU and UK will be, and how the relationship between the EU and UK will be once the negotiations are over.

As this was being written, the early signs were that the negotiations between the EU and UK looked set to be highly contentious and the scenario of a "disorderly" exit could not be ruled out. This would be a 'lose-lose' for both the UK and the EU, and how such a result would impact the European security order, which in turn would have ramifications for the EU's external relations, is still unclear. ASEAN and Singapore will thus have to follow closely the developments to deal with any disruptions or volatility.

Notes

1. Straits Times online news, "Markets Mauled, but it is not like 2008 crisis: Tharman", 25 June 2016 http://www.straitstimes.com/singapore/markets-mauled-but-its-not-like-2008-crisis-tharman (accessed 25 June 2016).
2. Channel News Asia online news, "Brexit vote a turning point, PM Lee", 24 June 2016 http://www.channelnewsasia.com/news/singapore/brexit-vote-a-turning/2901114.html (accessed 25 June 2016).
3. Alan Riley and Francis Ghiles, "Brexit: Causes and Consequences" CIDOB Brief 159, 10/2016 http://www.cidob.org/publicaciones/serie_de_publicacion/notes_internacionals/n1_159/brexit_causes_and_consequences (accessed 1 Nov 2016).
4. BBC Online News, "Net Migration to UK rises to 333,000 – second highest on record" 26 May 2016. http://www.bbc.com/news/uk-politics-eu-referendum-36382199 (accessed 14 Nov 2016); BBC Online News, "EU Referendum: Results in Maps and Charts" 24 June 2016 http://www.bbc.com/news/uk-politics-36616028 (accessed 14 Nov 2016).
5. Channel News Asia online news, "Brexit vote a turning point, PM Lee", 24 June 2016 http://www.channelnewsasia.com/news/singapore/brexit-vote-a-turning/2901114.html (accessed 25 June 2016).
6. Christopher Patten, "A British Tragedy in One Act" Project Syndicate, 24 June 2016 https://www.project-syndicate.org/commentary/brexit-political-suicide-by-chris-patten-2016-06?barrier=true (accessed 26 June 2016).
7. Kenneth Rogoff, "Britain's Democratic Failure" Project Syndicate, 24 June 2016 https://www.project-syndicate.org/commentary/brexit-democratic-failure-for-uk-by-kenneth-rogoff-2016-06 (accessed 26 June 2016).
8. Yeo Lay Hwee, "Why the EU matters to ASEAN" in ASEAN Focus, August 2016, published by ASEAN Studies Centre, ISEAS-Yusof Ishak Institute, Singapore.
9. Yeo Lay Hwee, "ASEAN-EU Dialogue: Moving Towards Strategic Relevance" in "50 Years of ASEAN and Singapore", edited by Tommy Koh, Chang Li Lin and Sharon Seah (World Scientific Publishing, Singapore: 2017).

CHAPTER 9

Brexit and Taiwan: An Opportunity for a New Agreement or Wishful Thinking?

Michael Reilly, Jyun-yi Lee, and Chih-mei Luo

Introduction

Of all the countries in East Asia, the one that might most welcome Brexit is Taiwan. As a small open economy, Taiwan depends on trade for its prosperity. Its diplomatic isolation has made its membership of the World Trade Organisation (WTO) disproportionately important in this respect as it is the only major international organization of which Taiwan is a full member. Its membership has enabled it to build strategic coalitions to advance its trading objectives while also asserting its sovereignty.[1] For Taiwan, therefore, the growth over the last 15 years of bilateral and regional trading agreements at the expense of multilateral progress has been a matter of major concern. It fears, with justification, being excluded from such agreements by Chinese pressure

M. Reilly (✉)
Taiwan Studies Program, University of Nottingham, Nottingham, UK

J.-y. Lee
Institute for National Defense and Security Research, Taipei, Taiwan

C.-m. Luo
Department of Public Administration and Policy, National Taipei University, New Taipei, Taiwan
e-mail: cmluo@mail.ntpu.edu.tw

D. W. F. Huang, M. Reilly (eds.), *The Implications of Brexit for East Asia*, https://doi.org/10.1007/978-981-13-0185-8_9

on third countries, to the detriment of both its own long-term prosperity and sovereign status. As part of its efforts to counter this risk, it has sought unsuccessfully for more than a decade to open negotiations on a free trade agreement (FTA) with the EU. The latter has expanded its engagement rapidly with the broader East Asian region during this period under its *Global Agenda,* which includes strategic dialogues, partnership and co-operation agreements and more. But Taiwan has been almost completely excluded from this growing engagement.

Despite the very limited engagement at the collective EU level, however, bilateral co-operation with some individual member states has been more fruitful for Taiwan, that with the UK especially. In 2002, the two signed agreements on cultural and educational co-operation and double taxation, followed in 2009 by the UK being the first western country to remove its visa requirement for short-term Taiwanese visitors, a policy rapidly followed by the rest of the EU. Since then, the UK has also signed bilateral agreements on air services, on working holidaymakers and on prisoner transfers, all signs in Taiwanese eyes of British acceptance of its de facto sovereignty. The UK has also been one of the very few member states to speak openly in support of an EU-Taiwan FTA.[2] This has perhaps encouraged Taiwan to see the UK as generally more sympathetic to its position than the rest of the EU.

For its part, the UK government has stated that it wants to use its departure from the EU to push for an open international trading environment. As Prime Minister Theresa May put it, the UK aims to be *the strongest and most forceful advocate for business, free markets and free trade anywhere in the world.* This stance is repeated in the government's formal position paper on future customs arrangements with the EU, in which it says it plans to pursue new trade agreements with 'old friends and new allies' by seeking 'ambitious new trade arrangements and comprehensive trade deals.'[3]

From Taiwan's perspective, therefore, it shares a like-mindedness with post-Brexit Britain as to the importance of free trade and this with a country which has already demonstrated its readiness to engage with Taiwan in many areas. It could therefore be excused for seeing a bilateral FTA with a post-Brexit UK as a realistic ambition and a major prize if achieved. In theory, this should be both straightforward to agree and attractive to both sides. Straightforward because most bilateral trade is already subject to only very modest tariffs if not completely tariff free; attractive to Taiwan because of the boost it would give to agreeing other FTAs by having one with a G7 country—it would no doubt hope for something of the impact the UK's removal of visas had on third countries—and attractive to the UK because the government would want to show quickly its ability to strike new bilateral trade deals in a post-Brexit world.

In practice, however, the obstacles to reaching such an agreement outweigh the potential mutual benefits, meaning it is unlikely to happen soon. In part, this is due to reasons of *realpolitik* and the inevitable reluctance on the part of the UK to offend China, especially as it makes its way in the post-Brexit world. But at least as big a stumbling block is likely to be the difficulty of reconciling the very different objectives Taiwan and the UK would have in negotiating such an agreement. It is not at all obvious that these can be overcome and Taiwan is likely to achieve greater success and more quickly by concentrating its efforts on concluding a bilateral investment agreement (BIA) with the EU.

Trade or Sovereignty? Taiwan's Pursuit of Free Trade Agreements

Taiwan is one of the most trade-dependent economies in the world, for its size almost certainly *the* most trade-dependent. Its 2014 trade/GDP ratio of 130.5 was surpassed only by city states such as Hong Kong and Singapore and trade has been the major contributor to its robust economic growth rates over the years.[4] So an open international trading system is of fundamental importance to the nation and with further liberalization of the multilateral system seemingly in baulk, it is no surprise that in recent years it has sought to pursue its own bilateral agreements instead. Since 2003 successive Taiwanese governments have signed eight bilateral FTAs, five with countries with whom it enjoys formal diplomatic relations and three 'economic co-operation' or 'economic partnership' agreements. But only two of these eight agreements were with major trading partners, one with Singapore and most notably the Economic Co-operation Framework Agreement (ECFA) signed with China in 2010.[5]

The ECFA is very much a special case and not just because China is Taiwan's largest trading partner. At first glance, it is heavily one-sided in Taiwan's favour, China offering far more concessions on tariffs or market access than it gained from Taiwan. The early economic benefits from the agreement were estimated to be approximately six to one in Taiwan's favour. Given widely held perceptions that China is adept at promoting or protecting its own interests in any agreements it negotiates, this has not surprisingly reinforced assumptions that China's primary motive in signing the ECFA was to increase Taiwanese dependence on its own economy in line with its long-term strategy of achieving sovereignty over the island.[6]

This perhaps understates the level of popular support that existed in Taiwan for the signing of the agreement: it was part of Ma Ying-jeou's manifesto for the 2008 presidential election campaign which he went on to win comfortably. Taiwanese companies were understandably worried that the ASEAN-China FTA which came into force in January 2010 would place them at a competitive disadvantage, the more so as China and Korea were also considering a bilateral FTA. But Taiwan's own considerations in negotiating the ECFA were strategic as well as defensive. Until then, China had blocked its attempts to sign bilateral FTAs with anyone other than its 'diplomatic allies,' or to join the growing number of regional trade agreements under discussion. It was hoped signature of the ECFA would remove this Chinese opposition, as well as redressing any disadvantages for Taiwanese businesses arising from the FTA between China and ASEAN.[7] This appeared to be the case, for following signature of the ECFA, Wang Yi, then the director of the People's Republic of China's (PRC) Taiwan Affairs Office, now the Chinese Foreign Minister, said that China would react to Taiwan's attempts to negotiate FTAs with other countries in a 'pragmatic' and 'appropriate' manner.[8]

If China saw the ECFA as a means of drawing Taiwan closer under its influence, Taiwan therefore appears to have seen it as a necessary step to upholding its own sovereignty, for agreements with Singapore and New Zealand, with neither of whom Taiwan has formal diplomatic relations, soon followed. Given Taiwan's near-total exclusion from international organizations and lack of diplomatic relations, the importance of these to Taiwan should not be understated. For Taiwan, any international agreements assume an importance beyond their direct impact. Trade agreements especially enable it to assert its de facto independence and act as a defence against being co-opted completely into the 'one-China' sphere. From this perspective, the existence of an agreement is of greater importance than the substance therein. One might therefore expect Taiwan to be flexible in its negotiating position or willing to offer generous concessions in its desire to sign agreements.

By this time the EU had moved beyond 'traditional,' tariff-focused, FTAs in its own bilateral negotiations to 'Partnership and Co-operation Agreements' embracing market access barriers, differing labour and environmental standards and more. The USA was following a similar approach, for example over the Trans-Pacific Partnership (TPP), (of which New Zealand was also an original member) described in one analysis as a *fairly heavy undertaking in terms of rules commitments...for relatively little...additional market access.*[9] In their most recent form, such as the EU's comprehensive agreement with Canada (CETA) or the now dormant if not abandoned Transatlantic Trade and Investment Partnership (TTIP), such agreements have gone even further, with provisions for transnational dispute settlements that could potentially override national legislation, one reason they have generated such strong populist opposition.[10]

Of particular relevance to Taiwan was the agreement concluded between the EU and Republic of Korea (RoK, or Korea) which entered force in 2011. At the time, this was groundbreaking in its coverage of non-tariff barriers, especially in the electronics and automotive industries. In these areas, Korea agreed to base hitherto distinct domestic standards on international ones, to accept EU compliance tests as equivalent to its own, or to allow mandatory testing to be undertaken within the EU rather than in Korea.[11]

By contrast, the agreements Taiwan was pursuing at the time focused almost exclusively on reducing or eliminating tariffs across a wide range of products. There was logic in this approach, for importers and exporters alike in Taiwan have identified tariffs as the single biggest obstacle to trade for Taiwan, lending weight to the focus on them in negotiations.[12]

Under the agreement with Singapore, for example, tariffs were removed on all Taiwan's exports to Singapore and 97% of Singapore's to Taiwan with immediate effect. Although both governments described the agreement as 'comprehensive,' in practice the chapters on market access and investment did not go significantly beyond either side's existing commitments under WTO agreements or national legislation.[13] Similarly, under the agreement with New Zealand, complete elimination of tariffs on bilateral trade was to be phased in over 4 years by New Zealand and 12 years by Taiwan. In this case too, both governments described this as a 'comprehensive' agreement but the remaining measures are confined mainly to air services and education, with some limited agreement on improving customs co-operation.[14] As an exporter primarily of agricultural products, however, New Zealand stood to gain significantly from tariff and quota reductions in these areas even without wider market access measures being agreed. By contrast, in the case of Europe, the European Commission has argued that the economic case for an FTA with Taiwan concentrating on tariffs is not compelling because most of the current bilateral trade is in areas where tariffs are already low or zero, so any agreement aimed mainly at reducing these further would have little impact on trade. Presumably, if the Commission had been willing to enter into negotiations with Taiwan, it would have only agreed to do so if a comprehensive agreement like that with Korea was to be considered.

For some years now, Taiwan's top trade priority has been accession to the TPP, notwithstanding President Donald Trump's withdrawal of the USA from it in January 2017. Now known as the Comprehensive and Progressive Agreement for Trans-Pacific Partnership, or CPTPP, in its original scope the TPP was much closer to the EU's Partnership and Co-operation Agreements than to Taiwan's existing bilateral agreements, including among other measures, sections on labour and environmental standards, transparency in respect of activity by state-owned enterprises and product-specific annexes covering areas such as product labelling and testing regimes. The previous Kuomintang (KMT) government in Taipei had identified 50 areas where domestic action would be needed to meet TPP requirements.[15] But Taiwan is by no means immune from the same populist opposition to new trade agreements increasingly common elsewhere, and action to date in implementing the necessary reforms has been limited. Prior to its own withdrawal from the TPP, the USA was insisting that Taiwan must demonstrate its intent by implementing reforms or market opening commitments before its application to join could even be considered. The most controversial of these was the insistence that Taiwan's ban on the use of the ractopamine additive in pork be lifted, a demand that has generated widespread protests in the country, in the face of which the government has so far taken no action.[16]

History and logic suggest that Taiwan will eventually yield to the demands of CPTPP members and implement the necessary reforms although without the USA as a member, these are unlikely to be as wide-ranging or extensive. Its accession to the WTO in 2002 was preceded by extensive reforms to its trading arrangements, including reducing the previously extensive range of prohibited imports, abolishing quantitative restrictions on trade and removal of multiple exchange rates.[17] And even without the USA as a member, the CPTPP will include countries with whom Taiwan's combined trade exceeds its trade with the whole of Europe, so the likely benefits from accession will likely far outweigh any domestic costs. This in turn suggests that in trade negotiations, Taiwan pursues a twofold objective, tempered by a measure of pragmatism. Where possible, it will use agreements first and foremost to assert its own sovereignty and reduce tariff barriers for its exporters but will be willing to pay the price of domestic reforms or market opening measures where the rewards justify doing so.

Assuming it was to enter negotiations with the UK, therefore, which model would prevail? Would it aim for a tariff-focused agreement like those it has signed to date or would it be willing to accept some removal of barriers or market opening if that was what the UK demanded? An agreement like those with New Zealand and Singapore would be of little direct economic benefit to Taiwan. The bilateral trade balance is heavily in its favour and the great majority of its exports to the UK are already tariff-free. The UK is an important trading partner but only at the second tier: it is Taiwan's 12th largest export market, 3rd within the EU, behind Germany and the Netherlands, and ranks 18th as a source of Taiwan's imports.[18] Given British government statements about pursuing free trade, it seems reasonable to assume that the UK would not suddenly start erecting tariff barriers against the rest of the world after leaving the EU.

On the other hand, an FTA with the UK like those with New Zealand and Singapore would be a major political prize. As its first such agreement with a G7 country, it would be a significant boost to Taiwanese sovereignty.[19] Taiwan would presumably also hope for a bandwagon effect like the one that followed the UK's lifting of visa requirements in 2009, which was followed in due course by the rest of the EU, Canada, the USA and other countries. Whether such a model would meet UK objectives or requirements is something to which we now turn.

'Taking Back Control': The UK's Trade Policy Priorities in a Post-Brexit World

The UK has long seen itself as committed to free and open international trade. Within the EU, for example, it was open in its support for granting China Market Economy Status in the WTO and ready to block anti-dumping measures against Chinese steel imports, even at the risk of the closure of its biggest steelworks.[20] Its detractors might argue that this is self-serving: it can adopt this stance because in reality trade is less important to the UK than it likes to believe. Its exports are a much smaller proportion of its GDP than they are for most of the EU. By contrast, services are relatively more important than for its neighbours: 80% of GDP and 45% of overall exports, the highest share in any G7 country, making the

UK the second largest exporter of services worldwide. Until now the UK has been obliged to accept priorities set by the European Commission in international trade negotiations, priorities obviously drawn up with the majority of EU member states in mind. In a post-Brexit world, assuming the UK leaves the Single Market and Customs Union in accordance with the stated intention of its government, it will be free to set its own trade objectives according to its priorities. The British government has already indicated that services are likely to feature high among these.[21]

But it should be no surprise that the first trade priority for the British government post-Brexit is to ensure the continuity of trade between the UK and EU. The EU is by far the UK's largest trading partner and if only because of geography will remain so. The British government also appears to recognize the extent to which modern manufacturing relies on extended transnational supply chains and the need both to preserve these and allow them to continue to grow. Thereafter, the government seeks continuity in existing trade and investment relationships, 'including those covered by EU Free Trade Agreements or other EU preferential arrangements'[22]

While reiterating its commitment to maintaining existing trade patterns and agreements, however, the government also states it wishes to boost trade relationships with new allies. Could this offer an opening to negotiate an FTA with Taiwan? At first sight, such an agreement may appear attractive. If it focuses on tariffs it should be quick and easy to agree as these are already low and confined to relatively few areas. For the UK, it would be a 'quick-win,' enabling it to demonstrate its own sovereign position in trade negotiations and giving its new trade negotiators valuable early experience. Taiwan would undoubtedly welcome such a deal.

But the UK will also need to demonstrate credibility in its approach to trade negotiations, not least for domestic reasons. It seems reasonable to assume that any deal would have to stand up to scrutiny against the UK's objectives as set out in its paper on future customs arrangements but also be comparable in benefits to UK businesses with what they might have gained from any deal that the EU may have negotiated. In the case of Taiwan, the European Commission's market access database currently lists just 3 areas in which barriers or impediments to trade have been reported, a reduction of 13 over the preceding year.[23] One of these, however, a ban on beef imports from the EU because of the historic problem of Bovine Spongiform Encephalopathy (BSE), would be of direct interest to British farmers. More broadly, market access barriers remain in many areas, the automotive industry being a good example. At 17.5%, average tariffs in the sector are among the highest in Taiwan on manufactured products, while imports are also subject to dual testing and local certification requirements, further hampering their ability to compete. The aim is to protect the domestic motor industry which is very inefficient and small by global standards, the total annual output of its seven plants being less than that of the UK's leading factory.[24] The UK motor industry might reasonably expect to see improved access on the table in any negotiations.

A bigger challenge for the UK may lie in its objectives for the services sector, given the emphasis it has already placed on this in its future trade objectives. The UK companies would certainly welcome progress in reducing barriers in Taiwan, especially in financial services, which in the past has been singled out by the EU for its regulatory barriers or restrictions. But this sector is currently dominated by state-owned institutions, which account for an estimated 60% of its overall output and to date the Taiwan government has resisted efforts to liberalize it.[25]

In short, the two sides are likely to have very different objectives in negotiating a bilateral trade agreement. Taiwan would want it first and foremost to enhance its sovereignty. Hitherto it has reluctantly agreed to domestic reform only as the price of entering multilateral trading arrangements. It seems unlikely that it would agree to any meaningful reform as part of a bilateral agreement, especially with a second-order trade partner and given the absence of reciprocal obstacles for Taiwanese exporters to the UK. For its part, the British government will be unwilling to enter negotiations with Taiwan on a tariff-only agreement, given the need for it to demonstrate its credibility in trade negotiations. But on its own, the UK simply lacks the leverage of the EU, the USA or Japan in negotiations and any market opening measures agreed would be subject to Taiwanese assessments of their impact on domestic industry or special interest groups. It seems unlikely that either side would be prepared to agree to the sort of concessions or requirements sought by the other side and talks would be more than likely to founder in the face of the very different objectives and requirements of the two sides.

In practice, other demands are likely to render such considerations academic. The UK has expressed its wish to maintain continuity in current trading agreements between the EU and third parties. Assuming all these third parties agree and are willing to sign new bilateral agreements without significant amendments, there are still 44 such agreements that the UK will need to sign, excluding ones currently being negotiated. Prime Minister Theresa May has also reportedly hoped that the agreement currently being negotiated between the EU and Japan could form the basis of a similar agreement with the UK, while one of her officials has said that the USA and UK have agreed to a bilateral trade deal 'as soon as possible' after the UK leaves the EU.[26] All this will impose considerable demands on the new trade negotiating team that the UK must first assemble and will take time to achieve.

As in the case of Taiwan's objectives for other FTAs, however, the biggest stumbling block is likely to be China, or at least the UK's perceptions of its position. Given the recent history of UK-Taiwan bilateral relations, Taiwan could be forgiven for thinking that the UK might be different to other countries in this regard. But while the UK has been willing to extend its co-operation with Taiwan, it has also gone to considerable lengths in recent years to court China, including hosting President Xi Jinping for a high-profile state visit in Autumn 2015 intended to herald a 'golden era' in bilateral relations. Its efforts prompted the withering criticism from a leading European think-tank that it pursued its own narrow interests in its dealings with China at the expense of a coordinated European approach and 'chose financial benefits over values in ... dealing with Beijing'.[27] China is also the only country mentioned by name in the British government's paper on future customs arrangements, a further indication of its likely priorities. Given that its bilateral trade with China far exceeds that with Taiwan and that UK services industries are especially eager to secure improved access to the Chinese market, the likelihood of the UK giving priority to negotiating an agreement with Taiwan over one with China is remote. So far, China has been prepared to accept other countries signing agreements with Taiwan provided they did so with China first. This was the case with New Zealand and Singapore; it was also the basis on which China joined the WTO.[28] As the UK appears keen to start such negotiations with China, unlike the EU, it does hold out the prospect that it may one day agree to open negotiations with Taiwan too but given the other reasons cited here, this is unlikely to happen for some years yet.

The Prospects for a Taiwan-EU Bilateral Investment Agreement

Given that the prospects of an early trade agreement with the UK therefore seem remote, Taiwan would be better served by focusing its attention on one with the EU instead. The way in which the EU will conduct its trade policies with other countries after Brexit remains uncertain: whether it will remain firm in its commitment to free trade or turn towards protectionism. With the USA under President Trump moving steadily away from multilateralism, the EU could become its flag-bearer and champion. Or it could follow the USA lead. At a time of such uncertainty, any opportunities for trade liberalization should be grasped. This is especially true for Taiwan, which in view of the declining USA commitment to multilateral trade, increasingly risks being excluded from new agreements. In these circumstances, an agreement with the EU is certainly worth pursuing.

In 2015 the EU was Taiwan's fifth largest trading partner worldwide and a major source of foreign direct investment. Trade between the two accounted for 9.13% of Taiwan's total trade. Taiwan's exports to the EU were 8.46% of Taiwan's total exports, and Taiwan's imports from the EU were 9.94% of Taiwan's total imports. Meanwhile, Taiwan ranked 22nd in terms of EU trading partners and was its sixth largest trading partner in Asia.[29]

Given this background, Taiwan has been making the case for a bilateral FTA with the EU for almost a decade but without success, notwithstanding the EU's willingness, eagerness even, to open discussions with countries such as Vietnam; and Taiwan seemingly meeting the European Commission's own criteria for opening such negotiations. Published in 2006, these include both market potential and the degree of protection against EU exports to the country.[30] Not surprisingly, the general assumption in Taiwan was that the EU was reluctant to move for fear of offending China. Then in October 2013, the European Parliament adopted a resolution on EU-Taiwan trade relations and urged the European Commission to begin talks with Taiwan over an agreement on investment protection and market access. The Commission in its 2015 report responded by saying *[B]uilding on the investment provisions under negotiation with China, the EU will explore launching negotiations on investment with Hong Kong and Taiwan.*[31]

In view of this positive statement and the absence of wider opportunities, a bilateral investment treaty with the EU serves as an ideal policy instrument for Taiwan to pursue. The title, with its specific reference to investment, is something of a misnomer, implying as it does a focus primarily on investment protection and therefore less ambitious than an FTA. Taiwan's own BIA with Japan signed in 2011 is a good example of such agreements, devoted as it is almost exclusively to mutual investment protection arrangements and with significant sectoral exclusions.[32] Just as recent years have seen an expansion in the scope of FTAs, however, so too

BIAs have become more ambitious and comprehensive, to the extent that a 'high standard [and] new generation BIA' such as the one currently being negotiated between the EU and China, covers such a wide range of issues that it almost amounts to an FTA.[33] At a time when the EU is divided internally between populist opposition to globalization and championing free trade, shown most clearly in protests against both the CETA with Canada and the TTIP and pressure to liberalize further in the light of the outcome of the UK's referendum, a BIA can be seen as a cautious, low-profile response, capturing the middle ground. On the one hand, it would show the EU's commitment to globalization and free trade. On the other hand, it need not involve more sensitive issues such as market access, government procurement, competition policy, the role of state-owned enterprises, environmental protection or labour standards and accordingly has a lower and less controversial profile.

This low profile should also suit Taiwan, always sensitive to the potential for opposition from China, and the EU's announcement was welcomed there, at the time by the KMT government of Ma Ying-jeou and again in 2016 by the subsequent Democratic Progressive Party (DPP) administration under Tsai Ing-wen. On receiving members of the European Parliament on 20 April 2017, Tsai expressed her gratitude for the parliament's promotion of Taiwan-EU trade and economic relations and laying down the foundation for a BIA.[34]

There are obstacles to agreeing a BIA between the two. A political one concerns the EU's acceptance of a 'one China policy,' and its lack of diplomatic or formal political relations with Taiwan. The Commission's stance of initiating investment negotiations with Hong Kong and Taiwan only after opening negotiations with China (and after several rounds of discussions) clearly indicates a 'China first, Taiwan (and Hong Kong) second' approach. This is consistent with China's approach to third countries agreeing FTAs with Taiwan, as noted above. It remains to be seen whether negotiations with Taiwan could make progress in isolation or whether they will be held hostage to progress in the negotiations with China.

There is a bigger question about China's attitude. Its relatively tolerant approach to third countries negotiating agreements with Taiwan, of 'reach agreement with China first, then talk to Taiwan but keep us informed' was set at a time when cross-straits relations were at their warmest since the founding of the PRC in 1949. Since then, Beijing's tone and attitude has hardened following Tsai Ing-wen's election victory in 2016. Whether the Commission will still be willing to negotiate with Taiwan at a time when cross-straits relations have cooled and China is again squeezing Taiwan's international space is as yet unknown.[35] But China's hardening attitude may paradoxically facilitate progress by encouraging a firmer stance on the part of the EU. In a review of China's strategy in July 2016, the EU's Council of Ministers affirmed its expectation that relations with China should be truly reciprocal. It also underlined its attachment to human rights and the rule of law. But the Council went further, explicitly expressing support for Taiwan and the values it shares with the EU.[36] Taiwan would therefore seem well advised to grasp the opportunity on offer from the EU and make the most of it, especially given uncertainty surrounding its ambitions of joining the CPTPP.

Potential practical difficulties also exist. For example, a legal obstacle concerns the lack of a dispute settlement mechanism. Typically, a BIA always contains two core elements: the substantive standards of investment protection awarded to covered investors and their investments, and the procedural mechanism to address investor-state disputes settlement (ISDS). The ISDS is a controversial issue as it has attracted criticism including, inter alia, arbitrators being biased in favour of investors, proceedings lacking transparency and arbitral awards imposing a chilling effect on state regulatory power over public interests.[37] In 2015 the EU proposed an 'Investment Court System' (ICS), which is an improved version of ISDS intended to be incorporated in all ongoing and future treaty negotiations.[38] Whether and how this design is negotiated between Taiwan and the EU is an important issue.

Rather than focusing on the obstacles, however, Taiwan should concentrate on the opportunities. Whatever the limitations of a BIA, at present this is the one concrete offer Taiwan has from a third party to negotiate a meaningful trade agreement. Given the flexibility offered by the European Commission's preference for 'comprehensive' agreements, Taiwan could indeed approach a BIA with the EU as something akin to the CPTPP, negotiating an agreement with the EU in parallel with CPTPP negotiations if its aspirations to join the latter make progress, or using the likely requirements of CPTPP accession as a benchmark for an agreement with the EU if not.

At the time of writing, it is not certain that the UK will even leave the EU. Since Mrs May set out her position in January 2017, envisaging a 'hard Brexit' with withdrawal not just from the Single Market but also from the European Customs Union, she has lost her parliamentary majority and the earlier rhetoric of some of her ministers is gradually being overtaken by a growing reality of the complexities and challenges ahead.

At a minimum, there will be a transition period before the final divorce but it is far from impossible, even probable, that the UK will end up in a closer relationship than first envisaged by Mrs May. This only reinforces the reasons for Taiwan to pursue a BIA with the EU ahead of any agreement with the UK. If the UK ends up remaining in the EU after all, or even in the Single Market, the BIA will apply to it as well as other members and it will be precluded from negotiating a separate agreement. Should the UK still eventually leave the EU, negotiations over a BIA could be well advanced or even completed before this finally happens. In this case, given the British government's desire for continuity in existing agreements, the BIA would serve as a ready framework on which to base subsequent bilateral negotiations with the UK.

Conclusion

The 'Leave' campaigners in the UK may have welcomed the referendum result as an opportunity, as they saw it, to 'take back control' and for the UK to carve out new international trading relationships freed from European concerns. As the euphoria wears off, however and reality asserts itself, so too will the realization that, if only for reasons of geography, the UK's most important relations will continue to be with its European neighbours. It is still possible that the referendum result will be reversed or overturned: that has happened before in France, Denmark, the Netherlands and Ireland after previous referenda on the EU. Should the UK press ahead and leave, however, its first task will be to rebuild the legal and regulatory agreements necessary to underpin its new arrangements. Only once this has been completed will the UK be able to consider new and wider trade priorities. As it does so, it will inevitably take full account of its own domestic interests, meaning it is likely to be both pragmatic and mercantilist in setting priorities. But it will wish to preserve as much as possible of existing EU agreements in the new bilateral ones it will pursue, if only so as to minimize the adjustments and negotiations required. Only once it has renegotiated these and agreed new terms with its biggest trade partners will it have the confidence and capacity to broaden its horizons. That could take several years.

The EU meanwhile remains committed to trade liberalization although the mounting opposition shown in the cases of the CETA and TTIP suggest that far from being assured, an open economy and free trade require constant promotion and protection. Perhaps ironically, popular antipathy to President Trump in Europe could yet strengthen the case for multilateral free trade, given his own aversion to both it and the EU.

Against such an uncertain background and faced with a hostile and increasingly assertive China, Taiwan should seek to strengthen its relations with the EU and prioritize these over any considerations of a new trade agreement with the UK. This points to a BIA with the EU as the recommended policy option for Taiwan. Combining as it does the EU's continued support for free trade with a lower profile and therefore less opposition than would surround an FTA, it is well suited to Taiwan's geopolitical position. It is also already on offer, whereas any new agreement with the UK is still several years away, even assuming the UK would have the capacity to negotiate one. Should this opportunity arise, then a BIA with the EU would provide a strong foundation on which to build.

Notes

1. Michael I. Magcamit, Alexander C. Tan: *Crouching tiger, lurking dragon*, International Relations of the Asia-Pacific, vol15/1, 2015.
2. At a lunch organized by the European Chamber of Commerce in Taipei in January 2009 the then UK Minister for Trade, Gareth Thomas, expressed British support for an EU-Taiwan FTA.
3. Theresa May: *speech at Davos, 2017*, https://www.weforum.org/agenda/2017/01/theresa-may-at-davos-2017-her-speech-in-full/, retrieved 23 August 2017; HM Government: *Future Customs Arrangements, A future partnership paper*, 15 August 2017, https://www.gov.uk/government/uploads/system/uploads/attachment_data/file/637748/Future_customs_arrangements_-_a_future_partnership_paper.pdf, retrieved 22 August 2017.
4. World Trade Organization, http://stat.wto.org/CountryProfile/WSDBCountryPFView.aspx?Language=E&Country=E28%2cTW, *retrieved 15 July 2016*.
5. The first of these was signed with Panama in 2003. Although Panama broke diplomatic relations in 2017 when it switched its recognition to China, to date the FTA remains in force.
6. Chris Hogg: *"Taiwan and China sign landmark trade agreement"* BBC News. http://www.bbc.co.uk/news/10442557, retrieved 23 August 2017.
7. Magcamit and Tan: *Crouching tiger, lurking dragon*, op.cit; Netina Tan, *ECFA's Regional Impact and the Taiwan-Singapore FTA Negotiations*, diplomacy.nccu.edu.tw/download.php?filename=668_85101b2d...FTA (PDF), retrieved 23 August 2017.

8. *Taiwan to pursue FTAs with other Trade partners,* Straits Times, 3 July 2010.
9. Tun-Jen Cheng and Wei-Chin Lee: *Wrestling over the Trans-Pacific Partnership: US strategic interests, China's responses and Taiwan's membership options* in Peter C.Y.Chow, ed.: The Trans-Pacific Partnership and the path to free trade in the Asia-Pacific, Cheltenham 2016.
10. For example: *Stop TTIP. European Initiative Against TTIP and CETA,* https://stop-ttip.org/, retrieved 5 October 2016.
11. DG Trade: *The EU- Korea Free Trade Agreement in practice,* Brussels, 2011.
12. A Di Battista et al., *Global Enabling Trade Report 2014 p294,* World Economic Forum.
13. IE Singapore: *The Agreement between Singapore and the Separate Customs Territory of Taiwan, Penghu, Kinmen and Matsu on economic partnership (ASTEP),* https://www.iesingapore.gov.sg/-/media/IE-Singapore/Files/Trade-from-Singapore/ASTEP/ASTEP_30_04_2014_V8_final.ashx?la=en, retrieved 23 August 2017.
14. NZ Department of Foreign Affairs and Trade: *About ANZTEC,* https://www.nzcio.com/en/anztec/about-anztec/, retrieved 23 August 2017.
15. Sara Yi-ying Lin: *TPP from Taiwan's Vantage Point: Political, Trade and Strategic Considerations,* Washington 2015.
16. The use of ractopamine as an additive in meat is permitted by the UN's Codex Alimentarius within specified limits. Taiwan prohibits it in pork on the grounds that Taiwanese are heavy consumers of it. The EU bans it in all meat.
17. Magcamit and Tan: *Crouching tiger, lurking dragon,* op.cit.
18. Ministry of Finance, Taiwan: *External Trade Statistics,* https://www.mof.gov.tw/Eng/Pages/Detail.aspx?nodeid=259&pid=64520, retrieved 23 August 2017.
19. Taiwan does already have a Bilateral Investment Agreement ('Arrangement') with Japan.
20. Michael Reilly: *The Burial of Thatcherism?* Chap. 2, above.
21. Ibid., HM Government: *Future Customs Arrangements, A future partnership paper,* op.cit.
22. *Future Customs Arrangements,* op.cit.
23. DG Trade: *Market access database,* European Commission, http://madb.europa.eu/madb/barriers_crossTables.htm, retrieved 24 August 2017.
24. Michael Reilly: *Towards an EU-Taiwan Investment Agreement,* Prospects and Pitfalls, 2018.
25. *National Statistics,* Republic of China (Taiwan), http://eng.stat.gov.tw/fp.asp?xItem=33339&ctNode=3570, retrieved 18 October 2016.
26. Anushka Asthana: *Trump expects trade deal with UK to be completed 'very, very quickly.'* The Guardian, 8 July 2017, https://www.theguardian.com/

world/2017/jul/08/theresa-may-in-bid-to-boost-post-brexit-trade-with-g20-meetings, retrieved 23 August 2017.

27. European Council on Foreign Relations, *Foreign Policy Scorecard 2016*, http://www.ecfr.eu/scorecard/2016, retrieved 24 August 2017.
28. China joined the WTO on 11 December 2001 and Taiwan on 1 January 2002.
29. Bureau of Foreign Trade, Taiwan, 'Taiwan-EU Economic Relationship 2016', http://www.trade.gov.tw/App_Ashx/File.ashx?FilePath=../Files/Doc/e730ac7a-9615-49f7-b068-366d309658c5.pdf, retrieved 24 April 2017.
30. *Global Europe, Competing in the World,* Commission Communication, 2006, http://trade.ec.europa.eu/doclib/docs/2006/october/tradoc_130370.pdf, retrieved 21 October 2016.
31. European Commission, *Trade for All*, p. 31.
32. *Taiwan-Japan Bilateral Investment Arrangement (BIA),* MOEA Taipei, 26 October 2011.
33. Chen Xin, 'The EU's Dilemma with China: Free Trade or Bilateral Investment?' *The Parliament Magazine*, 18 March 2014, https://www.theparliamentmagazine.eu/articles/feature/eus-dilemma-china-free-trade-or-bilateral-investment, retrieved 22 April 2017.
34. Chung Li-hua, 'Tsai Ing-wen: As Long as Taiwan and the EU Are Willing to Cooperate, There Are Unlimited Possibilities', *Liberty Times*, 20 April 2017, http://news.ltn.com.tw/news/politics/breakingnews/2042222, retrieved 24 April 2017[in Chinese].
35. Cf. Chien-Huei Wu, 'Toward an EU-Taiwan Bilateral Investment Treaty: A Roadmap', in J. Chaisse (Ed.), *China's Three-Prong Investment Strategy: Bilateral, Regional, and Global Tracks* (Oxford: Oxford University Press, forthcoming).
36. *EU Strategy on China,* EU Council conclusions, 11,252/16, 18 July 2016.
37. Cf. Pia Eberhardt and Cecilia Olivet, *Profiting from Injustice: How Law Firms, Arbitrators and Financiers Are Fuelling an Investment Arbitration Boom* (Brussels: Corporate Europe Observatory and the Transnational Institute, 2012).
38. European Commission, 'Commission Proposes New Investment Court System for TTIP and other EU Trade and Investment Negotiations', 16 September 2015, http://europa.eu/rapid/press-release_IP-15-5651_en.htm, retrieved 25 October 2016.

CHAPTER 10

Identity Mobilization, Path Dependence, and the Future of the European Union After Brexit

David W. F. Huang

INTRODUCTION

In a referendum on 23 June 2016, the British people voted for "Brexit," giving the government a mandate to leave the European Union (EU). While the "exit" result was somewhat anticipated in a number of polls prior to the referendum, the result nonetheless sent a shock wave around the world. Never before in the history of European integration had any major member state contemplated leaving the EU and acted to make it happen. There were, previously, occasions in which a country was extended an offer of EU membership but rejected the opportunity in a referendum, and cases in which EU treaty revisions were rejected by referendums of some member states, but there was no precedent for a major member state leaving the EU: Britain will be the first. What impact will Brexit have on the prospects of the EU? Will Brexit induce a crisis mentality in the remaining member states such that further integration is promoted, or will Brexit trigger a domino effect leading other EU member

D. W. F. Huang (✉)
Institute of European and American Studies, Academia Sinica,
Nankang, Taipei, Taiwan
e-mail: wfhuang@gate.sinica.edu.tw

D. W. F. Huang, M. Reilly (eds.), *The Implications of Brexit for East Asia*, https://doi.org/10.1007/978-981-13-0185-8_10

states out of the Union? These are the questions in which scholars and policy makers in East Asia are most interested.

This chapter seeks to answer the above questions by investigating the impact of Brexit on EU governance. Two theoretical concepts are introduced: "identity mobilization," derived from post-functionalism; and "path dependence," from historical institutionalism. I argue that the balance of forces between anti-EU sentiments embedded in national identities and the "path dependent" nature of EU institutions will shape the contours of post-Brexit EU governance. Although Brexit will not lead to a total collapse of the EU, the existing trend of "differentiated integration" will be more deeply entrenched. Without Britain, the EU will not become a more homogeneous entity. On the contrary, diversity within the EU will be highlighted given that there is now a precedent (or a credible threat) that dissatisfied member states might opt for exit. Nevertheless, the "stickiness" of EU institutions means that highlighting diversities will not necessarily provide sufficient momentum for disintegration. Multiple cores and peripheries will emerge among the member states, depending on the will and capacity of each member state to participate in different policy programs. The "Community method" will become much less effective in pushing for policy convergence. Instead, multiple modes of governance will be entrenched with no hope of later convergence. The future of the EU may well be locked into a limbo of "differentiated integration."

Two Theoretical Concepts: "Identity Mobilization" and "Path Dependence"

In an article, Liesbet Hooghe and Gary Marks claim that the issue of European integration has been politicized in elections and referendums, leading to an increase in the importance of national identity, public opinion, and political parties in deciding European jurisdictional outcomes.[1] They hypothesize that identity is causally important in EU governance when an issue has opaque economic implications, when obvious effects on community are debated in public forums, and when mass organizations rather than interest groups are mobilized.[2] They find that the legitimacy of decision-making on vital European issues has shifted away from insulated elites to the mass public since the 1992 Maastricht Treaty, and claim that European integration has moved "from permissive consensus to constraining dissensus," in which neo-functionalism no longer explains unfolding events.[3] Thus, they propose "a post-functionalist theory," highlighting the impact of identity mobilization on EU governance.[4]

To some extent, post-functionalists anticipated Brexit, given that British identity and parliamentary sovereignty played a fundamental role in shaping debate during the Brexit campaign. If the post-functionalism thesis was correct with respect to identity mobilization, what would be its impact on EU governance? One likely result is that EU institutions will have to pay more attention to public opinion and the national identity politics of the member states. The EU could respond by introducing more democratic elements, for instance including more stakeholders, in its decision-making processes. However, introducing more players into the system of EU governance, other things being equal, will create more veto points within the system, making it less efficient and more prone to deadlock at a time when institutional deadlock is the last thing that the EU wants. Such an outcome would certainly undermine the EU's "output legitimacy."

Hooghe and Marks suggest some possible strategies that European leaders may follow to overcome governance deadlock. For example, European leaders may avoid controversial referendums by repackaging EU reforms into smaller bundles, in which logrolling and side-payments across individual reforms are possible. Alternatively, EU-wide reforms could be advanced by "providing greater flexibility for recalcitrant member states to opt out, by making it easier for sub-sets of member states to cooperate, or by shifting decisions to non-majoritarian regulatory agencies."[5] Is it possible for the EU to push forward with EU-wide reform in order to rein in its ever-expanding institutions, or to provide some flexibility for those unwilling or incapable of participating to "opt out?"

The theory of historical institutionalism predicts that it would be extremely difficult for the EU to reform or dismantle its supranational institutions due to the "path dependent" nature of institutional development over time.[6] On the basis of this theory derived from rational choice theory, Paul Pierson argues that, while the initial design provided for weak supranational institutions and limited policy competencies, EU member states may find it increasingly difficult to exercise control over these institutions for the following four reasons.[7] Firstly, member states may have a high "discount rate" with respect to the future and may agree to EU policies that undermine their long-term controls over policies in exchange for short-term electoral gains. Secondly, even if member states do not apply a high discount rate to the future, they could be shortsighted in their institutional choices, leading to unintended consequences in institutional development.[8]

Thirdly, the preferences of member states may change over time, either through inheriting or through socializing *acquis communanutaire*. The preferences of member states are endogenously conditioned and shaped by what they have already agreed to within Europe.[9] Member states may seek to change EU institutions and policies only to find that they are "locked in" a "joint-decision trap," in which decision rules around unanimity and intergovernmentalism make it virtually impossible for any individual member state to promote institutional or policy changes in accordance with its own preferences.[10] Fourthly, as Pierson explains, EU institutions and policies may become "sticky" because there is an "increasing return" on their continuing operations.[11] On the one hand, EU institutions and policies are set up to reduce transaction costs of interactions among member states, and following the existing path of policy and institutional development, member states find it easier to reap the benefits of their continuing operations. On the other hand, institutions and policies may become self-perpetuating because the vested interests they create turn out to support them.[12] Rolling back the unintended consequences of institutional development has proven extremely difficult, either because original coalitions establishing them no longer exist, or because member states face prohibitive sunk costs associated with dismantling the existing EU institutions and policies.

Indeed, over the past six decades, the EU's supranational institutions and their policy competencies have expanded substantially, creating a complex web of governance. This complex system of EU governance is subject to institutional "path dependence," in that member states have invested so much in EU institutions to make sure they function well that they have few incentives to unravel them. Neither would member states have incentives to withdraw from the EU altogether, because doing so they would incur unbearable sunk costs. Nor would far-reaching institutional reform of the EU be likely.

What, then, will be the likely impact of Brexit on EU governance? Given that Brexit is a manifestation of post-functionalism, I argue that the likely impact of Brexit is a proliferation of various forms of "differentiated integration." The term "differentiated integration" first appeared in the 1976 Tindemans Report and encompasses various modes of governance in the EU context. What distinguishes this from differentiated integration with an exit option is that member states would highlight "diversity" within the EU in order to respond to domestic challenges stemming from identity mobilization, while at the same time consolidating various forms of governance, thus allowing for flexibility within the sphere of EU governance. In other words, an existing mode of governance which deviates from the "Community method" will be entrenched with no hope of policy convergence in the future.

Identity Mobilization in the EU

Brigid Laffan suggested 20 years ago that the prospects for further integration depends on the EU's ability to create a European identity,[13] but Fligstein's research shows that the minimal sense of European identity barely exists and has not changed much over time. From this, he concludes that the EU's future development would stall.[14] In fact, since the 1992 Maastricht Treaty, the EU project has shifted emphasis from economic integration to ever closer political union, and the policy competence of EU institutions has expanded to include not only economic but most social, cultural, and political matters. The expansion of the EU's authority and policy competence not only threatens national identities, but contributes to the politicization of European integration. This politicization of European integration is manifested by an increased level of resistance to EU policies, a declining support for the EU, and a revival of nationalism. Paradoxically, the very success of European project itself has pit European identity against national identities, reigniting nationalism in various forms to resist further European integration. Why should an increase in the EU's power not correspond to an increase in the prevalence of European identity?

As Vivian Schmidt suggests, national elites do not supply European discourses to facilitate development of European identity, and even if they do, they tend to blame the EU for their failures at the national level.[15] Thus, it is not surprising to find that Europeans are eager to reclaim their national identities and to rid themselves of "unnecessary" EU intervention. The increasing assertiveness of national identity has undermined citizens' support for the EU. Indeed, using survey data, Carey shows that regardless of whether national identity is conceptualized in terms of the intensity of feeling toward one's own country, level of attachment to the nation relatively to other territorial entities, or fear of other cultures invading the dominant national culture, his statistical results confirm that a stronger national identity leads to a lower level of support for the EU.[16] An increasingly assertive national identity, which has been observed in various opinion polls, is only a necessary condition for Europeans to withhold support for the EU. In order to have a real impact on the political system and EU governance, national identities have to be mobilized. Two notable indicators of identity mobilization are the use of referendum and the rise of extreme right parties in Europe.

The Rise of Extreme Right Parties

The rise of extreme right parties has been the most important political trend in Europe of the past two decades.[17] Most of the rhetoric of European extreme right parties is in line with an ethnic-culture version of national identity, with a specific focus on opposing immigrants given that they are regarded as "the others" and a potential threat to the national economy and culture. European extreme right parties appeal to voters who tend to be marginalized by globalization, trade liberalization, and the neo-liberal version of regional integration. These parties invite voters to focus on their ethnic or national uniqueness, and to subscribe to their Christian or cultural heritages as an excuse to exclude immigrants from outside Europe. They are essentially populist and anti-establishment parties, and frequently employ authoritarian rhetoric to mock the inefficiency and democracy of the EU and its member states.[18] Since the 1980s, extreme right parties in Europe have gained electoral momentum and found ways to influence policies (e.g. immigration and social benefits) in their respective national political systems. Previously regarded as marginal political groups, their recent, consistent electoral successes have gradually inserted their policy agendas into mainstream political discourse.[19]

Extreme right parties in Europe do not necessarily reject the EU as a whole, but they do fear a net loss of "national identity" if EU integration encompasses ethnic and cultural matters, or embraces multiculturalism.[20] "Eurosceptic" parties from the extreme right, such as the French *Front National* (FN), Italian *Lega Nord* (LN), German *Republikaner*, and the Belgian *Vlaams Belang* (VB), tend to support the basic principles of the EU, while at the same time harshly criticizing EU institutions and policies.[21] Such a position allows extreme right parties to present themselves as defenders of liberal democracy while justifying their anti-immigrant and exclusionary policies.

The extreme right agenda has gained support from a significant portion of the European public. For example, in the 2003 European Social Survey, 50% of respondents opposed admitting immigrants from a different race or ethnic group. In the 2004 Eurobarometer, 60% of EU citizens ranked "immigration" as the most important problem confronting Europe, higher than terrorism, pensions, taxation, education, housing, the environment, public transport, defense, or foreign affairs.[22] Figure 10.1 shows that for most of the time between 2005 and 2016 immigration ranked higher than those other issues.

Although none of the extreme right parties has been able to obtain a ruling majority in any national parliamentary election, these parties have formed coalition governments with center-right parties in Austria, Denmark, and Italy. Moreover, they have been able to push mainstream parties to adopt anti-immigrant rhetoric and to change immigration laws in Austria, Denmark, Netherlands, and France.[23] Mainstream center-right parties have tried to win back support by mimicking the anti-immigrant rhetoric of their extreme right counterparts, but have failed to squeeze out extreme right parties. In the end, mainstream parties have found themselves moving further to the right on immigration while allowing anti-immigrant, anti-EU, and anti-globalization sentiments spread throughout Europe.[24]

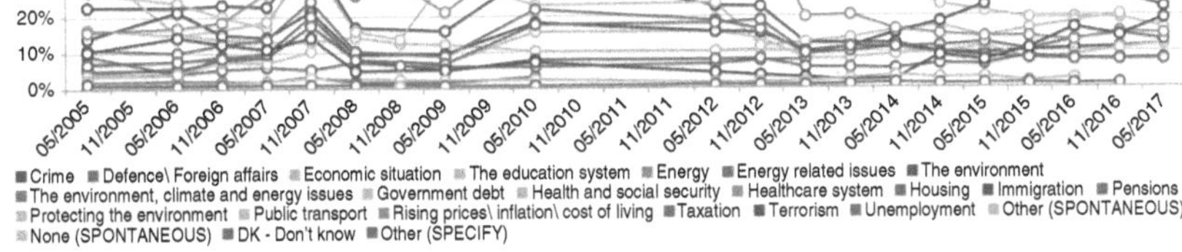

Fig. 10.1 What do you think are the two most important issues facing (our country) at the moment? European Union (from May 2005 to May 2017). (Source: Eurobarometer interactive, http://ec.europa.eu/commfrontoffice/publicopinion/index.cfm/Chart/getChart/chartType/lineChart//themeKy/42/groupKy/208/savFile/54)

Referendums on EU Matters

Political elites in Europe are not unaware of the impact of populism and extreme right parties on European integration, but they face a dilemma. On the one hand, if political elites attempt to depoliticize matters on European integration and continue business as usual with their bureaucratic/technical-driven method of policy making, then the EU's legitimacy and democratic credentials would be greatly undermined.[25] On the other hand, if political elites respond to populists' demands for more procedural and substantive inputs from stakeholders, and more referendums on EU matters, they risk a governance stalemate and might jeopardize the entire integration project. Nevertheless, in order to resolve domestic or intra-party disputes on EU matters, political elites in many EU member states have gradually conceded to demands for referendums.

Although referendums on EU matters have been recurrent and significant features of European politics since 1972, several studies suggest that there is an increasing trend for referendums to be used by European countries (especially post-communist states, the Netherlands, and the UK) in recent decades.[26] Since France held its first referendum in 1972 on the accession of Denmark, Norway, Ireland, and the UK to the (then) European Communities (EC), there have been in total 54 referendums (excluding Brexit and the Hungarian referendum on refugees) relating to European integration held in Europe.[27]

Until April 2016, 23 of the 28 EU member states had held at least one referendum on EU matters, while only Germany, Belgium, Portugal, Cyprus, and Bulgaria were yet to hold a referendum. According to Tilindyte's research, 24 of the 54 referendums were related to EU membership, 18 referendums were about treaty ratification, and 12 referendums concerned EU policies. Moreover, Ireland, Denmark, and Switzerland account for almost half (25) of referendums on EU matters held so far. Ireland is the only member state which has held a referendum on every treaty revision since 1972. Tilindyte's research also indicates that the approval rate in treaty referendums is significantly lower than that in membership referendums. Specifically, nine membership referendums preceding to enlargement of ten East European states in 2004 produced the highest approval rates. The UK is the only country which has held referendums and voted for "remaining" in the EC, in 1974, and for "leaving" the EU, in 2016.[28]

Referendums invite popular involvement in European affairs. Following active and intensive campaigns on a referendum proposition, people may be informed or misinformed about both sides of the argument.[29] Some observations of campaign rhetoric in two most recent referendums held by EU member states are provided. One referendum was introduced on 6 April 2016 by the Dutch government, followed by a successful signature drive of more than 450,000 people. The referendum asked the Dutch people whether they approve the EU-Ukraine Association Agreement. Sixty-one percent of those who voted rejected the agreement, and while the turnout rate barely reached 32.3%, it exceeded the 30% threshold for the referendum results to be valid. Nonetheless, it is the lowest turnout for an EU referendum thus far. Although the referendum result is non-binding, the "no vote" required the Dutch government to refer the EU-Ukraine Association Agreement back to its parliament for reconsideration.

During the referendum campaign, one commentator pointed out that this Dutch referendum was not about Ukraine. Rather, it was about distrust of national politics, and the growing Eurosceptic sentiment in the Netherlands. That said, she warned that a "no vote" meant that all future EU treaties with external countries could be held hostage by a single EU member state. It could make the EU less credible in negotiating trade deals and association agreements, and undermine the EU's ability to operate outside its borders. It would be a serious blow to the EU's image as a transformative force for its neighbors.[30] The president of European Commission Jean-Claude Juncker also warned that a Dutch "No" vote could lead to a "continental crisis."[31]

Immediately after the Dutch referendum result was revealed, the Dutch far-right leader Geert Wilders said that "it looks like the Dutch people said No to the European elite and No to the treaty with the Ukraine." Emile Roemer, leader of the Dutch Socialist Party, commented: "I am happy with the result. People wanted to tell the government that Ukraine is too corrupt to sign an agreement with. They also wanted to show that Europe is only there for the elite and multinationals."[32] However, Ukrainian President Petro Poroshenko countered that the "No camp" wanted to "challenge the power of the EU, not the association agreement with Ukraine."[33] On the other hand, his political opponent, Mustafa Nayyem argued that the referendum result was not about Ukraine, nor the Netherlands, but instead "a personal verdict to Petro Poroshenko" who had chosen the elite and oligarchs as partners, rather than ordinary people.[34] From the above reports of campaign rhetoric, we know that this Dutch referendum was portrayed as a battle between ordinary people and

European elites, between the Netherlands and the EU, with standard narratives of identity mobilization. Nevertheless, its impact could include a suspension of the EU-Ukraine Association Agreement, and damage the EU's capacity to negotiate external agreements.

In Hungary, a referendum was called by the government on 2 October 2016, asking people to decide whether Brussels should be allowed to compel Hungary to resettle immigrants without the consent of the [Hungarian] parliament. The turnout rate for this referendum was 43%, which falls below the statutory minimum threshold of (50%), but of those who voted, 98% voted "No" in support of Prime Minister Viktor Orban's position. Orban said that he would use the referendum result to renegotiate refugee quotas with Brussels. For some, this Hungarian referendum was unnecessary, given that few refugees had expressed a desire to resettle in Hungary, and so far the Hungarian government had not accommodated a single refugee out of its pre-assigned quota of 1294. This referendum was a part of the political maneuvers by politicians seeking to enhance their own domestic positions and strengthen their bargaining leverage against the EU. During the referendum campaign, Orban's ruling party, *Fidesz* spent tens of millions of Euros on negative advertisements targeting immigrants and refugees, linking them with terrorism. One researcher from a pro-government think tank explained, "the opinion of the [Hungarian] government is not against the migrants and refugees per se, but rather against the reactive, unconsidered, and poor responses of the European Union."[35] Fidesz deputy chairman Gergely Gulyas hailed the referendum result as "a sweeping victory for all those who believe that the foundations of a strong European Union can only be the strong nation states."[36]

A more negative campaign message was delivered in Prime Minister Orban's own words when he labeled refugees and immigrants "poison." His government also sponsored a poster aimed at mis-informing voters: "Did you know that since the beginning of the migrant crisis, harassment toward women has steeply risen in Europe?" This anti-immigrant rhetoric maybe rooted in Mr. Orban's ethnic-cultural version of national identity. He often talks about the Christian heritage of Hungary and refers to its glorious past as part of the Austro-Hungarian Empire. He believes that Hungary should take the leadership in promoting a future for the EU that is based on "common Christian values."[37] Tracing Orban's political career, one finds that he was initially a liberal politician, but he transformed his party into a conservative one in the 1990s. Now, he is shifting his party's position again by incorporating Eurosceptic, populist, and radical right ideologies as he believes these forces will determine the future of Europe. Orban's aim is to become a leader of these Eurosceptic and populist European forces.[38] Indeed, Orban has declared that his government would demand that more national power be returned from the EU if the majority of Hungarian voters supported his position on the referendum.[39] From the above reports, we find that Hungarian politicians, like their Dutch counterparts, deployed standard narratives of identity mobilization in the conduct of their referendum campaigns. What distinguishes Hungarian from Dutch politicians in their respective referendum campaigns is that the former explicitly embrace extreme right ideologies and demonize the "outsiders," that is, immigrants and refugees. While the Hungarian referendum failed to reach its 50% turnout threshold, Prime Minister Orban arguably has changed the tenor of the immigration debate in Europe.

Will Brexit Trigger a Domino Effect Leading to a Collapse of the European Union?

Given that identity mobilizations through extreme right parties and referendums on EU matters have become so prevalent and forceful in Europe, is it possible that the anti-EU sentiments and referendums will lead to one member state "leaving" the EU followed by another, resulting in a collapse of the EU? Will Brexit trigger such a domino effect?

In line with the post-functional theory of identity mobilization, we have selected a few conditions that make Brexit possible as a yardstick for comparison. We assume that favorable conditions for identity mobilization in Britain *could also be applied to those who wish to leave the EU*. Next we compare the favorable conditions in Britain with those in other member states, and identify those member states with conditions closest to those in Britain. Following the Brexit experience, in total, we select "net national identity," "net membership benefits," "attitude toward intra-EU immigrants," "years of EU membership," and "trade dependence on the EU," as potential influences on member states' decision to leave the EU. From the Eurobarometer survey conducted in May 2015 (see Fig. 10.2), we find that net national identity in Britain is 91%, while net national identity for the EU average is 82%. There are a few member states with net national identities closer to that of Britain, for example, Greece (97%), Italy (84%), Latvia (82%), and Cyprus (84%). Despite anti-EU rhetoric of

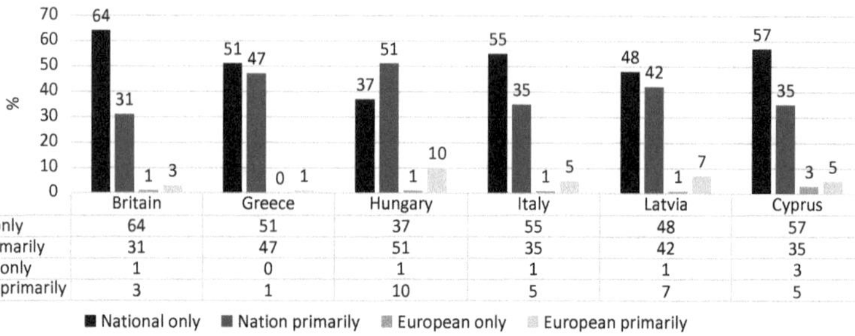

	Britain	Greece	Hungary	Italy	Latvia	Cyprus
National only	64	51	37	55	48	57
Nation primarily	31	47	51	35	42	35
European only	1	0	1	1	1	3
European primarily	3	1	10	5	7	5

Fig. 10.2 National identity versus European identity by selected countries. (Note: Net national identity = National (only + primarily) – European (only + primarily). Source: Eurobarometer interactive, http://ec.europa.eu/COMMFrontOffice/publicopinion/index.cfm/Chart/getChart/chartType/barChart//themeKy/41/groupKy/206/countries/UK/savFiles/129,179,555,47,554,112,143,184,193,201,632,698,662,3,7,49,186,190,192,195,196,187,197,646/periodStart/031992/periodEnd/052015)

Hungarian politicians, the level of net national identity in Hungary only reaches 77%, well below that of EU average. Therefore, it is less likely for Hungary to leave the EU if only net national identity is taken into account. In contrast, Greece seems to be more likely to leave the EU if a referendum is allowed.

People's evaluations of the negative consequences of EU membership for one's own country can be another condition that prompts them to choose to leave the EU in a referendum. The latest Eurobarometer data dealing with this question can be found in May 2011. As Fig. 10.3 shows, in Britain, evaluation of the net benefit of EU membership is −19, meaning that 19% more of British respondents believe that Britain receives a negative benefit from its EU membership. The European average evaluation of the net benefit of EU membership is a positive 15. In Greece, the perceived net benefit of EU membership is −2, in Hungary −9, Italy 3, Latvia −1, and Cyprus 1. Judging from this yardstick, we can speculate that Hungary, Greece, and Latvia are more like than Italy and Cyprus to follow Britain and leave the EU if referendums are held.

As shown in the Brexit and the Hungarian referendum campaigns, anti-immigrant rhetoric formed a central part in strategy of identity mobilization against the EU. As Fig. 10.4 (Eurobarometer survey of May 2016) shows, the net positive attitude toward intra-EU migrants for the EU taken as a whole is 22%, whereas in Britain it stood at 3%. In other words, people in

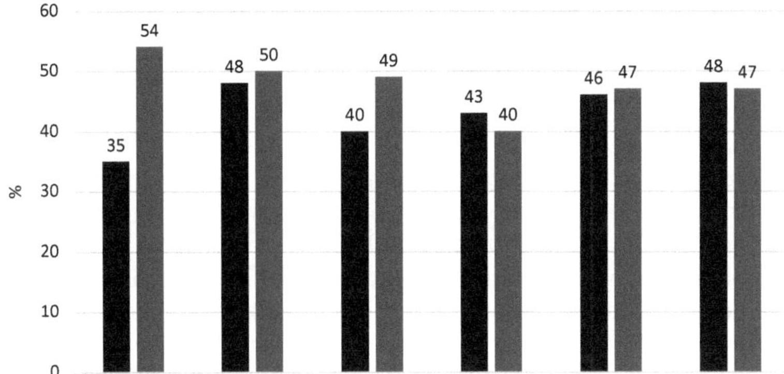

	Britain	Greece	Hungary	Italy	Latvia	Cyprus
benefited	35	48	40	43	46	48
not benefited	54	50	49	40	47	47

Fig. 10.3 Benefits of EU membership. (Based on the public opinion question: "Taking everything into consideration, would you say (your country) has on balance benefited or not from being a member of the European Union?" Source: Eurobarometer interactive, http://ec.europa.eu/COMMFrontOffice/publicopinion/index.cfm/Chart/getChart/themeKy/4/groupKy/4)

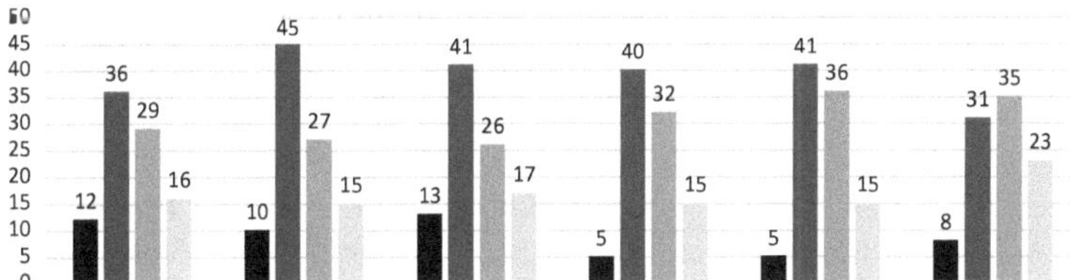

	Britain	Greece	Hungary	Italy	Latvia	Cyprus
very positive	12	10	13	5	5	8
fairly positive	36	45	41	40	41	31
fairly negative	29	27	26	32	36	35
very negative	16	15	17	15	15	23

Fig. 10.4 Attitudes toward immigrants outside the EU. (Source: Eurobarometer interactive, http://ec.europa.eu/COMMFrontOffice/publicopinion/index.cfm/Chart/getChart/themeKy/59/groupKy/278)

Britain were far less likely than people on average in the EU to favorably regard intra-EU migrants. Net attitudes toward intra-EU migrants are positive in Greece at 12%, and Hungary at 11%, and negative in Italy –2%, Latvia –5%, and Cyprus –19%. If attitude toward intra-EU migrants help determine whether to vote against the EU, then people in Cyrus, Latvia, and Italy are more likely to follow Britain's lead and choose to leave the EU.

None of the above findings point to any of these five EU member states following Britain's lead and leaving the EU, because we have not yet established a valid model to predict voter choice in the Brexit campaign. So far, our selection of explanatory variables is based on the thesis of identity mobilization. From the theory of historical institutionalism, however, we can identify other potential influences on Brexit. One reason why member states are reluctant to leave the EU is the sunk costs invested over the period of their EU membership. We can use the number of years since accession to the EU as a proxy to operationalize the concept of "sunk cost." The longer the state has been a member of the EU, the larger the sunk cost, and the less likely it will be to leave the EU. To date, Britain has been a member of the EU for 45 years, Greece for 37 years, Italy 68 years, and Hungary, Latvia, and Cyprus for 14 years. In terms of sunk costs to be paid upon leaving the EU, new member states like Hungary, Latvia, and Cyprus have least to lose. Nevertheless, if 45 years of EU membership does not prevent Britain from leaving the EU, then Greece should be seen as a likely candidate to leave the EU next.

Indeed, if we compared the variation of trade dependence of each member state on the EU market, we would speculate that Greece is likely to follow Britain and leave the EU. Data derived from Eurostat shows that 43.6% of UK trade is with other EU member states, while 46.6% of Greek's is intra-EU trade. Trade dependence on the EU market for Hungary is 77.9%, Italy 53.7%, Latvia 66.4%, and Cyprus 58%. The fact that these member states are highly dependent on the EU market for trade and economic growth makes them less likely to leave the EU. Even if they choose to leave the EU, the costs incurred as a result of trade disruption would be greater than that paid by Britain and Greece. Taking into account all of the above potential influences on "exit" decisions, we find that it is rather unlikely Brexit will trigger a domino effect.

The five member states selected in this section are most similar to Britain in the conditions for identity mobilization. However, none of their conditions are much more favorable for identity mobilization than those of Britain, and only in Greece do we find some similar conditions that might prompt its people to choose to leave the EU. Greece has a higher net national identity, and a negative attitude toward EU membership. Figures on sunk cost and trade dependence on the EU market in Greece are also similar to those of Britain. But most importantly, Greece (much like Britain) has a Eurosceptic party in power (at the time of writing), making it likely that the government will seek to shift blame to the EU and to call for a referendum to resolve its internal rifts. That said, a country's decision to join or leave the EU can be attributed to many factors, most of which (e.g. security interests) are not discussed in this chapter. Therefore, the conclusion reached here should be treated with caution, as it is based on partial theoretical speculation, not robust empirical evidence.

Differentiated Integration: European Union Governance with an "Exit" Option

Although Brexit *is unlikely to* trigger a domino effect leading to a total collapse of the EU, it can cause problems for EU governance. One need not to go beyond imagining the astronomic number of negotiations and legislative revisions that will be required in Britain and the EU to reach a final conclusion concerning the impact of Brexit on EU governance. Here we provide theoretical reasoning on how Brexit will affect the existing system of EU governance in the long run.

Since the establishment of European Coal and Steel Community (ECSC) in 1951, supranational institutions in the ECSC/EC/EU have expanded not only in the number of their governing units but also in their power and policy competence.[40] The development of EU institutions and policies creates path dependence, such that once established, it is difficult to unwind them.[41] As a result of the path-dependent development of EU institutions and policies, the functioning of the EU governance system has become too complex to be understood even by EU experts, let alone the general public. Instead of treating EU governance as a unitary system, we should distinguish different modes of EU governance.

Depending on the nature of the EU policies in question, the corresponding modes of EU governance could be different. According to Theodore Lowi (1972), public policies can be distinguished from regulative, distributive, and redistributive in nature.[42] Whereas regulatory policies in the EU tend to follow the mode of the "Community (or Union) method," distributive and redistributive policies are often pursued through the modes of "network governance" or "open method of coordination." The "community method" is used where the policy competence of member states has been transferred to the EU's supranational institutions. These institutions are entrusted with authority to ensure the compliance of its member states to the EU's treaties, secondary laws, regulations, directives, decisions, and recommendations.[43] The complex rules around decision-making among the Council, Commission, and European Parliament (EP) are usually applied to policies where the EU has the competence.[44] However, the "Community method" can be applied to distributive and redistributive policies as well, such as the EU's trade policy, and common agriculture policy (CAP) or common regional policy (CRP) respectively. Nevertheless, the corresponding format of decision-making also varies.

There are other EU policies that are administrated by "network governance"[45] or "open method of coordination."[46] The competence of these policies is either shared between the EU and its member states, or exclusively owned by the member states. The EU's environmental policy, for example, is dominated by an extensive policy network of environmental experts, industries, transnational interest groups, as well as bureaucrats from the EU and member states.[47] In contrast, the Common Foreign and Security Policy (CFSP), whose competence is still vested in member states, is dominated by a policy community of diplomats and foreign policy experts. Though CFSP has not yet been fully "communitarized," it is nevertheless "Brusselized" in a sense that much foreign policy deliberation and action has been moved to Brussels for better coordination.[48]

There are policies, such as Fiscal policy, employment policy, industrial policy, economic structure reform, and social welfare policies, whose competence largely belongs to member states. Some of these policies, together with policies concerning national identity like culture and education policies, are carefully managed by the "open method of coordination (OMC)." Through policy cooperation and coordination, the Commission and member states jointly produced norms and acceptable practices, which later were incorporated into Community legislation. Although there is no legal penalty against non-complying member states, the OMC seems to enhance policy cooperation through learning and peer pressure.[49] Given that it is operated under the precondition that member states' sovereignty not be infringed, the OMC could be a favorable option for European elites when public scrutiny over a given policy is intensive.

Multiple modes of EU governance listed above *is* a manifestation of differentiated integration. According to Dyson and Sepos, differentiated integration refers to a

> Process whereby European states, or sub-state units, opt to move at different speeds and/or towards different objectives with regard to common policies. It involves adopting different formal and informal arrangements (hard

> and soft), inside or outside the EU treaty framework. In this way, relevant actors come to assume different rights and obligations and to share a distinct attitude towards the integration process – what it is appropriate to do together, and who belongs with whom.[50]

With Brexit, the question is whether "differentiated integration" has been further entrenched. Will different modes of EU governance be institutionalized with no hope of eventual convergence? From the recent history of European integration, we know that crises in the EU tend to stimulate further integration schemes, but not conformity. For example, the recent government debt crisis stimulated various schemes of fiscal cooperation in the Eurozone. However, these alternative integration or cooperation schemes are not likely to be harmonized if participants feel they can withdraw from them at any time.

Moreover, the rejection of EU treaty revisions in Irish and Danish referendums allowed both countries to negotiate flexibility with the EU and secure options to opt out on some policies under Justice and Home Affairs (JHA). Such a tendency to cherry-pick policy items on which to cooperate could be reinforced given that the Brexit precedence allows other member states to contemplate the previously inconceivable "exit" option. Now member states may threaten to leave the EU altogether if not granted policy flexibility. When member states are equipped with an "exit" option, the EU is less capable of pushing for convergence through the Community method because strict convergence would force the laggard to leave the Union, leading to a process of disintegration.

In other words, the long-term implication of Brexit on EU governance is that the trend toward differentiated integration will be consolidated and existing modes of EU governance will be entrenched without any hope of convergence in the future. Intuitively one would think that the Union, without a reluctant member like the UK, would be more homogenous. But having the "exit" option may in fact prompt member states to highlight their national differences, despite European elites' efforts to urge unity and solidarity. As one sees from various news reports, Hungary is constantly challenging the EU's refugee policy, Greece and Spain continue to protest austerity policies in the Eurozone, Poland and some Eastern European members have not lived up to their promises on protecting human rights, and Italy, France, Greece, Portugal, and so on have continued to manipulate their fiscal policies in spite of warning from the Commission. If the motto of the EU is "unity with diversity," the implication of Brexit for EU governance could well be to increase pressures for more "diversity."

Conclusion

At the time of writing, the EU has published its negotiation directive for the first phase and appointed its chief negotiator, Mr. Michel Barnier for dealing with Brexit negotiations. Judging from the content of the negotiation directive and the statements of Mr. Barnier in press conferences of the initial rounds of negotiation, we find that the EU intends to ensure its citizens' rights are protected, Britain's financial obligations fulfilled, the Irish border issue resolved, the integrity of the single market preserved, and the autonomy and legal order of EU observed after the Brexit agreement takes effect. As the EU's negotiation directive prescribes, the Brexit agreement should ensure the necessary protection of the Union's interests in the UK, and should

> Include effective enforcement and dispute settlement mechanisms that fully respect the autonomy of the Union and of its legal order, including the role of the Court of Justice of the European Union (ECJ),…as well as appropriate institutional arrangements allowing for the adoption of measures to deal with unforeseen situations not covered by the agreement.[51]

Moreover, when the European Council decides that negotiations can proceed to the second phase, there will be transitional arrangements covering such matters as the future relationship between Britain and the EU. Any such transitional arrangements must be clearly defined, limited in time, and subject to effective enforcement mechanisms. If these transitional arrangements were to be prolonged, the Union's regulatory, budgetary, supervisory, judiciary, and enforcement measures would apply.[52] Although the Brexit agreement should set a withdrawal date no later than 30 March 2019, the UK and the EU could jointly agree to extend the period of negotiation. Finally, the UK will become a third country upon withdrawal.[53]

The EU's negotiation directive clearly envisions different phases of Brexit negotiation, and the potential for flexibility in governance within the EU during the transition period. However, the EU's legal order and governance structure cannot be challenged by whatever form the Brexit agreement takes. In fact, if there is a dispute settlement mechanism agreed by both Britain and the EU, the prerogatives of the ECJ should be maintained. The core institutional structure of the EU embedded in *acquis* is not negotiable, but various forms of future association of Britain with the EU can be negotiated in the second phase. Should Britain negotiate a different format of association with the EU beyond the EFTA (European Free Trade Association) model (single market without customs union), the Turkish model (customs union without single market), or others, then the complexity of EU governance would increase.

At the moment, the EU has set out three preconditions for Britain to accept in order to move on to the second phase of negotiation. Such a negotiation strategy is certainly based on the Union's interest and leverage, but it could also be seen as anticipating internal EU challenges, especially those derived from identity mobilization. On the one hand, the EU cannot be seen as too soft on Brexit, because a soft position could encourage other member states to exit the Union. On the other hand, the EU's demands cannot be too tough to make it impossible for a Brexit deal concluded in time. The preconditions set out by the EU are both tough and reasonable. What follows is how Mr. Barnier negotiates with his British counterpart, Mr. David Davis.

In a speech addressed to entrepreneurs, trade unionists, leaders of NGOs and civil society of the EU on 6 July 2017, Mr. Barnier highlighted the cost of Brexit and reiterated the EU's three preconditions for the initial phase of negotiation, namely, citizens' rights, financial settlement, and Irish border issues. Not only did he reject the possibility of sector-by-sector participation in the single market, but he also rejected the idea of achieving frictionless trade by building a customs union without a single market, as some in Britain had speculated. He told the EU's social partners that the UK could not be half-in and half-out of the single market and the UK must respect the EU's autonomy of making and implementing rules, standards, and regulations.[54] While he emphasized that there would be no punishment or revenge against the UK, he obviously attributed the dire consequences of Brexit to the choice made by the UK, not by the EU. Barnier warned that "no deal" would worsen the lose-lose situation resulting from Brexit because it would mean that UK would trade with the EU under basic World Trade Organization (WTO) rules. He said his responsibility was to limit the cost of Brexit for the 27 member states as much as possible, though he confessed that the Brexit negotiations would be no easy task. Finally, he argued that the preparation for Brexit negotiations had helped to build up a very strong sense of unity among the 27 and he pleaded for maintaining such unity throughout the negotiation process.[55] Barnier's statements are meant to demonstrate the transparency of the EU's negotiations, but his tough messages could well forestall identity mobilization in some member states.

In press conferences of the first three rounds of negotiations with the UK, Barnier reported some procedural progress in negotiations, such as coming to agreement on dates, organization, and priorities of the negotiations, as well as clarification of each other's positions, but he also highlighted substantial differences between the UK and the EU. For example, on the Irish border issue, Barnier felt that the UK wanted the EU to suspend application of its law to Northern Ireland, hence creating a new external border of the EU. He worried that the UK might use Ireland as a test case for the future UK-EU customs relations, but Barnier asserted, "This will not happen. Creativity and flexibility cannot be at the expense of the integrity of the Single Market and the Customs Union."[56] Another example of friction concerns citizens' rights, over which Barnier quickly pointed out that the UK disagreed that the ECJ had the final control over what its national court would do. On financial settlement, Barnier highlighted the differences of the UK's position. He said, "In July, the UK recognized that it has obligations beyond the Brexit date.... After this week, it is clear that the UK does not feel legally obliged to honor these obligations after departure."[57] At the end, Barnier noted that time was quickly passing to reach a Brexit deal in time. Barnier warned the UK, "We are far from being able to recommend to the European Council that there has been sufficient progress in order to start discussions on the future relationship (between the UK and the EU)."[58] The tough line in Barnier's statements reflected a mandated position of the EU, and served to strengthen the solidarity of the 27 member states.

In this chapter, we use two theoretical concepts, identity mobilization derived from post-functionalism and path dependence from historical institutionalism, to speculate on the long-term impact of Brexit on EU governance. Specifically, we argue that Brexit will not trigger a domino effect leading to a collapse of the EU, and, due to the path-dependent nature of EU institutions and policies, a pervasive and comprehensive reform of EU governance system is rather unlikely. Whether European integration continues depends on the balance of forces between "identity mobilization" originated in member states and the tenacity of EU institutions to resist such pressure. Given that Brexit is a manifestation of identity mobilization, we argue that the likely impact of Brexit is a proliferation of various forms of "differentiated integration." The "Community method" can no longer be used to push for policy convergence. Instead, multiple modes of governance will be entrenched with no hope of convergence in the future. Paradoxically, the EU will not become a more homogeneous entity without Britain. On the contrary, the diversity within the EU will be highlighted, given that the exit option is now conceivable and there is a precedent. Nevertheless, because of the "stickiness" of EU institutions, highlighting diversities will not give overly much momentum to the forces of disintegration.

Notes

1. Liesbet Hooghe and Gary Marks. 2008. "A Postfunctionalist Theory of European Integration: From Permissive Consensus to Constraining Dissensus." *British Journal of Political Science* 39(1): 1–23.
2. Hooghe and Marks, p. 13.
3. Ernst Haas. 1968. *The Uniting of Europe: Political, Social and Economic Forces, 1950-1957.* 2nd ed. Stanford, CA: Stanford University Press.
4. Hooghe and Marks, pp. 1–2.
5. Hooghe and Marks, p. 22.
6. Paul Pierson. 1996. "The Path to European Integration: A Historical-Institutionalist Analysis." *Comparative Political Studies* 29(2): 123–63; Pierson, Paul. 2000. "Increasing Returns, Path Dependence, and the Study of Politics." *The American Political Science Review* 94(2): 251–67.
7. Pierson (1996, p. 126).
8. Mark D Aspinwall and Gerald Schneider. 2000. "Same Menu, Separate Tables: The Institutionalist Turn in Political Science and the Study of European Integration." *European Journal of Political Research* 38: 1–36, p. 16.
9. Simon J. Bulmer. 1994. "The New Governance of the European Union: A New Institutionalist Approach." *Journal of Public Policy* 13: 351–80.
10. Fritz W. Scharpf. 1988. "The Joint-decision Trap: Lessons from German Federalism and European Integration." *Public Administration* 66(3): 239–78.
11. Pierson (2000).
12. Pierson (1996, p. 137).
13. Brigid Laffan. 1996. "The Politics of Identity and Political Order in Europe." *Journal of Common Market Studies* 34(1): 82–102.
14. Neil Fligstein, 2008. *Euroclash: The EU, European Identity and the Future of Europe.* Oxford: Oxford University Press.
15. Vivien A. Schmidt. 2011. "The Problems of Identity and Legitimacy in the European Union: Is More Politics the Answer?" In *Debating Political Identity and Legitimacy in the Europe Union*, edited by Sonia Lucarelli, Furio Cerutti, and Vivien A. Schmidt, 16–37. Abingdon, Oxon, UK: Routledge, p. 16.

16. Sean Carey. 2002. "Undivided Loyalties: Is National Identity an Obstacle to European Integration?" *European Union Politics* 3(4): 387–413.
17. Cas Mudde. 2007. *Populist Radical Right Parties.* Cambridge: Cambridge University Press.
18. Hans-Georg Betz. 1994. *Radical Right-Wing Populism in Western Europe.* Basingstoke, UK: Macmillan; Kitschelt, Herbert. 1995. *The Radical Right in Western Europe: A Comparative Analyst.* Ann Arbor, MI: University of Michigan Press.
19. Pippa Norris. 2005. *Radical Right: Voters and Parties in the Electoral Market.* Cambridge: Cambridge University Press; Hainsworth, Paul. 2008. *The Extreme Right in Western Europe.* New York: Routledge.
20. Mudde, Populist Radical Right Parties, 2007.
21. Ibid., p. 162.
22. Neil Fligstein, Alina Polyakova, and Wayne Sandholtz. 2012. "European Integration, Nationalism and European Identity." *Journal of Common Market Studies* 50(S1): 106–22, p. 115.
23. Norris (2005).
24. Fligstein, Polyakova, and Sandholtz (2012, p. 116).
25. Pieter de Wilde and Michael Zurn. 2012. "Can the Politicization of European Integration be Reversed?" *Journal of Common Market Studies* 50(S1): 137–53.
26. Sara Binzer Hobolt. 2009. *Europe in Question- Referendums on European Integration.* Oxford, UK: Oxford University Press, p. 3; Qvortrup, Matt. 2013. *Direct Democracy- A Comparative Study of the Theory and Practice of Government by the People.* Manchester, UK: Manchester University Press, p. 3; International Institute for Democracy and Electoral Assistance (IDEA). 2008. *Direct Democracy- The International IDEA Handbook.* Stockholm, Sweden: International IDEA, 47–49.
27. Laura Tilindyte. 2016. "Referendums on EU Issues." European Parliamentary Research Service. http://www.europarl.europa.eu/RegData/etudes/BRIE/2016/582041/EPRS_BRI(2016)582041_EN.pdf
28. Ibid.
29. Hobolt (2009).
30. Kateryna Zarembo. 2016. "Yes for Ukraine, Win for Europe." *Politico,* March 15. http://iwp.org.ua/eng/public/1972.html
31. Cynthia Kroet. 2016. "Viktor Orbán to call for EU Treaty Changes." *Politico,* September 21. http://www.politico.eu/article/viktor-orban-to-call-for-eu-treaty-changes/
32. Ibid.
33. Ibid.
34. David Stern. 2016. "Dutch Referendum Shakes Ukraine." *Politico,* April 7. http://www.politico.eu/article/dutch-referendum-shakes-eu-ukraine-association-agreement-petro-poroshenko/

35. Andrew Macdowall. 2016. "Voters Back Viktor Orbán's Rejection of EU Migrant Quotas." *Politico*, October 2. http://www.politico.eu/article/hungary-referendum-eu-migration-viktor-orban/
36. Ibid.
37. Lili Bayer. 2016. "Victor Orban's Vision of a Bigger, Looser Europe." *Politico*, September 6. http://www.politico.eu/article/viktor-orbans-vision-of-a-bigger-looser-europe-hungary-european-union-brexit/
38. Ibid.
39. Cynthia Kroet. 2016. "Dutch Reject EU-Ukraine Deal." *Politico*, April 6. http://www.politico.eu/article/low-turnout-as-dutch-reject-eu-ukraine-deal/
40. Philippe C Schmitter. 1996. Imaging the Future of the Euro-policy with the Help of New Concepts. In *Governance in the European Union*, edited by Gary marks, Fritz W Scharpf, Philippe C. Schmitter, and Wolfgang Streeck, 121–50. London, Sage; Wolfgang Wessels. 1997. An Ever Closer Fusion? *Journal of Common Market Studies* 35(2): 276.
41. Scharpf (1988) and Pierson (1996).
42. Theodore J. Lowi. 1972. Four Systems of Policy, Politics and Choice. *Public Administration Review* 32(4): 298–310
43. David Phinnemore and Lee McGowan. 2010. *A Dictionary of the European Union*, 5th ed. London: Routledge, p. 86.
44. Peter Moser, Gerald Schneider, and Gebhard Kirchgässner. 2000. *Decision Rules in the European Union: A Rational Choice Perspective*. London: Macmillan.
45. Gerda Falkner. 2000. "Policy Networks in a Multi-level System: Convergence towards Moderate Diversity?" *West European Politics* 23(4): 94–120; Frans van Waarden. 1992. "Dimensions and Types of Policy Networks." *European Journal of Political Research* 21: 29–52; Hussein Kassim. 1994. "Policy Networks, Networks and European Union Policy Making: A Sceptical View." *West European Politics* 17(4): 15–27.
46. Dermot Hodson and Imelda Maher. 2001. "The Open Method as a New Mode of Governance: The Case of Soft Economic Policy Co-Ordination." *Journal of Common Market Studies* 39(4): 719–46.
47. Thomas Gehring. 1997. "Governing in Nested Institutions: Environmental Policy in the European Union and the Case of Packaging Waste." *Journal of European Public Policy*, 4(3): 337–54; Elizabeth Bomberg. 1998. "Issue Networks and the Environment: Explaining European Union Environmental Policy." In *Comparing Policy Networks*, edited by David Marsh, 167–84. Milton Keynes, UK: Open University Press; John McCormick. 2001. *Environmental Policy in the European Union*. New York: Palgrave.
48. Christopher Hill. 1998. Closing the Capability – Expectations Gap. In *A Common Foreign Policy for Europe? Competing Visions of the CFSP*, edited

by John Peterson and Helene Sjursen, 18–38. London: Routledge; Michael E. Smith 2004. "Toward a Theory of EU Foreign Policy-Making: Multi-Level Governance, Domestic Politics, and National Adaptation to Europe's Common Foreign and Security Policy." *Journal of European Public Policy* 11(4): 740–58; Fraser Cameron. 2012. *An Introduction to European Foreign Policy*. 2nd ed. Oxon, UK: Routledge; Jolyon Howorth. 2007. *Security and Defence Policy in the European Union*. New York: Palgrave Macmillan.

49. Hodson and Maher (2001).
50. Kenneth Dyson. 2010. "'Euro' Europe: 'Fuzzy' Boundaries and 'Constrained' Differentiation in Macro-Economic Governance." In *Which Europe? The Politics of Differentiated Integration*, edited by Kenneth Dyson and Angelos Sepos, 215–32. Basingstoke, UK: Palgrave Macmillan, p. 4.
51. Negotiating directives for Article 50 negotiations, Council of the European Union, XT21016/17 ADD 1 REV 2 ANNEX, UKTF, Brussels, 22 May 2017, https://ec.europa.eu/commission/publications/negotiating-directives-article-50-negotiations_en. [Hereafter EU Council].
52. EU Council, p. 7.
53. EU Council, p. 4.
54. Michel Barnier, "Speech by Michel Barnier at the European Economic and Social Committee," European Commission, 6 July 2017, http://europa.eu/rapid/press-release_SPEECH-17-1922_en.htm
55. Ibid.
56. Michel Barnier, "Statement by Michel Barnier on the publication of the Guiding Principles for the Dialogue on Ireland and Northern Ireland," European Commission, 6 September 2017, http://europa.eu/rapid/press-release_SPEECH-17-3145_en.htm
57. Michel Barnier, "Speech by Michel Barnier at the press conference following the third round of Article 50 negotiations with the United Kingdom," European Commission, 31 August 2017, http://europa.eu/rapid/press-release_SPEECH-17-3043_en.htm
58. Ibid.

Index[1]

[1] Note: Page numbers followed by 'n' refer to notes.

D. W. F. Huang, M. Reilly (eds.), *The Implications of Brexit for East Asia*, https://doi.org/10.1007/978-981-13-0185-8

FSC
www.fsc.org
MIX
Papier | Fördert gute Waldnutzung
FSC® C083411

Kolibri 360 GmbH
Ferdinand-Jühlke-Straße 7
99095 Erfurt, Deutschland
produktsicherheit@kolibri360.de